HUMANITARIANISM AND THE EMPEROR'S JAPAN, 1877–1977

Humanitarianism and the Emperor's Japan, 1877–1977

Olive Checkland
Honorary Research Fellow
University of Glasgow

St. Martin's Press

First published in Great Britain 1994 by
THE MACMILLAN PRESS LTD
Houndmills, Basingstoke, Hampshire RG21 2XS
and London
Companies and representatives
throughout the world

A catalogue record for this book is available
from the British Library.

ISBN 0–333–60089–4

Printed in Great Britain by
Ipswich Book Co Ltd
Ipswich, Suffolk

First published in the United States of America 1994 by
Scholarly and Reference Division,
ST. MARTIN'S PRESS, INC.,
175 Fifth Avenue,
New York, N.Y. 10010

ISBN 0–312–10258–5

Library of Congress Cataloging-in-Publication Data
Checkland, Olive.
Humanitarianism and the Emperor's Japan, 1877–1977 / Olive
Checkland.
p.   cm.
Includes bibliographical references and index.
ISBN 0–312–10258–5
1. Nihon Sekijūjisha—History.   2. Red Cross—Japan—History.
I. Title.
UH537.J3C49   1994
361.7'634'0952—dc20   93–26984
                                                             CIP

For
Seibi Ota
and the spirit of the
volunteer
in the
Japanese Red Cross Society

Emperor Meiji (reigned 1867–1912) in whose name the
Japanese Red Cross Society was founded (1877) to adopt
humanitarianism and so confer legitimacy, in the eyes of
the world, on the new Japanese regime

Contents

PART IV 1945, AND AFTER

List of Tables

List of Maps

List of Illustrations

Preface

Images of Japanese humanitarianism are fixed in Western minds by the violence shown to Allied prisoners of war, between 1941 and 45; but, during the Russo–Japanese struggle of 1904–5, the Japanese were world leaders, caring with humanity for Russians as prisoners of war. For the present purpose the word humanitarian is used in a limited sense to mean reducing suffering and promoting welfare during time of war.

The Red Cross Society of Japan (JRC) was the brainchild of Hirobumi Ito and Tomomi Iwakura who in 1873, in the course of the Iwakura Mission, spent time with the Red Cross people in Geneva, studying the nascent humanitarian movement there. Did the wily Ito see the Red Cross as a form of legitimation for Japan in her struggle for international recognition? He certainly encouraged the initiative. Tsunetami Sano, who was acting as a Japanese diplomat in Vienna from January to September 1873, and who met members of the Mission during that time on several occasions, was put in charge of the endeavour.

From the beginning the Red Cross Society was associated with and encouraged by the imperial house. It was appropriate that a movement which involved the 'Emperor's Children', the armed forces, should receive the Emperor's blessing. It was also the case that such a society could, in the Emperor's name, command in Japan absolute obedience from all its members.

Sano's opportunity to launch a benevolent society, which was the forerunner of the Red Cross Society, came in 1877 when the South West Civil War, or Satsuma rebellion, broke out. At this time a rudimentary aid service to the wounded on the battlefield was launched under the name of the *Hakuaisha*.

By the early 1900s, the JRC had 900 000 nominal members, roughly one in ten of the population, and was the largest such society in the world. In Japan the Red Cross was a super-patriotic society, into which local public service employees and others were drafted. The spirit of 'voluntaryism', so vital at so many levels of Western society, was not the principle motivating the Red Cross in Japan until after 1945 when American Red Cross Societies workers introduced it. In times of peace membership levels of Red Cross Societies in other countries could slump embarrassingly but this did not happen in Japan where membership remained, by Western standards, startlingly high.

The Meiji Emperor, by 1900 a powerful figure, undoubtedly obtained the humanitarian objective he had espoused. The battles against the Russians were bitter, bloody and hard-won, but once captured, the defeated Russians were treated with care and consideration. The imperial message had been carried through the officer corps to the common Japanese soldier; do not maltreat the Russian prisoners of war. According to Russian figures, of the 70 000, some 500 died of their wounds or of illness during their imprisonment. During the First World War the Japanese held some 5000 German prisoners or internees, who had been captured in German enclaves in Shantung in China and elsewhere. They also were well treated.

The Japanese achievement in caring for the Russians was widely acknowledged in international circles at that time. It was particularly impressive because there were at that time no Geneva conventions outlining the treatment expected for war prisoners; indeed the Red Cross as an international body had declined to widen its commitment, which had originally been for wounded soldiers, to cover prisoners. The Japanese proceeded by using the rules for caring for such men worked out at the International Peace Congress organised at The Hague in 1899 (see Appendix C).

The early recognition in 1886 by the International Red Cross movement, of Japan as an equal, had a special significance in Japan. This approbation, coming at a time when Japan was struggling to reverse her 'unequal treaties', and was generally patronised by the West, made a great impact. The fact that the International Committee of the Red Cross did *not discriminate against* Japan brought an exceptional reward in humanitarian endeavour to the international community.

But the Meiji Emperor, by encouraging the Japanese to adopt modern humanitarian ideas, had overturned and rejected an earlier and powerful military code of honour which had motivated the *samurai* for hundreds of years. These ideas may have been discounted and submerged but they were far from dead.

With the death of the Emperor Taisho in 1926 the way was clear for the re-emergence of narrow nationalistic views, as earlier values re-asserted themselves. In this way a terrible inconsistency between modern humanitarianism and a ruthless military code was exposed. Although during peace-time it was possible for both sets of ideas to flourish, the huge Red Cross Society – eagerly supported in Japan because it was a subsidiary arm of the military – was, overseas, praised as a strong and powerful humanitarian society, a signatory from the beginning of the earliest Geneva conventions which attempted to control the excesses of war. The Second World War was to demonstrate the irreconcilability of the two positions as Red Cross benevolence, to those other than Japanese, faltered and faded when confronted by the brutalism of Japanese military might.

In Japan the semi-official status of the JRC ensured that it was well represented in the provinces as well as in Tokyo. Prefectural governors, *ex officio* responsible for the successful organisation of the Society in their own areas, rallied local pride to ensure that their regional Red Cross was the best in Japan. Provincial centres usually boasted an imposing Red Cross Headquarters while later, Red Cross hospitals were built. Relief Detachments, consisting of doctors, nurses, pharmacists and orderlies, were recruited from regional Red Cross hospitals to serve together as units either at home or overseas in temporary wartime military or Red Cross Hospitals. Several of the units during the Russo–Japanese War served in hospitals nursing prisoners of war.

The Red Cross Society was probably the first body in Japan to offer women professional training as nurses. The ladies who joined the Auxiliary movement, which recruited aristocratic women to appear in nurses' uniform and to 'serve' in Red Cross hospitals, were probably token 'volunteers'. Their nursing work was intended to encourage respectable girls to offer themselves for training. Although these girls (often in early days, war widows, and so war-heroes) were rigorously disciplined and controlled, they were educated as nurses and enjoyed a status and respect, as well as a financial competence, the significance of which may be difficult for Westerners to comprehend.

The JRC expanded and flourished during the 1890s and 1900s. Later in the First World War, when Japan was allied to Britain and America it continued to grow. After the First World War the JRC – backed by its fine reputation – would probably have succeeded in its ambition to host the International Conference in the 1920s but for the disaster of the Tokyo Yokohama earthquake on 1 September 1923. It was not until October 1934 that the Red Cross movement agreed to hold its four-yearly conference, previously always held in Europe, except for 1912 when it was held in Washington, in Tokyo. This Congress, which brought numbers of foreign guests to Tokyo, was the first major international gathering ever held in Japan. The visitors were astonished by Japanese efficiency and perhaps overwhelmed by the unremitting hospitality.

At the Tokyo meetings the discussions of Red Cross work were congratulatory, mostly referring to past achievements. Publicly it was a rosy picture. There was no mention of the Manchurian incident, of 18–19 September 1931, staged by the Japanese army to authenticate their Manchurian intervention, or of the subsequent imposition of the puppet regime of Manchukuo. Japan's walk out from the League of Nations in March 1933, consequent on the Lytton Commission's critical report on Japanese activities in Manchuria, was ignored. And there was no recognition that the Kwantung Army of Japan, which was preparing for the Great Asian War and was soon to carry its aggression from Manchukuo south into China proper, was operating on the Asian mainland effectively out of control of the Japanese government in Tokyo.

The optimism of the International Red Cross Congress in Tokyo provided a hollow victory for humanitarianism, for, despite the compliments and platitudes, internationalism had become, for Japan, in the run-up to the war, an irrelevance.

The First World War had revealed major problems between the belligerents with regard not only to the sick and wounded but also to uninjured prisoners of war. In the light of this two Geneva conventions had been agreed in 1929, and that which related to prisoners of war was never ratified by Japan. The war between 1941 and 1945 brought large numbers of prisoners, many of whom were badly treated, into Japanese hands. Far from the Japanese occupying the high moral ground as they had during the 1904–5 Russo–Japanese War and the Great War of 1914–18, older values re-emerged. Honourable Japanese would die, rather than become prisoners. When Japanese families bade farewell to their soldier sons they parted with them forever and would have been ashamed to have them surrender as prisoners of war. The figures speak for themselves. At the end of 1944 there were some 8658 Japanese as prisoners, although by the end of July 1945 the figures had jumped to 15 959, against some 200 000 Allied prisoners of war.

The Japanese treated their prisoners of war, Australian and New Zealanders, Americans and Canadians and British, as prisoners had been treated for centuries in Japan. They put them to work. Prisoners had traditionally been given the most brutalising jobs; white men laboured in mines and factories in Japan, in Manchuria and in Burma and elsewhere in South-East Asia. Such work, in extreme climates, barely sustained as they were by an inadequate rice diet, was beyond the strength of many. There were frequent accidents and many deaths.

The JRC was in an impossible position during the 1941–5 war. To its critics, its servants seemed to be tools in the hands of the military; to its friends, Red Cross personnel did what little they could to ease international tension. When it was all over the International Red Cross in Geneva, in a face-saving statement, assured the JRC authorities that they had not themselves done anything of which they had cause to be ashamed.

Negotiation on behalf of prisoners of war was done during the war years by neutral representatives, usually Swiss, of the International Committee of the Red Cross (ICRC). The Japanese military authorities could have been accused of non-co-operation; they certainly followed a policy of delay and obstruction. Representatives of the ICRC, either resident in Japan or sent from Geneva, strove to establish communications through which they could argue for better conditions for the POWs. It was all to no avail. Visits to POW camps organised after months of interminable negotiation were wasted as camp commandants harangued the Red Cross men at length about the high standards which they maintained. In the end the Red Cross man was allowed only a short – two minute – strictly controlled talk with one or more prisoners, always in the presence of and within the hearing of Japanese guards. Occasionally Red Cross parcels were delivered to camps. Occasionally they found their way into prisoners' hands. All this produced much bitterness. The known brutalism, as applied to POWs, played some part in determining the ferocious American saturation bombing of Tokyo towards the end of the war. Would atomic bombs have been dropped on Hiroshima and Nagasaki had the standard of behaviour applied by the Japanese to their war prisoners during the Russo–Japanese War of 1904–5, and the First World War of 1914–18, still applied in the 1940s?

The end of a disastrous war came with an unprecedented radio broadcast on 15 August 1945 by the Emperor. This brought the news of defeat, shocking to the Japanese people, nurtured as they had been on years of propaganda promising victory, and of the acceptance of the Allied Joint Declaration. The Emperor told them that they must 'endure the unendurable and suffer the insufferable' and that this would 'pave the way for a grand peace for all the generations'. Japan is still considered an aggressive nation, but prior to the Meiji period warlike behaviour had been confined to power struggles within her own closed borders. It had been the guns of western steamships which had forced her into the modern world: tragically she had proved herself a model pupil, only too easily tempted by the blandishments of imperialism.

The 1941–5 war destroyed the old Red Cross Society of Japan. Salvation came, with much help from the American Red Cross Society (ARC), through the development of regional Red Cross hospitals into a civilian hospital service. The Red Cross Society now provides throughout Japan a network of health services, including general hospitals, maternity hospitals, pharmaceutical services, clinics and other ancillary services. In Tokyo and elsewhere the Red Cross still trains nurses and runs a large hospital complex at Shibuya. The national Blood Transfusion service of Japan is effectively provided by the Red Cross Society.

Overseas the Red Cross Society has set up projects in India, South-East Asia and elsewhere in the Third World. The new 'non–military' Japan has for some years been searching for a role, willing to share with others less fortunate than themselves the benefits of modern medicine and health care.

Was the Cross, the Christian symbol adopted as a metaphor for the humanitarian work of the Red Cross organisation based in neutral Geneva, embraced so eagerly in Japan because of an urgent need to join a world club rather than as an expression of genuine concern? Even if this view is accepted, nothing can detract from the early achievements of Japan in rendering aid to Russian and German prisoners, although it is hard to forget the appearance of emaciated prisoners emerging from camps all over South-East Asia in 1945.

It was due to the support offered to me in 1990 by Tadateru Konoe, then the head of the International Division but now a Vice President of the JRC, that it was initially possible to pursue Red Cross affairs in Japan. The Daiwa Anglo–Japanese Foundation made a grant which greatly eased the expense of a period of residence in Tokyo. Keio University generously provided the necessary status as Visiting Professor and the environment to make steady work possible. Norio and Setsuko Tamaki, Norikazu Kudo, Chuhei Sugiyama and Yoshitaka Komatsu have never failed to provide invaluable encouragement and support. Great benefit has resulted from the critical reading of the work by Margaret Lamb, Norio Tamaki and Oswald Wynd. From Kamakura, Seibi Ota has proved a devoted researcher into the ways and work of the Japanese Red Cross which he has served for forty years. At Nihombashi, Tokyo, Kenichi Matsumoto, the chairman of Sakura Fine Technical Co. Ltd., has provided otherwise unobtainable information on the manufacture of sophisticated artificial legs, arms and eyes by his company in Japan during the Russo–Japanese War of 1904–5. In Edinburgh, James McEwan has kindly made available his unpublished diaries as a prisoner of war at Ohama, Japan. In Surrey, Veronica Marchbanks has diligently trawled the British Red Cross archives at Barnett Hill for references to Japan. In Geneva, Florianne Truninger has patiently combed the archives of the *Comité International de la Croix–Rouge*, to which direct access is not permitted, in response to a stream of enquiries. In Washington, where all Red Cross material between 1881 and 1946 is kept in the National Archives, Tab Lewis has searched carefully for material which might be relevant. In Brantwood, Tennessee, Margaret Duffy of the American Red Cross, who served in Japan, has provided much help on 'voluntaryism'. In Glasgow Isabel and Bill Burnside have transformed the written word into an impeccable typescript. My thanks to them all.

Cambridge, England   OLIVE CHECKLAND
Cellardyke, Fife, Scotland

Author's Note

Japanese names are rendered with given name followed by family name.

Dates are in Western style.

List of Abbreviations

AAMC	Australian Army Medical Corps
AIF	Australian Imperial Force
ARC	American Red Cross Society
ASJ	Asiatic Society of Japan
BRC	British Red Cross Society
ICRC	International Committee of the Red Cross, Geneva
IJA	Imperial Japanese Army
IJN	Imperial Japanese Navy
IMS	Indian Medical Service
JAS	*Journal of Asian Studies*
JRAMC	*Journal of the Royal Army Medical Corps*
JRC	Japanese Red Cross Society
JSL	*Japan Society of London* (now *Japan Society*) *Proceedings and Transactions*
MD	Doctor of Medicine
MM	Military Medal
MN	*Monumenta Nipponica*
NAGC	National Archives Gift Collection, Washington, USA, for American National Red Cross Records pre-1946
POW	Prisoner of war
RA	Royal Artillery
RAF	Royal Air Force
RAMC	Royal Artillery Medical Corps
REME	Royal Electrical and Mechanical Engineers
RN	Royal Navy
R Sigs	Royal Signals
SSUF	Straits Settlements United Force
USSR	Union of Soviet Socialist Republics

Chronology of Humanitarianism and the Japanese Red Cross

Japan   *Elsewhere*

1859   Battle of Solferino, observed by horrified Henri Dunant.

1862   Henri Dunant published *Souvenirs de Solferino.*

1863   United States Army, General Order No.100 Instructions for the Government of Armies of the United States in the Field, 'Francis Lieber's Code', 24 April 1863

Red Cross Society founded, Geneva Committee for the relief of wounded soldiers, 1 September.

1864   First Geneva Convention for wounded and sick on land.

1867   Paris Exposition Red
Cross display seen and
admired by Tsunetami
Sano.

                          1868   St Petersburg
Declaration on
Prohibited Weapons.

                          1870   London, National
Society for aid to the
sick and wounded in
war, founded; later
British Red Cross.

1873   Vienna Exhibition,
Red Cross display seen
and admired by
Tsunetami Sano,
Tomomi Iwakura and
Hirobumi Ito visited
Red Cross in Geneva.

                          1874   Brussels Conference,
Rules of Military
Warfare, draft code
prepared.

                          1876   10 February, title
'International
Committee of the
Red Cross' (ICRC)
adopted.

1877   *Hakuaisha*, precursor
of Red Cross Society in
Japan (hereafter JRC)
established during
Satsuma Rebellion to
assist casualties of both
sides on battlefield.

		1880	Institute of International Law's Manual of the Laws of War on land, 'The Oxford Manual'.
		1881	American Red Cross Society founded.
1886	15 November. Japan adhered to the Geneva Convention.		
1887	2 September. The Society was recognised by the ICRC. The Red Cross Voluntary Women's Service Corps was organised.		
1888	15 July. JRC Medical Teams sent for relief of sufferers after eruption of Mt Bandai, Japan.		
1890	1 April. JRC Nurse training started.		
1892	17 June. The JRC Central Hospital in Tokyo was opened.		
1894	Medical teams were dispatched to aid sick and wounded in the Sino–Japanese War.	1894–5	Sino–Japanese War, 17 April 1895; Treaty of Shimonoseki ended war.
		1899	1st Hague Conference on Peace and Disarmament, Conventions, agreed;

	Land War Regulations and Declarations.
1904	JRC Medical Teams sent to Asian mainland to aid sick and wounded in the Russo–Japanese War. 70 000 Russian POWs in Japan well treated. 175 artificial eyes, arms and legs provided by Japanese for Russian prisoners of war.
1904–5	Russo–Japanese War September 1905; Treaty of Portsmouth, USA, ended war.
1906	18 April. International Relief Activities of the JRC on the occasion of the San Francisco earthquake.
1906–7	2nd Geneva Convention, Wounded and Sick on land and sea.
1907	Red Cross International Conference, London.
1907	2nd Hague Peace Conference, Conventions and Land War Regulations.
1909	London Conference, Declaration on the Rules of Naval Warfare.
1912	HM The Empress Shoken contributed ¥100 000 to the International Red Cross. The National Headquarters moved to the present site.
1912	Red Cross Societies, International Conference, Washington.

		1913	9 August, Oxford Manual on Naval War.
1914–18	5000 Germans held as prisoners or internees in Japan, well treated.		
1915–17	During the First World War Japanese Red Cross teams were dispatched to Russia, England and France.		
1919	Japan, one of five founding members of League of Red Cross Societies.	1919	May, League of Red Cross Societies, federation of all National Societies, formed, now called International Federation of Red Cross and Red Crescent Societies.
1920	The first Florence Nightingale Medals were awarded to three JRC nurses.		
1922	The first Junior Red Cross formed in Shiga Prefecture. Relief works for Polish refugees organised.		
1923	1 September. The great earthquake took place in the Kanto Area causing casualties of about 140 000, JRC teams involved.	1923	The Hague Rules for Aerial Warfare.

1925   Geneva Gas Warfare
        Protocol.

1926   The Second Oriental
        Red Cross
        Conference was held in
        Tokyo.

1929   Geneva Conventions
        on Sick and wounded
        on land and sea,
        POWs in War
        (September).

1931   Manchurian
        Incident.

1933   Japan left the League
        of Nations.

1934   October. The 15th   1934   Large gathering of
        International   Red Cross luminaries
        Conference of the Red   from all major
        Cross Movement was   nations, an
        held in Tokyo.   impressive publicity
                                          scoop for Japan.

1930s   During these years,
        despite appearance or
        normality, Japanese
        Red Cross had been
        subverted by the
        military authorities
        into working primarily
        for them.

1937   Invasion of China by
        Japan, always known
        as the 'China Incident'.

1941	The Pacific War broke out and the Society 'made every possible effort in medical relief'.	1941	7 or 8 December, Pearl Harbor attack. USA in war with Allies, including Britain and China against Axis powers of Germany, Italy and Japan.

1941–45   Nearly 200 000 Allied POWs (American, Australian, British, Canadian, Dutch and New Zealanders) held in deplorable conditions throughout Japanese-held East Asia; incidence of brutality high, as were casualties. Other Asiatics cruelly treated although some co-operated with Japanese hoping to benefit from Greater Asia Co-Prosperity Sphere which Japan planned for the region.

Some 15 000 Japanese POWs held in New Zealand and Australia. From Featherston, NZ and from Cowra, NSW, the Japanese prisoners organised suicidal camp outbreaks; many POWs died.

		1945	6 and 9 August, atomic bombs dropped by Americans on Hiroshima and Nagasaki, Japan.

1945   6 and 9 August, atomic bombs dropped by Americans on Hiroshima and Nagasaki, Japan.

15 August, Emperor broadcast to the nation, war ended.

2 September, surrender signed, USS Missouri in Tokyo Bay.

1946   The New Statutes of the Society were made.

1946–8   Tokyo War Trials.

1947   The Junior Red Cross was reorganised and the Red Cross Volunteer Service Corps were organised. Water Safety Course was restarted.

1948   First Aid and Home Nursing Courses were started.

1949   4th Geneva Conventions, included wounded and sick on land and at sea, also prisoners and civilians.

1952   April. The first Red Cross Blood Bank was opened in Tokyo.

August. The Society's
Law was enacted.

1953 Repatriation of
Japanese nationals
. from the Soviet Union
and China was started
by the Society.

1956 ICRC draft rules for
the protection of
civilians.

1959 Repatriation of
Koreans in Japan to
the Democratic
People's Republic of
Korea was started by
the Society.

1960 Aug.–Nov. A Japanese
medical team was
dispatched to the
Congo, for the first
time after the Pacific
War.

1963 Jul.–Aug. 'Konnichiwa
'70', Technical Seminar
for the South East
Asian and Pan-Pacific
Region in the Field of
Red Cross Youth was
held.

1968 International Year of
Human Rights,
Secretary General
begins enquiry into
'Human Rights' in
armed conflicts.

1971 10 October. HM the
Emperor and HM the
Empress, Hon. Pres. of

the Japanese Society,
visited the ICRC,
Geneva.

1972   1 April. Mrs Sachiko
Hashimoto,
ex-Director of Junior
Red Cross Department
of the Society, was
awarded the Henry
Dunant Medal.

1974–7   Geneva Diplomatic
Conference for the
Re-affirmation and
Development of the
Law of Armed
Conflict.

1975   3 October. HM the
Emperor and HM the
Empress, Hon. Pres. of
the Society, visited the
American National
Red Cross,
Washington.

1979   Diplomatic
Conference at
Geneva on
Prohibited Weapons.

HOKKAIDO

.Sapporo

Hakodate

Aomori

Akita

HONSHU ISLAND

Yamagata

Niigata

Nagano

Toyama

Tsuruga
Fukui
Shiga
Toltoii
Gifu
.Kyoto
Shizuoka

Tokyo

Aichi

Okayama
Osaka
Nara
Hiroshima
Yamaguchi
Kagawa
Wakayama
Matsuyama Tokushima
Saga Oita
Kochi SHIKOKU
Nagasaki KYUSHU
Kumamoto

Kagoshima
Miyazaki

Okinawa

N

Locations underlined had
Red Cross Hospitals by 1911

0   500 km

Map 1 Japan, 1877–1977

Part I

Establishing the Emperor's Credentials

1 The Red Cross in Japan

OF BATTLEFIELDS, BARBARITY AND BENEVOLENCE

The date, 24 September 1877; the scene, a battlefield[1] near Kagoshima, in south-west Japan, where a rebel army was facing the newly conscripted imperial army. The rebels, indifferently armed, were variously attired, traditionally in the fearsome array of a *samurai* warrior, or contemporaneously in a motley arrangement of various items of western uniform. The Emperor's well-armed soldiers were neatly kitted out in modern soldierly gear and, disciplined and trained as they were, they routed, for the last time, a *samurai* army from the field.

After the carnage was over, in one part of the bloody arena the wounded leader Takamori Saigo,[2] was himself committing *seppuku*,[3] following which his head was severed and buried by a faithful retainer. Elsewhere, others were endeavouring to succour the wounded, whether rebel[4] or not, in the spirit of *Hakuaisha*,[5] or Humanity Society, the precursor of the Red Cross Society in Japan, which had just been formed.

The inconsistency and irreconcilability of these two positions, the old *bushido* and the new humanity, is the theme of this work. For many years from 1877, humanitarianism in Japan was in the ascendant, only to be routed by the old barbarism during the Pacific War of 1941–45.

Takamori Saigo, the rebel leader, became, in after years, the Great Saigo who, gaining nobility from failure, was judged to have fought for, and never betrayed, his *samurai* principles. Even during the period when the humanitarian work of the Japanese Red Cross Society (JRC) was in the ascendant, Saigo, as a national hero, was pardoned in 1891, for his rebellion, and his more than life-size statue stands proudly to this day in Ueno Park not far from the Yasukuni[6] National shrine for the war dead in Tokyo.

HENRI DUNANT AND THE RED CROSS

The first humanitarian intervention had come nearly twenty years earlier in Europe when, on Midsummer Day 1859, Henri Dunant[7]

3

(1829–1910), a Swiss citizen, had cried, 'Tutti Fratelli' ('Brothers All') as he helped the citizens of Castiglione in north Italy tend the wounded, whether they were 'friends', in this case Italians or French, or 'enemies', Austrians, after the battle of Solferino. Henri Dunant, eager to seek an interview with the French Commander-in-Chief, Louis Napoleon, found himself at the battlefield where he was not only horrified at the carnage – 38 000 men were killed or wounded within the space of 15 hours[8] – but overwhelmed by the inhumanity of leaving casualties to suffer and to die where they had fallen. As a result, he wrote *A Memory of Solferino* (1862),[9] copies of which circulated widely throughout Europe.

It was the introduction of large national armies and of compulsory military service which, together with the ever-increasing destructiveness of weapons, had led to a terrible escalation in the scale of war. These factors inspired those in Europe and in America who felt that some concerted effort must be made 'to *restrain* the destructive force of war'.[10]

Thus associations were formed in several countries to assist the wounded in time of war. The first Red Cross conference was held in Geneva in October 1963 at which thirty-one European delegates, including Dr W. Rutherford,[11] Inspector General of Hospitals of Great Britain, attended. At a meeting on 20 December 1875, the Geneva Committee of the Red Cross adopted the name The International Committee of the Red Cross. On 18 September 1888 the motto *Inter arma caritas*, 'caring between armies', was first adopted. The Cross is a Christian[12] image but it is also the symbol of the neutrality of Switzerland, and a white cross on a red background (as distinct from the Red Cross on a white background) is the Swiss flag.

The struggle to restrain the Gods of War and ensure reasonable treatment for its casualties had another aspect, relating to medical services on the battlefield. During the Crimean War (1854–6), when the British and the French challenged the Russians over their attempted push for a Mediterranean outlet, the work of Florence Nightingale[13] and her associates was widely publicised. Facilities for dealing with wounded and sick soldiers, fighting in areas far from home, were, despite conscientious medical officers, woefully inadequate. Thus in the Crimea, as elsewhere in war, unsatisfactory conditions guaranteed heavy casualties from disease, rather than battle. The intrusion of Nightingale and a group of female medical auxiliaries into the battle zone, and the military hospitals behind the lines, marked a revolution in expectations for the common soldier. The legendary 'lady with the lamp', an angel of mercy, was more than an important symbol, for she brought relief and good health to thousands who would otherwise have perished.

In Britain the National Society for Aid to the Sick and Wounded in War, which shortly afterwards became the Red Cross Society,[14] was formed in the summer of 1870 in response to the outbreak of the Franco–German War. In the United States the Red Cross Society[15] was founded in 1881 by Clara Barton who had herself, as a relief worker, experienced the horrors of the aftermath of battle during the American Civil War of 1861–4.

HUMANITARIANISM IN JAPAN

On 1 July 1859 (when, in Italy, Henri Dunant was at the battle of Solferino), in Japan, William Keswick[16] (of the trading house Jardine Matheson) was landing with a small group of Western merchants at Yokohama, a small purpose built treaty port south of Tokyo. The permanent intrusion of Westerners into Tokyo Bay, within a few miles of the centre of the Shogun's capital, broke the seclusion by which Japan had kept herself isolated from the rest of the world. The arrival of the Westerners in three Japanese ports, Yokohama, Nagasaki and Hakodate, signalled the end of the bankrupt Shogunate.

Some Japanese had already become sensitive to changing attitudes in Europe. As early as 1867 Tsunetami Sano[17] had noticed a display publicising Red Cross ideas at the Great Exhibition in Paris. Later he saw, and other members of the Iwakura Mission had also seen, other Red Cross publicity at the Vienna exhibition in 1873.[18] At the same time, between 29 June and 15 July 1873,[19] during their visit to Switzerland, Tomomi Iwakura, the leader of the Japanese Mission to America and Europe, and Hirobumi Ito had visited the Red Cross in Geneva where it was reported that the Japanese ambassadors 'paid serious attention to the explanations which we had provided, during several successive meetings', and 'accepted the presentation of our publications'.[20] Aimé Humbert (acting for the Japanese) wrote a letter explaining the Japanese position (Neuchâtel, 20 September 1873) saying that the Japanese Army was modelled on European lines and that each regiment had surgeons and ambulances and that a Sanitary Corps was being formed. M. Humbert argued that 'the time was propitious for the Mikado to adhere to the principles of the Convention at Geneva'.[21]

As a result of Ito and Iwakura's interest Tsunetami Sano was requested to take responsibility for the introduction of humanitarian ideas to Japan. The opportunity for action came in 1877 when, during the South West rebellion of that year, the *Hakuaisha* Society was established, probably through doctors working on the battlefield, and some succour was given to wounded men. Out of this came the JRC which was re-organised in 1886, and later recognised by the Red Cross in Geneva. What is remarkable is that Japan should embrace Western humanitarianism, based as it was on Western ethics and Christian values, in defiance of the old *samurai* code of battlefield behaviour.

IDEAS BEHIND HUMANITARIANISM

In Europe there was much discussion of humanitarian ideas. Henry Dunant,[22] the original founder and inspirator of the Red Cross, was forced to wander, penniless, around Europe, for his business ventures had proved disastrous, and had plunged him irretrievably into debt. In Geneva, Gustave Moynier, a lawyer by training who had worked for the Geneva Society for Public Welfare, took over the leadership of the burgeoning Red Cross movement.

At a philosophical level Jean Jacques Rousseau had discussed the pursuit of war, writing in 1762,

> The object of war being the destruction of the enemy State, one has the right to kill its defenders only when they have weapons in their hands; but immediately they put them down and surrender, thus ceasing to be enemies or agents of the enemy, they once more become ordinary men and one no longer has any right to their life. Sometimes one can extinguish a State, without killing a single member of it; moreover, war confers no right other than that which is necessary for its purpose. These principles are not those of Grotius . . . but they flow from the nature of things and are founded upon reason.[23]

Rousseau's reference to Hugo Grotius is particularly apposite because in his famous work, *Justice in Peace and War* (*De Jure Belli et Pacis*) of 1625, he had explained that for practical purposes it is the fate of prisoners of war (POWs) to be treated as slaves. Japanese behaviour towards their prisoners of war between 1941 and 1945 reflected these old ideas.

But Rousseau's brave words were not easy to interpret; do surrendered enemy personnel become neutral? How then can neutrality be defined? How can neutral elements on the battlefield be protected? It was a German American jurist, Francis Lieber,[24] who took the lead in producing a remarkable statement, which gained widespread recognition, in defining the conduct of war for the Americans during the Civil War. 'Lieber's Code' was issued as 'Instruction for the Government of Armies of the United States in the Field'.[25] Lieber had a special personal concern as three of his sons were involved in the fighting, two in the north on the Union side and one, who was killed, in the south, for the Confederate army.

Lieber's definitions were carefully worded and precise: 'a prisoner of war is a public enemy armed or attached to the hostile army for active aid, who has fallen into the hands of the captor, either fighting or wounded, on the field or in hospital, by individual surrender or by capitulation' (Article 49). This is elaborated (in Article 56): 'A prisoner of war is subject to no punishment for being a public enemy, nor is any revenge wreaked upon him by the intentional infliction of any suffering, or disgrace, by cruel imprisonment, want of food, by mutilation, death or any barbarity.' Even so, as Article 59 makes clear, 'All prisoners of war are liable to the infliction of retaliatory measures.' To sum up, in Article 76, the Code states that the POW is to be 'fed upon plain and wholesome food whenever practicable, and treated with humanity'.[26]

In Europe at the Brussels Conference on the proposed rules for Military Warfare (1874) (convened at the request of Russia, as was the conference of 1899) further clarification was attempted: 'prisoners of war are not criminals but lawful enemies. They are in the power of the enemy's government, but not of the individuals or of the corps who made them prisoners, and should not be subjected to any violence or ill-usage.'[27]

THE PRISONER OF WAR

The Red Cross movement, already conservative, was at this time only concerned with the wounded on the battlefield; it refused to involve itself with the war prisoners.

In 1899, under the personal guidance of Tsar Nicholas II, The Hague Peace Conference attempted to consider all matters relating to 'the laws and customs of war on land'. The Convention agreed 'detailed provisions for the treatment of prisoners of war reflecting the more humane ideas prevailing at that time and in particular the idea that they should be treated in a manner analogous to that of the troops of the Detaining Power'.[28] This was the first time anybody had outlined a formula for dealing with this difficult problem. It was on the basis of these arrangements that the Japanese cared for the Russian POWs between 1904 and 1905. The 4th Hague Convention of 1907, which largely re-stated the early Convention, applied to prisoners of war during the First World War and remained in force until 1929.

THE RED CROSS IN JAPAN

On 6 June 1886 Japan became a fully recognised member of the Red Cross movement, an astonishingly precocious act for a nation which thirty years earlier had been effectively closed to the outside world. Elsewhere in Asia, Siam, the only other independent Asian nation, ratified on 29 June 1895, Korea, by then effectively a Japanese colony, on 8 January 1903, and China on 29 June 1904.

There seems no doubt that Japanese involvement with the Red Cross was seen as a form of legitimation. In a world which seemed, to the Japanese, discriminatory, the recognition by the Red Cross movement of Japan as an equal had a special significance. It was 'a standard early sign of statehood',[29] and brought an extraordinary and disproportionate response. The fact that this was a humanitarian endeavour designed to ease the horrors of war was in one sense irrelevant. Even so, within twenty years nearly 70 000 Russian prisoners of war were to benefit from the benevolence of the Japanese at war (see Chapter 5 below).

It must also be emphasised that the JRC was not a society made up of volunteers, as were other Red Cross Societies in Europe and America. As one distinguished Japanese scholar has explained,

> the Meiji government, eager to bring the universal conscription system into effect, contrived to supplement compulsory enlistment by persuading both females and males who were not to join the army or navy to be members of the Red Cross in order to contribute to the success of the imperial objectives. Accordingly, local public service employees as well as local bosses were urged to persuade as many householders as possible to be members of the

Red Cross. It is possible that the association of army reservists may have participated in the canvassing. Ordinary members of the Red Cross were assured that these membership fees were an important contribution.[30]

The Society in Japan was not immediately successful. A programme of development was worked out 'in concert with the Minister of War' which postulated a membership of 100 000, or one member from every 400 Japanese. With this level of membership, and the subscriptions which would accrue, the authorities were confident that they would have sufficient funds. There was some increase in the membership when, in 1888, Mount Bandai (in Japan) erupted; the Empress, urged on by Sano, agreed that the Japanese Red Cross should assist the casualties and clear up the damage and so act as a national relief organisation. The outbreak of the Sino–Japanese War in 1894 provided further stimulus as patriotic Japanese rushed to join and the membership, 36 700 in 1893, swelled by 1895 to 160 000 members, each of whom paid at least 3 yen per year.

There were three categories of members: regular, special and honorary. As it was reported, 'each of them is given a distinctive medal, awarded with the Imperial sanction, which the recipients are permitted to wear on public occasions just as much as other Imperial decorations'.[31] By 1903 the Japanese Society was the largest in the world, with 900 000 Red Cross members, and a total income of almost 3 million yen. By October 1913 membership stood at 1 620 530, of which 67 768 were women and 17 187 were foreigners.[32]

The JRC was highly organised, authoritarian and centrally controlled. Unlike Societies elsewhere, where local autonomy was considered important, in Japan

the Local Sections formed in the prefectures have no separate existence, but are entirely subject to the will and control of the central governing body in all that concerns the finance and work of preparation and relief in time of war. The chief business of the Local Sections is the recruiting of the members and the gathering of the subscriptions but the income so obtained is taken to the central treasury . . . A portion of the personnel and supplies of the Society is provided for in the provinces but is entirely at the disposal of the headquarters, and no relief of the sick and wounded in time of war or political disturbance can be carried out unless under the control and guidance of the governing body in Tokyo.[33]

It is true that business was transacted at the General Assembly which was held in Ueno Park before an audience of some 30 000 to 40 000 members. But on these occasions all measures were carried 'by acclamation'.[34] In this way the Standing Committee of 30 members was quickly re-elected especially as 'almost the same names appear in the list from year to year with occasional and isolated changes caused by death or absence'. The Standing Committee was the governing body which elected '8 Administrators of whom one is President and 2 are Vice-Presidents'. These officials were the decision makers of the JRC.

Count Tsunetami Sano remained as President until his death in 1902. The new President was Count Masayoshi Matsukata,[35] whose wife had long been one of the active members of the Ladies' Committee of the Red Cross. His appointment, however, had little to do with his wife, for Matsukata was appointed because of his financial skills. He had been made Minister of Finance in 1881 at a time of serious financial crisis in Japan. His distinction as a finance minister rested on the unpalatable financial measures which he had initiated, and which had caused much hardship in Japan in the 1880s, but from which the country emerged with a strong currency in the 1890s.

The Red Cross Society was not financially stable in 1902 when Matsukata took over the leadership; its income was modest and its outgoings high. Despite the generous support provided by the Emperor and the contributions of its large membership, the Society did not have the resources to fund a major effort in time of war. Thanks to Matsukata's efforts the financial position of the Red Cross was greatly improved. Is it fanciful to suppose that he had been assigned to the post to establish the financial stability of the Red Cross in anticipation of the Russo–Japanese war?

The climax of Japan's humanitarian effort came during the Russo–Japanese War when Japan, with nearly 70 000 Russian war prisoners in her care, did treat them with fairness and humanity. Medical units of the JRC served for long periods nursing sick and wounded Russians. Observers from many countries noted with satisfaction the demonstration of Japanese humanitarianism in action. The Russian authorities, themselves astonished at Japanese care of their men, sent a large contribution to the JRC as a token of their appreciation.

After the First World War there was a struggle in Japan between those who held the new outward-looking ideas and the traditionalists who had always been suspicious of Japan's headlong rush into the modern world. Over a period of several years it became clear that those who believed in the old values, especially in the military, were steadily strengthening their hold on government. Japan was involved with the Red Cross from 1886; and as one of the great powers she signed, on 27 July 1929, both Conventions, dealing with sick and wounded and prisoners of war. That which related to POWs was never ratified.

The wars with which Japan was involved, from the 1930s through to the Pacific War which culminated in defeat in August 1945, revealed a terrible and brutal side of the Japanese. High standards of humanity in war, which the Japanese earlier had espoused so eagerly, were abandoned. Indeed the international aspect of JRC work fell into decay. In the aftermath, during the occupation of Japan by the Americans, the JRC was rehabilitated, largely by the devoted service by members of the American Red Cross Society (ARC). The Americans were particularly keen to introduce the idea of volunteers, who commit themselves of their own volition to the Red Cross, and so take their share of responsibility for the integrity of the movement.

The principles of the Red Cross, proclaimed again at the twentieth international conference in Vienna in 1965, are humanity, impartiality, neutrality, independence, unity, universality and voluntary service.

In the light of these objectives it is clear that Japan herself benefited from the impartiality and lack of discrimination practised by the Red Cross as an international organisation. The JRC, before 1930, did try to think in terms of humanity and universality, and was much praised for generous behaviour in time of war. But it was never independent and was always subject to the will of government: in effect, a state agency. Prior to 1945 a coercive Japanese state determined the response of the Red Cross Society. Humanitarianism in time of war was approved as official policy during the Russo–Japanese War (1904–5). During the 1930s, and the build-up to the Pacific War, humanitarianism was abandoned. That the Japanese should have such control over its people might astonish Westerners unfamiliar with the discipline, or conformism, which is even now the hallmark of the Japanese people. The JRC, effectively destroyed during the Pacific War, was re-created after 1945, partly on the American model.

2 The 'Emperor's Children': Army and Navy Health Care

A STATE OF PREPAREDNESS

Because the Emperor was said to depend on his 'children'[1] under arms for the maintenance of the independence and security of Japan, the soldier or sailor was, by 1890, taught, that 'his body is a fighting machine which is the property of his Emperor'.[2] Humanitarian concern was self-interested: sick soldiers and sailors were a danger and a liability.

In time of peace physical health had to be maintained and improved, and serious consideration given to the provision of nutritious food and pure water. In time of war supplies had to be ensured, first aid units, stretcher bearers and field hospitals made ready and, in the newest development, hospital ships or hospital trains prepared to handle the inevitable casualties.

Europeans had long known of the high costs, in terms of sickness and of lives lost, which were inevitable when military, or civilian, personnel were sent to live and work in climates other than their own.[3] Europeans and Americans readily fell victim to tropical diseases while they in their turn brought their own killer diseases to the people of the tropics. Until the twentieth century it was an inevitable cost that more fighting men were killed by disease than in battle. The Russo–Japanese War of 1904–5 was the first war in which more men died in battle, or later from their wounds, than died of disease.

The intellectual curiosity of the Age of Enlightenment, at the end of the eighteenth century, encouraged army medical officers to keep records of diseases as they affected the men in their care. This increased interest reflected, following the French revolution, the beginnings of humanitarian concern. It was also the case that pensions had to be paid to the dependants of those who died of disease on active service as well as those who died in battle.

12

Increasingly, especially in the British and the French armies, statistics were kept and research was undertaken, which built up a valuable body of information on the impact of disease on the men.[4]

Japanese medical military personnel became aware of these important matters when studying in Germany, France or in England. In the late nineteenth century they shared in research into serious infections, whether affecting civilian or military personnel, and were naturally anxious to transfer their knowledge to Japan.[5]

Despite the lessons about health and hygiene, supposedly taught by Florence Nightingale[6] during the Crimean War (1854–6), during the South African War (1899–1902) the British army suffered terrible losses from disease, impure water and bad food. The Americans[7] were humiliated, before a shot was fired, both during the Spanish–American War, in Cuba and Puerto Rico (1898), and in the Philippine campaigns of 1899, by having thousands of casualties behind the lines, from bad food and water. The major Japanese problem, in addition to those common to soldiers and sailors in the West, proved to be the incidence of beri-beri, which was later discovered to be a deficiency disease, due to the inadequacy of a rice diet.

It should be noted that information about Japanese preparedness in these matters comes not only from Japanese research papers, but also from American and British commentators. Dr Louis Livingston Seaman,[8] a former American army surgeon, in *From Tokio through Manchuria with the Japanese* (1905) and *The Real Triumph of Japan* (1906) spelt out what he saw as the Japanese achievement. The British Red Cross nurse Ethel McCaul,[9] and her friend Nurse Elaine St. Aubyn, who were shown war-time hospital Japanese arrangements in Japan and on the Asian mainland during the Russo–Japanese War, were also greatly impressed.

INFECTIOUS DISEASE

The military medical services, by utilising generally available measures to improve hygiene and by new ways of combating individual diseases, succeeded between the 1890s and 1914 in producing 'the steepest percentage decline of the whole century in the death rate of soldiers at home and abroad'.[10]

Although many intractable problems remained, medical science was making enormous strides. Malaria[11] (still a killer disease today in the tropics) had since the 1840s been controllable, but not curable, by the use of quinine. By the late 1890s medical research work had proved beyond doubt that malaria was transmitted by various sorts of mosquitoes. Thereafter attempts were made to destroy the mosquitoes and their breeding grounds, although the hundreds of species of the insect made this operation difficult.

Tuberculosis,[12] until the 1950s and the discovery of sulphonomides, was difficult to cure. Military personnel suffering with TB might benefit from the warmer climate when sent overseas; this, in modern parlance became known as 'relocation benefit'. Other pulmonary diseases were difficult both to diagnose correctly and to cure.

Diseases like cholera, discovered in 1849 to be water borne, were researched by Robert Koch in Germany who, in 1883, succeeded in isolating *Vibrio cholerae*. It is worth noting that Shibasaburo Kitazato (1853–1931),[13] working with Koch in Germany between 1885 and 1891, achieved a breakthrough, in 1892, in isolating the bacterium which causes tetanus, *Clostridium tetani*. Japanese bacteriological research was thereafter significant and sustained. Other 'common waterborne intestinal infections' included many kinds of dysentery, including ameobic, and diarrhoea. In 1898 Kiyoshi Shiga[14] was successful in isolating one of the bacilli responsible for capillary dysentery, this first example now being known as *shigella*. Drugs such as ipecacuanha were effective but it was even better to have pure water and proper sewers.

Typhoid fever, typhus and other fevers were classed as 'continuous' fevers, rather than 'paroxysmal', like malaria. *Typhosus* was identified by Karl Joseph Eberth in 1880. In army terms, a campaign to provide clean water had succeeded in increasing awareness of hygiene, although these diseases remained dangerous until proper waste disposal systems were installed. Venereal diseases were another category which exercised army doctors although deaths from syphilis and gonorrhea, in the early stages, were rare. The success of the efforts against infectious disease grew out of improved scientific knowledge which allowed the development of more effective treatment.

The measure of an army's anticipation of the hazards of a military campaign rests on the probable number of fatalities from disease set against those from the enemy's bullets. Dr Seaman claimed that the Spanish–American campaign in Cuba was 'a ghastly tragedy' and that 14 men died from disease for each 'who died a soldier's death on the field of honour'. He believed that the Japanese lost 'four men killed by bullets to one who dies from disease'.[15] How did an army achieve such extraordinary progress?

In the case of the Imperial Japanese Navy (IJN), with sailors isolated on board ship infectious disease should be more easily controlled, but shore leave and confined space created their own problems. The Japanese navy used vaccination to keep smallpox (then endemic in Vladivostok, Russia and Korea) at bay, and they also inoculated against typhoid fever. Their main method of control was the use of quarantine stations, established under naval authority at Sasebo and Maizuru naval bases. Except during time of battle and the immediate preparation for engagement, hospital ships cruised around the fleet almost daily, taking off officers and ratings suspected of having contracted infectious disease. Venereal disease was also prevalent in the IJN although men on naval vessels could be cured by abstention.

THE MEDICAL SURGEON IN ARMY AND NAVY

In Japanese terms, in the late nineteenth century, the army doctor had three main functions: to select recruits by physical examination, to preserve their health and to care for the sick and wounded. Ideally he required the expertise of a sanitary inspector, the diagnostic skills of a general practitioner, the careful precision of a surgeon, as well as high grade scientific training which enabled him to operate as an infectious disease specialist, chemist, microscopist, x-ray operator, and – because insects like mosquitoes were known to spread disease – entomologist.[16] Clearly such a wide range of skills could hardly be covered by one man, but the Japanese did by 1904, during the Russo–Japanese war, have sufficient personnel available to organise some facilities in all these areas.

In the IJN, men lived in a controlled environment aboard ship in close proximity to one another and in conditions which were markedly dissimilar to those of the army on land. The underlying health problems may have been the same but because circumstances were so different the navy's response might differ from that of the army. Other differences – and tensions – arose because the Imperial Japanese Army (IJA) was modelled on German lines while the IJN looked to the British Royal Navy. Although the medical profession in Japan was generally inspired by German medicine, the first Director General of the Medical Department of the Imperial Japanese Navy before 1914, K. Takaki, was a Fellow of the Royal College of

Surgeons of England (1880), trained at St Thomas's hospital in London. It is certainly the case that the campaign to improve health in the navy, especially as regards diet, was markedly different from that instituted in the army.

PURE WATER

By the beginning of the twentieth century armies in the field understood the importance of securing a supply of either pure spring water, or of boiled water. A. B. Cottell, who had served in the Royal Army Medical Corps (RAMC) in the South African war also commented on the importance of 'preserving as pure as possible an already existing, fairly satisfactory source of supply' of water.[17] His argument was that it was of vital importance to take 'every possible sanitary precaution' and he stressed even more the need for every single individual to take all the known necessary precautions at all times.

Dr Cottell concluded his brief account of the action he took in South Africa with four recommendations. These were, 'to preserve immediately all existing good sources of water from contamination by men and animals, and to boil all water when possible and fill water bottles with tea whenever occasion permits'. In addition a non-commissioned officer, from the Royal Engineers, should be available at all times to check (with the medical officer) all sources of water 'and supervise the conservancy of existing supplies'.[18] Dr Cottell condemned water carts (as used by the British army in South Africa) for they often, he believed, harboured disease and were not thoroughly cleaned out. He advised that a reliable and trustworthy man should always be in charge of the water cart, be required to clean it out and to procure clean water whenever possible.

In the case of the Japanese army operating in northern China, in 1904–5, the discipline was severe. All local sources of water were scientifically tested by the medical officer's staff, then clearly labelled so that every man knew whether the supply was forbidden altogether or for drinking, food preparation, or washing only. One of the British attachés with the Japanese army in Manchuria in July 1905 commented on the way in which the water supply was labelled. He also noted sentries, 'always one of the Red Cross men',[19] being posted at wells which were on a highway or a public place. Boiling water kettles were used communally, not only for water but also for rice boiling; no doubt the rice water was also used for drinking.

The effectiveness of discipline (in the Russian as well as the Japanese army) over drinking water is shown in an instance recounted by Lieutenant Tadayoshi Sakurai who, while interrogating a dying Russian soldier during the siege of Port Arthur, responded to the Russian's request for a drink by handing him 'a glass of spring water'. The Russian declined it: 'There is boiled water in my bottle; give me that.' As Lieutenant Sakurai comments, 'I do not know whether this Russian ... disdained to receive a drink from the enemy, but I was struck with his carefulness in observing the rules of hygiene and not drinking unboiled water.'[20] Sakurai in his narrative refers frequently to the discomfort and suffering of soldiers unable to replenish their water bottles during the course of a battle. Louis Seaman claimed that each Japanese soldier had his own water kettle in which to boil emergency supplies. Sakurai emphasises rather more the intense thirst suffered by men at the front line.

The supply of pure water was partly dependent on the efficiency of the disposal of human excreta over which the army doctor had wide powers. The Japanese built model latrines behind the lines but inevitably, despite good intentions, conditions during active service soon deteriorated. Sakurai himself suffered from dysentery brought on by being 'drenched to the skin and chilled through and through ... excessive work night and day, the insufficiency of sleep and the drinking of the worst possible water'.[21] In this case there was a pause in the battle, so Sakurai and his comrades could be properly attended to; they recovered in time to take part in the continuing struggle. Sakurai's narrative is a useful corrective to Dr Seaman's uncritical praise.

Later, during the invasion of China in 1938, one exhausted Japanese soldier explained how he broke all the rules, writing: 'the water was muddy and filthy but I filled my water bottle and dosed it with the medicine with which we were issued and had a long drink. As a preventative I also took some creosote tablets, but I was so tired I was soon drinking the water without any precautions'.[22] In this way, in difficult circumstances, even the most conscientious soldiers broke the rules.

Sailors on their ships were usually provided with distilled water, produced in excess as steam by the engines. Normally therefore, unless they were severely bombarded or shipwrecked, the navy could rely on a good source of drinking water. The complicated logistic problems faced by the army in providing drinking water could apply to the navy in battle.

A RICE DIET

The Japanese were the first nation to present a modern army on the field of battle nurtured on a rice diet. Rice is a valuable food, easily digested, and as cooked, packaged and issued to Japanese soldiers, readily carried; but of itself it does not provide the variety of nutrients necessary to maintain good health. It was Vitamin B_1, thiamin,[23] which was missing, although at this time research had not isolated vitamins as essential elements of diet. During military campaigns, soldiers often survived on rice alone, without the accompaniment of vegetables and pickles to which they would normally have had access. This led to the occurrence of *Kak'ke*, a disease known elsewhere as beri-beri. *Kak'ke*, which had been known in Japan and elsewhere for centuries, could weaken many men simultaneously leaving Japanese army units dangerously depleted. It may have become even more damaging in Japan in the nineteenth century following the new custom of machine milling or polishing rice – brown rice normally retained its vitamin B_1, but the preferred white rice did not.[24]

Kak'ke took two forms, 'dry' and 'wet'. In the case of 'dry' beri-beri there was a degeneration of the nervous system and sufferers may have been diagnosed as having 'neuritis' or a 'disease of the nervous system' or even 'diseases of the brain'. 'Wet' beri-beri produced cardiovascular difficulties and a tender liver, but was chiefly characterised by dropsy or excessive retention of liquids.[25] The disease seriously incapacitated those affected and could cause death.

The devastating effects of *Kak'ke* sent Japanese army surgeons hurrying to their laboratories, for scientific research must be able to provide the answers as to why the rice diet was inadequate. One of those involved in this nutritional enquiry was Ogai Mori[26] (1862–1922) who, as a senior army doctor, worked in Germany on diet for the Japanese soldier.

Ogai Mori arrived in Berlin on 11 October 1884 and left Germany in the summer of 1888. He spoke excellent German and so was able to benefit greatly from his studies. He worked particularly on a study of the diet of Japanese soldiers, and knowing that in terms of cost a rice diet was essential, he argued in its favour. He noted that while barley might have a higher protein content it was more difficult than rice to digest. Ogai published in October 1886, in *Archiv fur Hygiene*, 'Uber die Kost der niponischem Soldaten' which argued these matters; much of the research was not his alone.

Later in Berlin (from April 1887) – where he found his fellow Japanese students dull and inward-looking – he worked with Robert Koch at the Hygienisches Institut of Berlin University. This work was making good progress until the appearance of his non-German speaking superior Ishiguro required Ogai to turn interpreter. In the autumn of 1887 Ogai was in attendance with Ishiguro at the Red Cross meeting at Karlsruhe which formally set up an international Red Cross body and he left Germany on 5 July 1888.

Despite the reservations of those who claimed that the 'Western' diet was disliked by Japanese and that moreover the addition of 'beef' was too expensive, the army diet did change. At the time of the Russo–Japanese war the British Red Cross (BRC) delegation, who had enjoyed the biscuits containing barley and seeds, noted that sacks of barley and rice, together with 'tinned meat, prepared vegetables and dried fish were on their way to the troops'.[27] One British military attaché recalled sitting watching Japanese engineers building a bridge in Manchuria when 'an officer gave me a cup of tea (he called it) made from roasted barley which his men drank as a preventative against berberi. It was a very palatable beverage.'[28]

It was in 1884 that the IJN was forced to recognise the inadequacies of the diet of naval seamen. During the Korean disturbances[29] of that year the problems in manoeuvring IJN ships became acute because many of the crew were incapacitated by *Kak'ke*. In February 1890 Navy Dietary Regulations were introduced which required naval personnel to eat the food provided as standard on board ship. Previously sailors had used their small money allowance to buy food as they wished.

The man who took it upon himself to enquire into the incidence of *Kak'ke* in the naval service was Dr K. Takaki[30] who was appointed in February 1882 to be Vice-Director of the medical department of the Navy. He had become a Fellow of the Royal College of Surgeons in England (FRCSE) in 1880 and had spent years in training in London during which he had become familiar with Western food. He came to believe that the sailors' diet, when on board ship, was deficient in protein, and over-rich in carbohydrates.

The urgency of the task became clear when in 1883 the Japanese warship *Ryujo* returned from a foreign tour of 271 days during which she had visited New Zealand and South America, calling at Wellington, Valparaiso, Callao and Honolulu. During the voyage, out of 350 men on board, over 100 had been seriously ill. Dr Takaki knew that he had never heard of cases of beri-beri occurring among the crews of ships of Western navies and that Japanese ships themselves, usually made in Europe or America, were identical with those of other navies. Therefore, if Japanese naval men lived and worked in conditions similar to those of the Royal Navy, the disease must be related to Japanese food.

He resolved to organise an experiment which would require a change in the seamen's diet. The *Tsukuba*[31] was sent on an identical voyage to that undertaken by the *Ryujo*; but the diet prescribed was no longer typically Japanese, as can be seen from Table 2.1.

The substitution of a Western style diet, including bread, beef and ships' biscuits, must have been unpopular with the naval ratings. As a later compromise, it became obligatory to mix barley grains with the rice and this proved to be more acceptable.

Table 2.1 Diet of naval ratings on board *Ryujo* and *Tsukuba, c.* 1883

	On board Ryujo (in grams)	*On board* Tsukuba (in grams)
Rice	782	648
Bread	–	600
Ships' biscuits	–	490
Fish	96	15
Beef	73	300
Vegetables	215	450
Milk		
Sugar	18	75
Miso (bean sauce)	16	50
Flour	–	75
Beans	–	45
Pickles	145	75

Source: L. L. Seaman, *The Real Triumph of Japan* (New York, 1906), p. 238.

The *Tsukuba* arrived at Honolulu with three cases of beri-beri on board, whereas the *Ryujo* had had 125. In all the *Tsukuba* had, throughout the journey, 16 cases of the disease while the *Ryujo*, with the unreformed rice diet, had had 160. It was a remarkable breakthrough for a naval medical officer, who could subsequently claim that ultimately the success of the IJN against the Russian fleets in the war of 1904–5 depended in part, at least, on his determination to rid the Japanese naval personnel of the scourge of beri-beri. It is now known that Dr Takaki's new diet was successful because of its variety, for it included the necessary – but at the time unrecognised – vitamins. The naval authorities noted that those other workers who were involved with seamen and ships, including shore workers, coolies, crews, boatmen and members of the Red Cross Relief Corps, who were not covered by the navy's Dietary Regulations, continued to fall ill from *Kak'ke* in considerable numbers.

FIELD HOSPITALS

Japanese field hospitals behind the lines were staffed either by the army medical corps or by Red Cross Units. The old tradition in Europe had been for the army surgeon to undertake operations immediately behind the battle lines, but with improved transport, hospital trains and ships could move casualties away from the front. The surgical revolution of the 1860s[32] had made operations on men who had serious wounds much more likely to succeed; and so it became common practice, once any fragments had been removed, to cover wounds with an aseptic dressing which was left in place while the patient was moved back to a base hospital.

There are two startlingly different accounts of field hospitals at the time of the Russo–Japanese war. A visiting BRC nurse wrote of a field hospital at Fang-hwang-cheng, before battle, and Lieutenant Sakurai reported on a first-aid station, after battle, near Taipo-shan.

As Miss McCaul writes:

On arrival we found that a temple had been appropriated and transformed into a temporary hospital, and with a few ingenious alterations it answered the purpose admirably being large, airy and clean ... In the wards all the patients looked extremely comfortable on so-called bedsteads, which were in reality iron stands at head and foot; down the centre were boards or stretched canvas to support the thickly-wadded mattress, while a round chaff pillow and scarlet blanket completed the bed.

A neat but simple wooden contrivance to suspend an ice bag over a patient was pleasing to see. Everywhere were beautifully arranged vases of wild flowers which, I was told gave more pleasure to those sturdy little soldiers than any amount of books. The vases were constantly replenished and the patients entered largely into the joy of arranging them. .... A wing or corner of this hospital was set apart for dysentery cases. The most stringent rules are observed and

every precaution taken . . . I saw one or two cases dressed and all
the orderlies were in white overalls . . . The operating table was of
iron and folded for packing . . . Dr Kimura showed me . . . many
clever things made by the instrument man, who is always attachéd to
the military hospitals, and is responsible for the sharpening and
repairing of instruments . . . Biscuit tins play an important part . . .
These are large, very much the same shape as those that strewed the
camping-grounds in Natal. Out of them are made . . . the following
articles, kettles, basins, pails, soiled dressing tins and appliances for
nursing as well as many culinary utensils . . . when worn out they
are carefully buried. The refuse which cannot be burned is treated in
like manner, this accounts for the scrupulous cleanliness of the
camps. Charcoal was used extensively for heating purposes, especially in the ingenious little stove invented for the steriliser . . . I had
only one regret that our army doctor had not been allowed to see all
this.[33]

Sakurai's account of the dressing station behind the lines but within
the range of Russian guns is rather different. As he explained:

While the fighting is going on the Red Cross flags here and there
beckon to those who are wounded on the field. The brave men who
die on the spot receive no benefit from the great charity but the
wounded receive and monopolize its benefits . . . As soon as a battle
begins, the stretcher-carriers go about the field with stretchers on
their shoulders, pick up the wounded and carry them to the first aid.
These coolies – or carriers – must be as brave and earnest as real
combatants, else they could not do their work in an extremely
dangerous place and moment. They are entrusted with the philanthropic and perilous business of braving sword and shot, searching
out the wounded and carrying them to a safe place. They must share
their scanty food and precious water with their patients, and must
take every possible care of them and comfort and cheer them with
loving hearts. The stretcher bearers' hard toil and noble work
deserve our unbounded gratitude.

as Sakurai continues,

In the summer when I took part in actual engagements, large
armies of flies attacked the wretched patients, worms would grow
in the mouth and nose, and some of them could not drive the

vermin away because their arms were useless. Hospital orderlies would fain have helped these poor sufferers, but their number was so small that there was only one of them to a hundred of the wounded. And the patients were exposed to the scorching sun in the day and to the rain or dew of the night without covering. Sometimes the patients, after lying long in the field, were in an indescribable condition, and it was necessary to soak them in a stream and scrub them with a broom before dressing their wounds. These horrors were solely due to an unexpectedly large number of casualties produced by the unforeseen severity of the fighting. Those in charge of the surgical work were eager to take care of all as quickly as possible . . .; but as they had to crowd more than 1,000 patients into a hospital intended for 200 they were powerless to give any better care to the sufferers.[34]

Is it unfair to contrast Miss McCaul's account of a field hospital with that of Sakurai's view of a first aid station? Yet both descriptions, demonstrating ideal and actual conditions, may be valid. The flowers in the field hospital were no doubt put there to please the Red Cross lady visitors from England. Sakurai also noticed flowers, writing, 'Here we had some green grass, and some lovable blossoms also smiled on us. We would pick these flowers and arrange them in empty shells or put them in our button-holes and enjoy their fragrance. The tiny blue forget-me-nots made us sometimes fly in imagination to our dear ones at home.'[35]

The marked difference between the foreign and the Japanese account can be explained to some extent. As Sakurai noted,

In a march for practice, or in a march in time of war, but not for an actual engagement, as much rest and as ample a supply of provisions as possible are allowed. But when we march to a fight, we go on even without food or water, or in spite of a heavy storm. Each soldier carries a knapsack about ten *kwan* [just over 82.5 lbs] in weight, and has only one bottleful of water to drink. When he has emptied it he cannot get one drop more.[36]

Lieutenant Sakurai, after he and his men had been engaged in battles to gain ground from the Russians, referred frequently to the emaciated condition of himself and his men. The stark contrast between preparations for war and war itself are a reminder that the foreign commentators were never actually at the front.

HOSPITAL SHIPS

The provision of hospital ships,[37] a logical development of medical care, remained, in humanitarian terms, controversial. In 1868 it was agreed that military hospital ships 'remain subject to the laws of war' and 'become the property of the captor',[38] thus denying them any protection. In 1899, at the Peace Conference in The Hague, hospital ships were given the status of being 'neutral' vessels, not subject to capture by the enemy. Three types, which should be painted white, with large Red Crosses on them, were recognised: those belonging to individual states, those equipped and despatched by private consortia and those maintained by the relief societies, that is the Red Cross.

It was during the Spanish–American War in 1898 that hospital ships were first used, following the agreement of the naval commanders on both sides to respect their neutrality. It was the ARC who were the pioneers, the ICRC writing to them (9 June 1898):

> We were very happy to learn . . . that thanks to the acceptance of the Additional Articles to the Geneva Convention you are preparing for naval activity. Your Society will thus be the first to have flown its flag at sea and the example it will set will inaugurate a new and fruitful era for the Red Cross. We would like to congratulate you.[39]

The ARC had three hospital ships in action, the *Moynier*, the *Red Cross* and the *State of Texas*.

The necessity for hospital ships, properly equipped and staffed, became clear to the Japanese during the course of the Sino–Japanese War of 1894–5 when casualties had to be transported from the battlefields in mainland China to Japan in poorly-modified mercantile vessels. The fatalities which resulted from these makeshift arrangements were sufficient to demonstrate that something better must be provided. The expense of such custom-built ships which would only be used in time of war was prohibitive for any national Red Cross Society: as a result the Japanese worked out an arrangement, between the shipping company, NYK, and the Red Cross which, based on a lease-lend arrangement, proved satisfactory to both parties.

Two ships, the *Hakuai Maru*[40] (of 2636 tons) and the *Kosai Maru* (of 2627 tons) were ordered (17 August 1897) by NYK, at a cost of £54000 each, from Lobnitz Shipyard at Renfrew on the Clyde, Scotland. They were made of steel, had electric light, two decks and a spar deck and were registered A1 at Lloyds.

The 'hospital ships' were used by NYK as ordinary cargo ships with the proviso that 'the moment they are called for by the Red Cross Society they are to be restored to their original form and colour'. Generally NYK were to be allowed 30 days in which to prepare the ship for Red Cross service 'but only seven days in time of war'.[41]

The new hospital ships were first used at the time of the Boxer rebellion in 1900, when they lay off Taku, flying the Red Cross flag. During this emergency the *Hakuai Maru* carried 1536 patients, making seven trips back to Japan, while the *Kosai Maru* also made seven journeys and carried 1523 patients.[42]

Each ship could accommodate 208 patients, 154 in 3rd class beds, 12 in 2nd class beds and 36 in 1st class beds, there were also six beds for those with contagious disease. The contrast between the space available for ordinary soldiers and their officers was striking. The 154 beds of the lowest class were contained in two wards, each containing 77 beds; these were in the form of two-tiered bunks fastened together in sets of 5, one up and one down. There did not appear to be any way in which nursing staff could reach the six innermost patients, except at their head and their feet. Washing facilities would appear to have been a hand-basin on a stand, but other basins may have been strategically placed within the ward although not immediately visible. It is worth noting that no bathrooms are listed in the accommodation of the ship. From the dishes and containers shown in the 3rd class ward it would seem that food was also served in this room. In contrast the 36 officers' 1st class beds were allocated eleven wards while there were three 2nd class wards taking four beds each.[43]

It was acknowledged that:

Service of relief in different parts of the ship was not equally easy, but the treating of patients in officers' wards and operating rooms, usually situated in the most comfortable parts of the vessel, was far more pleasant than service in dark ill-ventilated steerage and cargo rooms, so that it was not fair to make a set of Nurses and Attendants, do their work always in the same place. Hence a new allotment of service was made every two or three voyages'.[44]

During the course of the Russo–Japanese War the hospital ships *Hakuai Maru* and *Kosai Maru* were in great demand, constantly plying between the mainland war zone and Japan. During the course of 1904 and 1905 the *Hakuai Maru* made 52 voyages and the *Kosai Maru* 54 voyages, during which they not only met with storms and high seas but were also delayed by dense fog as well as encountering floating mines. The *Hakuai Maru* transferred 13 077 patients from the battle zone to Japan, of whom 140 were Russians. The Japanese made great use of their hospital ships[45] and also of other cargo ships adapted for carrying battle casualties.

A VERY PROPER CONCERN

In 1912 the *Journal of the Royal Army Medical Corps* (*JRAMC*) published a translation of an article by the Russian army doctor, N. Kozlovski, on the Rusian Army losses over the period of the Russo–Japanese War of 1904–5.[46] These figures shown in Table 2.2 make a comparison between the experience of the Russian and the Japanese army during the 18 months of fighting. They may not be reliable but they indicate a Russian view.

Table 2.2   Casualties during the Russo–Japanese War, 1904–5 (Russian figures)

| | Actual Numbers | | | |
	Killed or died on battlefield	Wounded	Missing and prisoners	Died of wounds
Russian Army	25 331	146 032	59 218	6 127
Japanese Army	47 387	173 425	6 700	11 425

| | Per 1000 average strength | | | | |
	Killed	Wounded	Missing and Prisoners	Died	Died Per 1000
Russian Army	37.7	217.4	82.2	9.1	4.19
Japanese Army	72.9	266.8	10.3	17.6	6.58

Source: N. Kovlovski, 'Losses of Russian Army, 1904–5', *JRAMC*, Vol. 18 (1912), p. 331.

In interpreting this table Dr Kovlovski made the following comment:

> The Japanese army furnishes the highest actual and relative figures for killed and wounded, the Russian Army the highest for prisoners of war. The first result is accounted for by the stubbornness of the fighting, the great numerical strength of the armies engaged and the long duration of the campaign; the second result is partly accounted for by the large number taken prisoner at the capitulation of Port Arthur.
>
> Japanese army losses were exceptionally high partly at least because so many men sacrificed themselves as 'human bullets' in unavailing attacks, spread over many weeks, on the fortress of Port Arthur.

During the 1904–5 conflict the Russians stated they had lost, per thousand, 12 men from disease, 6 from wounds and 25 dead. They believed that the comparable Japanese figures, per thousand, were, 27 from disease, 11 from wounds and 47 dead.

The Japanese statistics were differently categorised and this makes comparison difficult even if the figures could be relied upon (see Table 2.3).

It should be noted that 'loss' means total casualties, and may include those who were incapacitated from infectious or other diseases as well as the wounded. 'Unknown' may refer to those Japanese who had the misfortune to be taken prisoners of war, a category to which the Japanese never referred and could not acknowledge.

Table 2.3 Casualties during the Russo–Japanese War, 1904–5 (Japanese figures)

	Instant Death	Wounded	Unknown	Loss	Total
Officers	1 657	5 307	53	7 017	14 034
Petty Officers and men	41 562	48 366	5 028	194 956	389 912

Source: Compiled from figures given by Baron K. Takaki, 'Military Hygiene of the Japanese Army', *New York Medical Journal*, Vol. LXXXIII, No. 23 (9 June 1906).

There can be no doubt that the work done by the Japanese army and navy medical corps to keep soldiers and sailors in good health was very successful. That casualties on the battlefield were extraordinarily heavy reflects rather the determination of the Japanese, 'the Emperor's children', to win rather than any lack of care by medical officers.

After the Russo–Japanese War Japanese soldiers and sailors continued to enjoy the benefits of new medical knowledge. Injections to guard against various diseases became routine; vitamins, as an essential ingredient of diet, were recognised and understood and, in general, servicemen's health improved. However, much later, between 1941 and 1945, the strains of the Pacific War and the extended supply lines of the Japanese resulted in a serious decline in standards of both food and hygiene. The Pacific War of 1941–5 left many military and civilian personnel undernourished and suffering ill-health.

3 The Red Cross and Health Care for the Nation

RED CROSS HOSPITALS

In Japan in the late nineteenth century there was no system of voluntary or charitable hospitals in the cities, no network of cottage hospitals in smaller towns and villages and no specialist hospitals at all.[1] The Japanese, like most of humankind elsewhere, did not have at this time opportunities for residential, or indeed any other health care. The first Great Hospital (Daibyoin),[2] originally on the site of the earlier Fujita villa (at Shitaya, Tokyo), which had perhaps housed imperial troops who had been wounded in the Civil War of 1868 in Tohoku (N. Honshu), was later incorporated into the Imperial University of Tokyo's Medical Faculty as an early general hospital.

As a result the JRC became a major provider of health care through the medium of its own hospitals, first in Tokyo, and later in centres throughout Japan. This could be considered a form of humanitarianism, offering medical care to the Japanese civilian population. Notwithstanding the importance of the hospital's role in treating civilian patients, the objectives of the Red Cross Hospital remained 'To care for the sick and wounded of the army in time of war and to train members of the relief services in time of peace.'[3] It should be noted therefore that civilian patients were being treated as a necessary element in the arrangements for the training of Red Cross personnel.

It was Baron Dr Hashimoto[4] who, as Surgeon-General of the JRC, recommended that the organisation should have its own hospital in Tokyo. When he had been in Germany, to study the Army Medical Services there, he had seen that civilian hospitals were necessary, at the very least, in time of peace to train military personnel. On his return the Ministry of War allowed the Red Cross to lease a piece of land in Tokyo and the *Hakuaisha* Hospital, built 'with funds contributed by the Army medical staff', was opened by the Empress on 17 November

Ill. 1   Early emblems of the Japanese Red Cross Society, designed by the
            Empress, showing the Red Cross, the paulownia, bamboo and the
            phoenix

1886. The hospital aimed to train Red Cross relief staff, to broaden the
experience of physicians and surgeons by having a larger number of
patients to treat and, ultimately, to be ready in the event of war. Large
numbers of patients were attracted by Dr Hashimoto's reputation and
the hospital soon proved too small.[5]

On the fifth anniversary of the first ICRC Societies in Geneva the
Empress granted a large piece of land, part of the imperial estate at
Shibuya in the suburbs of West Tokyo, to the Red Cross together with
a generous gift of ¥100 000. The new hospital[6] was modelled on that of
University Hospital, Heidelberg, Germany, and was opened by the
Empress on 10 May 1891, on which occasion she made a further gift of
¥5000. This sum was to be given by the imperial couple annually for
ten years, although in fact the amount was increased to ¥10 000 a year
for 20 years in 1899. In this way the Red Cross Society in Japan was
indebted to the throne for their fine hospital, which is still today the
site of the Red Cross Hospital complex.

In 1891 the hospital had four departments, Medical, Surgical,
Obstetrics and Gynaecology and Opthalmology, but other special

departments including Otology (1891), Pediatrics (1910), Dermatology (1912) and Dental Surgery (1923) followed. A large operating theatre was opened in 1905 as well as rooms for physiotherapy and orthopaedic surgery, while further facilities for housing patients with infectious diseases were constructed in 1906. The hospital accommodated paying and charity patients (see Table 3.1).

Table 3.1   Patients treated at the Red Cross Hospital, Tokyo, 1887–1933

Year	Out-patients			'Ward' patients in residence		
	Charity	Paying	Total	Charity	Paying	Total
1887	109	1 423	1 532	27	288	215
1892	172	2 355	2 527	65	648	713
1897	197	4 655	4 852	93	1 166	1 259
1902	271	7 148	7 419	314	1 376	1 690
1909	255	12 180	12 435	413	1 938	2 351
1912	531	16 518	17 049	457	1 978	2 435
1916	689	21 190	21 879	537	1 904	2 441
1921	913	21 230	22 143	521	1 867	2 388
1926	1 418	31 706	33 124	506	2 629	3 135
1933	2 672	31 092	33 764	696	3 750	4 446

Source: *The Japanese Central Red Cross Hospital* (Tokyo, October 1934) p. 15.

The buildings, of one storey, were always too small, and extensions, consultation rooms for day patients, extra wards, and a new nurses' home were added. Eventually it was decided to rebuild and the corner stone of a new three storeyed 'ferro-concrete' hospital was laid in January 1934. Since that date there have been several rebuildings and expansions on the same site.

Because the JRC had semi-official status, the prefectural governors, throughout Japan, were given responsibility for organising Red Cross activities in their own areas. Thus by the early years of the twentieth century there were impressive Red Cross buildings in various regional centres (see Table 3.2) and by 1914, Red Cross hospitals in thirteen centres other than Tokyo. In time of war the facilities became part of the military provision.

In this way the JRC provided the first and sometimes the only hospital beds available over a large area.

Table 3.2   Red Cross hospital beds in 1911

	Beds
Central Hospital, Tokyo	276
Hyogo Branch Hospital	114
Miye	86
Shiga	118
Nagano	191
Toyama	92
Wakayama	100
Kagawa	199
	1176
Red Cross Hospitals also run by Japanese at:	
Formosa	69
Kwantoshu (Liaotung pen)	45
Mukden (Manchuria)	42

Source: *Red Cross in the Far East* (Tokyo, May 1912), p. 35.

THE RED CROSS MATERNITY HOSPITAL

The first Maternity Hospital in Japan was founded in Tokyo by the Red Cross in 1921.[7] This initiative followed the recommendation of the League of Red Cross Societies which, anxious not to lose the enthusiasm for Red Cross work engendered by the recent war, suggested that in time of peace national Red Cross Societies might consider further efforts which would improve the health of women and their children. In Japan nothing could have been more urgent given 'the terrible situation of infant mortality'.[8] The death of many babies and many mothers reflected widespread ignorance.

Accordingly on the recommendation of Baron Hirayama (then JRC President) in July 1921 work was started on the building of a Maternity Hospital at Shibuya, close to the Central Red Cross Hospital, on a hilly site 'surrounded with trees and favoured with good air, quiet environs and traffic conveniences'.[9]

It was a new idea in Japan that babies might be born in hospital rather than at home, and when the hospital opened on 9 May 1922 it was not immediately apparent who would wish to enter as patients. All this changed when on 1 September 1923, the Great Kanto earthquake devastated a huge area of Tokyo and Yokohama.[10] The earth tremors which continued for several days sparked off hundreds of fires as thousands of the flimsy houses, already flattened, were also burned.

The disaster proved indirectly providential, for the empty Maternity Hospital was besieged by homeless pregnant women and by mothers with small infants and children. The staff responded to the crisis with notable initiative; for they had no supplies, and they were short of food. Fortunately 'a motor car came to fall into their hands' and they lost no time 'in driving it from nook to nook' to collect supplies from whatever source they could.[11]

It is also specially noted that:

> the midwives and nurses here in this Maternity Hospital were wonderfully calm and self-possessed . . . amidst such terrible rockings and shakings from the earthquake, carrying patients out of the wards to a safety zone in the open air nearby . . . Amidst the great and fearful shaking of the buildings, the midwives and nurses, as if in the battlefields . . . discharged their duties so excellently.[12]

On 9 May the Maternity Hospital instituted 'Mothers' Day' when the whole establishment was open to the general public. It became a popular day out, for 'mothers are entertained with lectures, physical examinations and motion-picture shows, which are designed for the education of mothers in child hygiene and child welfare'.[13] The hospital also established a special office which in 1933 received 2775 enquiries. There can be no doubt of the goodwill in attempting to improve health care for mothers and babies, but the numbers catered for in Tokyo were very small.

A NEW FEMALE PROFESSION

The launch in 1890, by the JRC of a systematic three year training programme for nurses was the first such initiative in Asia. The idea of teaching being necessary for the modern nurse had been much publicised by Florence Nightingale[14] when she and her team of nurses had made strenuous efforts to save the lives of wounded and sick soldiers during the Crimean War. Florence Nightingale herself had trained as a nurse at the institution for Protestant Deaconesses, in Kaiserworth,[15] on the Rhine in Germany, the place of origin of modern nursing training. After the Crimean War, Miss Nightingale used the funds collected and presented to her by the British nation to establish, in 1860, the Nightingale School for Nurses at St Thomas's

Hospital in London.[16] Thereafter nursing slowly came to be recognised as being a respectable, and indeed an honourable, profession for young women.

Japanese doctors knew of Florence Nightingale's public demonstration of the importance of good nursing but, as they were often German-trained, they also knew of pioneering German efforts. During their study time abroad they had enjoyed the support of well-trained German nurses and knew that for Japanese medicine to progress along Western lines they must establish something similar in Japan.

In the late 1880s when the idea of the trained nurse was discussed in Japan, those medical men who were involved understood that, as in the West, many difficulties lay ahead. As late as 1867 Florence Nightingale still claimed that nursing was done by those 'who were too old, too weak, too drunken, too dirty, too stupid or too bad to do anything else',[17] for nursing was still considered a menial occupation to which any female servant could aspire. It was difficult in all countries to establish the concept of an intelligent woman nurse, medically educated to work with the doctor to ensure that patients were helped back to health.

One barrier lay in attending to the intimate male body services which were necessary in nursing and which were regarded as unseemly for unmarried and carefully brought-up girls. In Britain, Florence Nightingale, armed with the confidence of her upper class upbringing, had become a national heroine following her war efforts, and later she had struggled, with varying degrees of success, to fashion a profession for women in nursing by working out new rules for health care. Was her work made easier because of the association in the West of nursing with the Christian ideal of service? She imposed a strict code of conduct and training on her nurses, and they emerged as the 'Angels' of the hospital ward. In Japan, women's lowly status militated against their being trained or indeed being respected as professional women.

RED CROSS NURSES

In an attempt to create a Japanese female nursing Corps the JRC, imbued with high principles and inspired by Western objectives, worked out the following conditions for teachers of those who would train the nurses,

One hundred and fifty silver yen are to be paid over the period of employment of two years, high-class travel fees [presumably between home and the Tokyo hospital]. While working, a house is to be lent but girls will provide their own bedding although a money grant will be given for some furniture. All the girls are to be under the administration of the hospital director. Applicants must be women of good conduct and they are expected to have been trained at the Augusta Hospital in Germany or at some similar institution. They should be able to understand German, French and English, or at least English beside German.[18]

No candidates offered themselves.

On 2 June 1887 the Ladies' Volunteer Nursing Association[19] (*Tokushi Kango Fujin Kai*) was launched in Tokyo by a group of wives and daughters of nobles and Ministers of State, led by ladies of the imperial family. Her Imperial Highness Princess Komatsu became chief administrator of the Society, and by 1904 there were 538 lady members. It was an exclusive club designed to encourage the ladies to act as role models for ordinary girls who would come forward to train as nurses. The girls of the aristocratic school, *Kazoku Joggakko*, were also involved.[20] They inspired a generation of *jugun-kango fu* (or military nurses) to train for a profession.

The Voluntary Ladies of the JRC in Tokyo 'subjected themselves to a fixed course of training' which involved 'the dressing of wounds, preparation of bandages', usually under the direction of Army medical officers. The ladies occasionally helped with actual ambulance or hospital work.[21] This Society, which brought the wives and daughters of distinguished men together for a purpose which was for the public good, was unprecedented in Japan. The real purpose, to encourage the idea of nursing as a worthwhile profession for women, may have been concealed, but it was nevertheless important and urgent. The publicity given to the ladies' committees aroused much interest and allowed the idea of a nursing profession to become more familiar in Japan. Although the distinguished lady 'nurses' were highly visible to the Japanese public through newspaper reports, it seems highly unlikely that they were ever seriously engaged in unpleasant menial nursing tasks.

The Red Cross Society continued to plan for the future. They appointed a surgeon from the army as Director of Nurses' Training; he was to work with the doctors who were to teach the nurses. On

Ill. 2 Aristocratic ladies of the Japanese Volunteer Nursing Association receiving a lecture on first aid, *c.* 1897

24 June 1889 they agreed 'Rules for the Training of Nurses' and planned to start the nurses training course on 1 April 1890.

The main points of the rules can be summarised as follows: 'Girls should be between the ages of 20–30 years, of sound health, good behaviour and gentle nature. They should be able to read ordinary letters, write sentences using 'Kana' and have some knowledge of mathematics. They must have two guarantors in Tokyo.' The training was to take place over three-and-a-half (later shortened to three) years. The first year was taken up 'with an outline of anatomy, physiology and antiseptic methods, the second with how to nurse, treat and bandage patients and the third with First Aid, carrying and moving patients and clinical practices'. After graduation girls were required to make themselves available as 'Relief Nurses' for the Red Cross. Their terms of engagement were for 15 years after which they could, if they were in 'good health and bodily strength' and under the age of 50, enter into a further contract. The contract was short, straight-forward and binding.

Written Oath

Now that I am engaged as (nurse or attendant or other functionary) according to the Regulations for the nomination of Relief Staff of the Japanese Red Cross Society, I solemnly promise that, imbued with the principle of paying my debt to my country through love of its soldiers, I will not only strictly follow the regulations of the Society, but will also promptly respond to the calls of the Society and devote myself to the work of relief.

Name, Seal, Personal Status, and Domicile.[22]

There was no restriction on marriage although the fact that 'Relief Nurses' had to respond without delay to Red Cross demands made marriage (given the mores in Japan at that time) virtually impossible. However, the nurses did have advantages; when not required by the Red Cross they were permitted to take on private nursing for which there was a steady and increasing demand and for which they were reasonably well-paid. For some years after the training scheme started girls did not receive their salary directly for it was paid to Red Cross officials and issued to the girls on request.[23] It is not known how long this practice lasted or how much questioning the girls had to undergo before they were issued directly with their hard-earned money.

In 1890 there were 25 applicants, of whom, after entrance tests, 10 were accepted for the Red Cross nursing course which began in April.

In October of the same year another five girls were admitted (from Tokyo) who, together with four more from the provinces (2 from Kyoto, 1 from Ehime and 1 from Hiroshima), made up the autumn intake. As the governors of the 47 prefectures in Japan were themselves responsible for the organisation of their local Red Cross it was relatively simple to encourage governors' wives to head local Red Cross Ladies' Committees. By 1904 there were 36 such Ladies' Committees nation-wide, with a membership of 3366. The Ladies' Committees were important channels guiding suitable girls from the regions to Tokyo and later, as the prefectures themselves opened their own hospitals, into their local Red Cross hospitals for training.[24]

In the early days it was essential for girls to continue their education to the higher grade if they wished to have the opportunity to apply for nurses' training. In 1894, it was believed that there were three main reasons for girls to apply for places in these schools. These were that the girls themselves were keen to learn, or that they came from poor homes and had to take any opportunity which would produce earnings, or that they were plain girls who would not easily find husbands.[25]

Following the Sino–Japanese War of 1894–5, efforts were made to recruit war-widows who were already regarded as heroines in Japanese society, to train as Red Cross nurses. This plan was remarkably successful and brought great benefits both to the Red Cross and to the widows, who had hitherto had no option but to remain a burden on their male relatives. To become a qualified nurse turned a widow into an earning asset, improved her status and gave her respect as well as providing a professional qualification. Such a breakthrough for those hitherto a liability was a boost for women in Japan. These nurses, who were usually slightly older, often became senior nurses or lecturers at the Red Cross Nursing College. Later, during the Pacific War, war-widow nurses were from 1941 to 1945, *Gun-Koku no haha*, or 'Mothers of the Nation'.

Male nurses, often those who had retired from army service, were also recruited. In 1880 the 'Rules on Male Nurses' were established and the training of men for Red Cross service was begun. This was continued until 1888 and intermittently thereafter until 1933 when it ceased. The total number of male nurses trained was 1600. Men were also used as 'carriers' or 'transporters' to carry the injured from the battlefield, behind the lines, or indeed anywhere else.

For over a century the JRC has been training nurses;[26] there are now 40 Red Cross Centres for this work in Japan. The course of study has changed over the years; subjects such as philosophy, aesthetics, foreign languages, pharmacology and social welfare (especially as relating to Red Cross work) have been added to make the curriculum more appropriate for modern times, and to take account of Japanese legislation such as the law of 1948 relating to nurses, including midwives and those in public health.

Nowadays applicants for training as Red Cross nurses (the phrase 'Relief Nurse' was abandoned in 1947) must be graduates of Senior High School, be single, under the age of 23, willing to live in the College dormitory and must conform to the Red Cross height and weight requirements. The Red Cross Society in Japan allocates large resources to this educational work: over 85 per cent of the girls trained are financed by the Society. In 1988 the amount spent on nurse training reached the sum of almost 4000 million yen (£16 million?). During the century since 1890 nearly 80000 women were trained, almost all of whom continued their careers in Red Cross hospitals although they were not obliged to do so.[27]

Also of great importance was the training of midwives undertaken by the Red Cross from 1922.[28] The rules for those applying for the course were similar to those of other Red Cross nurses. Initially candidates were accepted who had done well in the Higher Course in Primary School but by the early 1930s most applicants came from Girls' High Schools. The dormitory itself was a new building, on the Shibuya complex:

> a four storeyed ferro-concrete construction well equipped with steam-heat and electric apparatus. In the basement there are kitchen, dining room, laundry and basement. On the fourth floor there are two rooms, one for social meetings and amusements, the other for lessons in manners and Japanese etiquette. The rest is entirely given to the rooms to be occupied by the midwives, probationers and nurses.

The girls, living in the dormitory, cooked their own meals. In 1934 they were said to 'choose their own food and make their own bill of fare so that they may be able to enjoy more or less a home-like life, and may learn domestic economy themselves'.[29] Efforts were also made to see that girls who lost sleep by working at night could enjoy sound sleep during the day. The period of training was two years. In Japan now, there are three Red Cross Colleges at which midwives are trained, and of these the Tokyo centre is the most important. Since 1946 over 4600 women have qualified.

Since 1907 advanced or post-graduate training has been available for a selected few. The number so educated is something over 1500. For a few years from 1929 over 100 girls were trained as public health nurses although this work was abandoned, and not resumed, following the Japanese military campaigns in China from 1937. A handful of girls were selected for a special education in modern languages but this also was discontinued in 1937.

From the early days of the Red Cross in Japan much time and energy was spent in teaching 'moral values' to Red Cross nurses who were to have qualities of 'loyalty, patriotism, philanthropy, charity and benevolence, secondly, the virtue of sincerity, thirdly, industry and patience, fourthly, consideration and tolerance . . . particularly towards the patients, fifthly, self-control and stability of character, next gentleness with which the patient's heart has to be gained'.[30]

The extraordinary length (of which only a part is quoted here) of Baron Ozawa's discussion of the qualities necessary for the Red Cross nurse is a reminder of how thorough was the indoctrination of the Japanese people, including the Red Cross nurses. Does the emphasis on high moral values also suggest that, given the long-held custom of poor families selling daughters for prostitution, there were difficulties in establishing the status of these women as nurses, rather than as prostitutes? The Baron concludes his piece by remarking that those doctors who lectured on physiology or anatomy or any other subject must be men 'of noble inspiring character who are sure to impress the students with high purposes and high ideals'.[31]

The question remains how far the JRC succeeded in creating a corps of modern professional nurses. Certainly during the Sino–Japanese War of 1894–5 nurses were 'blamed' for their inefficiency, but standards had improved greatly by the Russo–Japanese War of 1904–5. Nevertheless it was probably the case that many would have agreed with the male stretcher bearer that 'he did not like nurses for they were not feminine and they were all hussies'.[32]

After the Russo–Japanese War and before the 'China incident' of 1937, it seems clear that nursing standards in the Red Cross were not high. There was a re-appraisal in 1933 of entrance qualifications and, from that date, a serious attempt to improve the quality of the teaching and training which nurses received. However when, on 7 July 1937, the North China War broke out, there was a serious shortage of Red Cross nurses and difficulty in finding the requisite number to staff the 'Relief Units' sent to China.

The Red Cross contribution to health care, encouraged by the imperial family who were 'the source of charity and philanthropy from which all the public and private humane enterprises spring',[33] was considerable, but there can be no doubt that until 1945 it flourished because it was an adjunct of the Japanese military services. To foreigners the organisation seemed feudal, its attitude towards its female staff coercive, yet it could be argued that, for those women who escaped from oppressive conditions at home, Red Cross nursing represented a kind of freedom, a release from familial authority.

Part II
Accolade for an Emperor

4 Japan, Humanitarian World Leader, 1894–1905

JAPAN, WITH RED CROSS PARAMOUNT

At the time of the Sino–Japanese War of 1894–5 Japan was the only fully accredited (since 1886) country in Asia which belonged to the Red Cross.[1] There was no corresponding society in China, although the outbreak of war was followed by a flurry of activity by resident Western missionary doctors who hoped to organise a Red Cross Society in China should the international Red Cross people agree.

From Geneva the Red Cross wrote dismissively,

> We cannot officially recognise the existence of a Red Cross Society in a State which is not a signatory to the Geneva Convention. As long as China's accession to this treaty (through the intermediary of the Swiss Federal Council) has not been diplomatically concluded, recognition of any kind of Chinese Red Cross Society will be refused.
>
> Until now we have done nothing to bring about this accession because it seemed to us premature. We do not believe that the Chinese people are sufficiently civilized, from the point of view of the laws of war, to observe faithfully the Geneva Convention, even after their Emperor has signed it. It would consequently be rash to complete this formality and to contract commitments which would be illusory.
>
> And now I must add that, in the case of China's acceding to the Geneva convention, the society of missionary doctors does not seem to me qualified to be affiliated to the Red Cross, despite its size and its usefulness.
>
> We can only recognise a single society per state, and this Society must have a national character; yours, being composed exclusively of foreigners would not satisfy this essential condition.[2]

The Chinese Red Cross Society dates from June 1904, after the Chinese had ratified the earlier Geneva conventions and a decade after the war with Japan.[3]

In contrast, the Japanese had been involved with Red Cross affairs almost from the beginning, at a time when the infant Red Cross movement was glad to accept any country which applied for membership. During the visit of the Iwakura Mission[4] to Geneva in the summer of 1873, contact had been made. According to the people in Geneva, Japan had thereafter enacted military regulations, inspired by the Geneva Convention. In 1886, 'Judging that the army had undergone the necessary transformations, the Japanese Government acceded to the Geneva Convention.'[5] Once the war had broken out in 1894 the Japanese Red Cross was ready; 'its large and well qualified staff, and its plentiful resources, made it a subsidiary on which the army could rely'.[6] It performed invaluable services on the battlefield and undertook many duties for the sick and wounded brought back to Japan.

There were no arrangements made for the housing and care of prisoners of war, which were not at this date considered the responsibility of the Red Cross authorities in Geneva. It may be the case, as the Japanese report, that sick and wounded Chinese were brought back to Japan and were nursed in the Red Cross Hospital in Tokyo, but there are other accounts of Japanese brutality to Chinese in China during this war.

However, the Sino–Japanese War was but a preliminary to the Russo–Japanese war of 1904–5, which was to demonstrate to the world at large Japan's national commitment to humanitarianism.

Russia had earlier ratified the Geneva Conventions and the Russian Red Cross had by 1904 'accumulated vast resources'. Unfortunately it soon became clear that mismanagement, if not corruption, was preventing the Russian Red Cross from fulfilling its role. There was a public outcry and the operation was speedily put on a more efficient footing. As was reported, 'from St. Petersburg to Harbin the Red Cross set up an unbroken chain of 95 field hospitals, and 28 staging posts; it controlled 28 mobile units, 12 disinfection units and two bacteriological stations. To evacuate the sick and wounded it had numerous hospital trains and several hospital ships.'[7] In fact the Russian Red Cross was able, to some extent, to make up the shortcomings of the official military medical service.

But because Japan was the victorious power she became responsible for much more of the humanitarian work. It was a challenge to which Japan and the Japanese responded with dignity, dedication and compassion. As a result there can be no doubt that Japan emerged as more experienced in the practice of humanitarianism in time of war than any other nation at that time.

It is possible to examine Japanese behaviour in more detail by looking at the Japanese take-over in Port Arthur and the arrangement of parole for some Russian prisoners, hospital ships, and artificial limbs for both Japanese and Russians. In the subsequent chapter the lives of the Russians as POWs in Japan will be discussed.

PORT ARTHUR

Port Arthur capitulated to the Japanese on 2 January 1905 after a long and bloody struggle. The Russians who had surrendered were to march out on 6 January. One British commentator described the scene:

> First came the officers carrying their swords, some mounted, others trudging wearily. The officers were all splendidly dressed and in their light blue overcoats and patent-leather boots looked more as if they had just come from an Emperor's parade than from a siege of six months' duration. As for the soldiers, their clothes and especially their boots, were in poor condition, and many wore Chinese costumes and sheepskin coats; but physically they appeared in excellent condition and in the best of health. Never were prisoners more lightly guarded. Here and there in the procession, through the cloud of dust raised as it passed along, you caught a view of a few little khaki-clad figures with red blankets on their backs and rifles in their hands, apparently swallowed up in the dense column of Russians . . . It was almost comic to see so few Japanese guarding those thousands of Russians.[8]

The Japanese instituted a parole system whereby some 400 Russian officers, including General Stoessel,[9] the Commander-in-Chief, were returned directly to Russia on their word of honour not to engage again in the war. Tzar Nicholas wrote to his officers in Manchuria, 'I allow each officer to profit by the reserved privilege to return to Russia under obligation not to serve or to take part in the present war, or to share the destiny of their men. I thank you and your garrison for their gallant defence.'[10] It was a generous gesture which, according to British observers, the Russian officers ill-deserved. One contemporary comment will suffice to indicate attitudes. The scene was the railway station at Chorashi, a few miles north of Port Arthur on 12 January 1905, a few days after the port had fallen to the Japanese.

I went to Chorashi Station . . . with a feeling of sympathy for the
Russians; for so great had been their downfall and humiliation that
common humanity could not but sympathise with the individual,
whatever we felt towards the nation. But after watching the crowd of
generals, colonels and lesser magnates, arrayed in costumes more fit
for a ball than a tragedy, and seeing how lightly they felt their
position and how contemptuously they received the assistance so
readily given by their adversaries, all sympathy quickly evaporated,
and its place was taken by a sense of justice done and judgement
richly deserved.[11]

For those Russian casualties not able to march out of the Fort
stocks of food, clothing and medical supplies had been made ready.
The reality proved to be far worse than had been thought and
immediately plunged both the Japanese military authorities and the
Red Cross into crisis. Within the Fortress at Port Arthur there were 34
buildings in emergency use for wounded and sick Russians. The
Japanese found they had over 17 000 patients on their hands of whom
6000 were wounded, over 9000 suffering from scurvy, nearly 500 from
infectious diseases and 1500 from other diseases.

The first requirement was that the personnel of the Russian Medical
Service should remain on duty so that the Japanese could organise in a
more systematic manner. They soon found that, because methods of
treatment varied, it was impossible to proceed by using Russian and
Japanese medical personnel side by side. They therefore designated the
units of the hospital as being either under the care of Russian or of
Japanese medical teams. In a remarkable display of generosity, which
they afterwards regretted, the Japanese allocated to the Russians the
best hospital units, leaving for themselves the make-shift buildings and
temporary accommodation. They were thus doubly disadvantaged;
this brought complaints from the Russians who found themselves at
once under strange Japanese care in the most dilapidated buildings.
The Japanese claimed that their prisoners recovered as well as those in
Russian hands, but they did admit the extra worry which this work
imposed upon their Red Cross Relief Detachments forced to cope with
these conditions.

Of the 34 sites at Port Arthur at which hospital patients were kept,
only three – the Red Cross Hospital of the Community of St Mary, the
Central Military Hospital and the Naval Hospital – were purpose-
built. The Japanese found conditions elsewhere unsatisfactory: often
patients were lying on the floor, their wounds dressed with ordinary

cloth with nothing but their overcoats for blankets. There were vigorous attempts to rationalise the 34 hospital sites and, when this had been done and some order had been restored, the hospital complex was renamed the Fortress Hospital of Port Arthur.

Elsewhere some 12 Relief Detachments of the Red Cross were assigned to service on the Chinese mainland during the course of the Russo–Japanese War. They did not have an easy time. Red Cross Detachment No. 102 reported as follows:

> We were assigned to a garrison building on the slope of the Peihosan which had belonged to a Russian Artillery Regiment. It was a large building, but everywhere inside and out there were heaps of dirt, rags, broken utensils, and fragments of shells, so that there was no place to set our feet on. There was not a window pane that was not broken, and there were big holes here and there in the roofs and walls through which projectiles had passed, and it seemed quite beyond human power to arrange such rooms as hospital wards. Still it had to be done, and working through the whole night we cleaned and swept, pasted cloth over the broken windows, burnt the broken boxes as fuel to dry the rooms and brought in what beds could be found in the fortress.[12] (The sick and wounded non-commissioned officers from the battleship *Poltawa* were assigned to this unit.)

There were difficulties especially when there were few interpreters. Temporary Relief Detachment No. 41 reported, 'The Russians regarded us with suspicion and although we intended to do our best to make them comfortable and easy, differences of manners and customs often caused misunderstanding and dissatisfaction.'[13] Once, however, the Japanese had explained that they were a Red Cross, as distinct from an army, detachment, the situation eased. Indeed the Japanese were pleased to record that 'Our disinterested kindness, springing from the depths of our heart' so won over the Russians that when they had to be moved, they petitioned to be allowed to continue under the care of the JRC. The captives proved a great trial to the medical staff in charge, not least because of their 'lack of discipline and of a sense of cleanliness'. According to the Japanese, the Russians 'spat upon the floor, mended their shoes or clothes, cooked and ate things in their wards, or even on their beds'. Something had to be done to convince the Russians of the need to keep up standards of hygiene. The Japanese decided to institute a system of self-government; this they did by having the Russian patients select one of their number to take responsibility for the enforcement of the sanitary rules.[14]

The Red Cross detachments worked in concert with Japanese army medical services. Between January and the end of March 1905, out of the 17 000[15] Russian prisoners, 800 died, over 10 000 were restored to health and sent to Japan and over 4000 were invalided out and returned home via Chefoo to Russia. The Russian 'sanitary' personnel of medical officers and their staff, including a large number of prisoners who had volunteered to become hospital orderlies, were also allowed to go home. By 22 May 1905 the Red Cross Relief Detachments serving in northern China had finished their immediate task with the Russians and were then returned to Japan.

HOSPITAL SHIPS

Hospital ships were used by the Japanese during the Russo–Japanese War to carry Japanese casualties and Russian prisoners to Japan (see Chapter 2 above and Table 4.1 below). It was believed by one commentator that: 'The Japanese employed eighteen hospital ships and these vessels were fitted out with every appliance necessary for the comfort of the sick and wounded. Each vessel had a head surgeon and a surgical staff, with as many as twenty or thirty Japanese hospital nurses, trained by the Red Cross Society of Japan.'[16]

Earlier in 1898, it had been the ARC which had first flown the Red Cross flag at sea when, during the Spanish–American war, the *Moynier*, the *Red Cross* and the *State of Texas* (all three marked in white and red as neutral non-combatant vessels) initiated humanitarian work afloat.

However, inevitably, the use of hospital ships by two belligerents in time of war was not a straightforward matter. Prior to the naval engagement in May 1905 two Russian hospital ships, the *Orel* and the *Kostroma* which were taking their stations as part of Admiral Rojestvensky's fleet, were intercepted by the Japanese cruisers and escorted into the Japanese naval base at Sasebo, where they were held for two weeks.[17]

The Japanese action produced an angry response from Russia. Despite requests from the International Red Cross neither the JRC nor the IJN were able, or willing, to give any explanation. The matter was fully aired in the *Bulletin* of the International Red Cross and threats were made to take the matter to 'the tribunals set up at The Hague', but in the event the matter was dropped. This incident reflects one aspect of 'neutrality', as seen by two opposing sides, in time of war.

Ill. 3 Japanese-made steriliser used by the Japanese Red Cross during the Russo–Japanese War

Table 4.1   Converted 'hospital ships'* used by Japan in the Russo–Japanese War, 1904–5

Name	Weight (tons)	Beds	Patients carried	Russians	Fatalities including Russians
Yokohama Maru	2372	318	13549	55	51
Rosetta Maru	3875	427	18124	119	47
					(1 Russian)
Rohira Maru	3899	?	9848	478	49
				(& 184)	
Miyoshino Maru	3455	?	16603	314	61
Chosan Maru	1984	210	7555	230	23
Koun Maru	2876	290	9498	88	30
Kawanoura Maru	2185	228	7060	27	43
Doyo Maru	2066	?	7463	158	26
Karafuto Maru	2500	?	7509	15	12
Toyei Maru	2807	?	6826	18	9
				& 160	
Robina Maru	4000	?	8896	78	15
Jingu Maru	2616	252	6556	173	12
Ugo Maru	2300		4299	99	8
				& 59	
Kissho Maru	2478		5101	530	2
Omi Maru	2501		5912	?	3
Kompira Maru	3723	442	8048	322	4

*These ships were primarily cargo vessels hastily, and perhaps inadequately, modified to take wounded soldiers and sailors.

Source: N. Ariga, *The Japanese Red Cross Society and the Russo–Japanese War* (1907), pp.144–74.

Less controversially, Sir Ian Hamilton, who returned to Japan in February 1905, noted

Yellow Sea, 9 February 1905, I am in a fine ship by Harland and Wolff of about 6,000 tons. We have 1,000 prisoners on board under charge of a Japanese corporal and twelve men. There are no officers among the Russians and the men do not at all know what to make of my uniform.

The Japanese treat them most considerately and kindly. No assumption of superiority or swagger of any sort. The Russians for their part are obedient; indeed they seem astonishingly docile and easily managed, in comparison with Anglo-Saxons. There are 300 sailors amongst the crowd, who strike me as being far and away above the standard of the soldiers in physique, bearing, alertness and intelligence. Some of the prisoners are playing the concertina. Others are dancing. They are excellently and warmly clad, and have lots of flesh on their bones. Very different is their condition from that of our poor fellows after Ladysmith.[18]

ARTIFICIAL LIMBS

The terrible wars of the twentieth century brought an enormous increase in the demand for artificial arms, legs and eyes.[19] This development had in its turn been dependent on the surgical revolution of the late nineteenth century, which by providing anaesthetics and then developing anti-, and later a-septic, surgery, allowed many more amputees to survive. During the Russo–Japanese War of 1904–5 there were large numbers of limbless men, both Japanese and Russian, who could benefit from the fitment of prostheses.

Artificial limbs had been made for hundreds of years but the modern developments can perhaps be dated from the time of the Marquess of Anglesey,[20] who survived the loss of a leg following injuries sustained at the battle of Waterloo in 1815. It was James Potts of Chelsea who registered a patent for an artificial leg, articulating at knee, ankle and toe joints, which became known as the 'Anglesey' leg. This prototype was carried to America in 1839 by a Dr Palmer, himself an amputee.

In 1851, at the Great Exhibition, Dr Palmer's wooden leg was the only one to receive honourable mention. In the years following, an improved Palmer 'American leg' was developed; artificial tendons permitted muscle action for knee and ankle joints while spring action effected some toe movement. From the late 1850s it is believed that over 1000 such limbs were in use in Britain and similar limbs remained in use until the First World War.

Tragically the American Civil War created further heavy demand, and Messrs Marks Company of New York became famous for their 'rubber foot' as they moved away from the wooden 'peg' leg. Also in America, Douglas Bly (1858) of Rochester, New York, created a limb with a ball and socket ankle mechanism. The suction socket and roller knee, presented by Dubois Parmalee, another American, also helped, as did the efforts to avoid using body straps to keep the artificial limb in position.

Some 175 of these arms and legs, together with artificial eyes, were fitted and presented to Russian war prisoners. It is not known how many of these body parts were provided for disabled Japanese; the photographs which have been found are of Russian prisoners with their new limbs. The firm of Matsumoto[21] were manufacturing these limbs, following models obtained from Messrs Marks of New York, and they were specially commissioned by the Japanese Government and the Imperial house. The Japanese were the innovators and thanks to their generosity, their own soldiers and sailors as well as Russian prisoners benefited from this. It was Detachment No.80 of the JRC from Ehime who 'were charged with the work of procuring artificial arms and legs and eyes for the patients, and bestowed much labour in measurements'.[22]

Messrs Matsumoto had been provided with drawings of the positions necessary from which to measure length and size of leg. A piece of paper was put upon the ground and various shapes and measurements recorded there. Interestingly and importantly the Japanese were particularly concerned with flexibility in the artificial leg because it was vital for Japanese who, universally, sat upon their legs and wore 'Geta' sandals which required movement in the artificial ankle. Was it these two specific local requirements which propelled Japanese into the forefront of the manufacture of sophisticated articulating artificial limbs?

It is worth noting that at this time there was no liaison between the operating surgeon and the prosthesis maker. The surgeon cut off the leg or arm, leaving part of the limb and or a flap of flesh as he judged best. The craftsman working on the replacement limb had to proceed with whatever the surgeon had left him. Co-operation between the two did not then exist.

The replacement limbs and eyes[23] provided for the Russians were usually presented by representatives of the Empress Shoken. The money for this work appears to have come from imperial sources.

THE NEW JAPAN TRIUMPHANT

Much has been written about the Russo–Japanese War which, because of the Japanese victory, astonished the world. There were apparently other remarkable features relating to ballistics. In the fighting in Manchuria the Russian bullet was 7.62 mm while the Japanese was 6.5 mm but, as the International Red Cross reported, 'This weapon amazed the medical corps. The wounds it caused healed with incredible speed. Soldiers whose rib cage and lungs sometimes even those whose

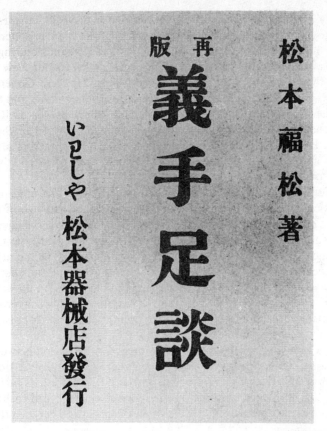

Ill. 4   Front cover of Fukumatsu Matsumoto's book *On Artificial Arms and Legs*, Tokyo, 1904. The information in the book, and the expertise, came from Messrs Marks & Co., New York

skull and brains had been penetrated through and through could often return to the battle a few hours later'. On 31 March (no year) in a letter to the Russian Red Cross, Dr Wreden noted, 'I am now convinced that the Japanese gun merits the appellation of a humanitarian weapon in so far as such an expression can be justified when speaking of war'. Dr Wreden had heard that, 'one month after the battle of Turenschang 32.4 per cent of the wounded Russians had taken up arms'.[24] No further reference has been found to this extraordinary report of the Japanese bullet.

例子に腰を掛け足部を平に紙の上に置き足の

れば圖に示す如く四個の大小圓第十二十三十

第一十圖

Ill. 5b From Matsumoto's *On Artificial Arms and Legs* showing the measurement of patients needing artificial legs

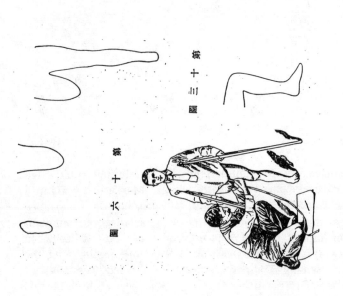

第十六圖

第十三圖

Ill. 5a From Matsumoto's *On Artificial Arms and Legs.* Apparently these measuring techniques came from the United States, where Civil War casualties had needed artificial limbs

There can be no doubt about the success of the various measures taken to prevent disease before battle; indeed it is now known that no war had previously had so few casualties due to preventable illness. Both the Russians and the Japanese inspected and controlled the water supply used by the forces, food supplies were kept clean, battlefields were cleared up, field hospitals inspected and high standards demanded.

The Japanese were particularly assiduous in these matters (see Chapter 2). The historian of the International Red Cross believed, as did many, that the Japanese had, since 1894, improved their 'battlefield' medical services. As he wrote, 'The official medical services and those of the Red Cross worked in perfect harmony and inspired the admiration of all observers. Everyone agreed that the Japanese hospitals, both at the front and behind the lines were models of their kind. The Japanese nurses were considered the best in the world.'[25]

Japanese efficiency and preparedness in time of war contrasted markedly with the perceived disorganisation of the Russians. After the revolution in 1917 it became government policy to revise the views held in Russia on the War of 1904–5 on ideological grounds. According to one Russian naval man, who had served at the battle of Tsushima, and whose book was published in 1936, a small table could be constructed comparing the fire power of the two forces.

	Russian	*Japanese*
Number of shots fired per minute	134	360
Weight of metal fired per minute	20,000lbs	53,000lbs
Explosives in 12 inch shell	15lbs (paroxylin)	105lbs (shimose)
Fired, per minute	500lbs	7,500lbs'[26]

Those Russians who thought in political terms, particularly members of the Baltic Fleet, were convinced that the disastrous train of events had reflected the current state of Russia, which

with her obsolete feudal system, and suffering from the curse of tsarist autocracy, did not meet the tests imposed by the battle. She is senile, whereas capitalist Japan, rejuvenated by reforms introduced from the West, has subdued the warlike pride of our admirals and generals. What is to blame for our defeat? Not individuals but our

Ill. 6 Idealised picture of Japanese mother and her son, who is dressed in the uniform of the Imperial Japanese Navy, celebrating Japan's victory; note the prominence of the Red Cross flag

whole political system. We have had our *Tsushima* in other places besides the Korea Strait. The Japanese bested us no less effectively on land. We have sustained a *Tsushima* defeat also, perhaps less glaring, but no less indubitable on our railways in our factories, our naval dockyards, our education – the whole misconducted and disordering life of one country. Yet Japan has conquered, not the working classes of Russia, but the detested and corrupt government of our country.[27]

The Russo–Japanese War enabled the new Japan to regain a self-respect which she felt had been challenged by the overbearing behaviour of America and the European powers since the opening-up of Japan in 1859. She had demonstrated to the world not only her vigour in battle on land and sea but also her achievements as a humanitarian power.

As a Red Cross leader Japan received great praise from contemporaries for her impeccable behaviour towards the Russians, especially as prisoners. Indeed, despite some stories of atrocities which may well have been true, both Russia and Japan were praised by the international community. The Red Cross in Geneva believed that 'the conduct of the belligerents was by and large praiseworthy: both sides genuinely tried to abide by their commitments, and, to a very large extent, they succeeded. The two armies received very precise instructions concerning the treatment of enemy medical personnel, the wounded and prisoners-of-war.'[28]

But these memories were to fade quickly as the Western powers contemplated the new powerful Japan. After the battle of Tsushima there was a wariness in Britain, especially in the Royal Navy, towards their erstwhile pupils. In America they felt that the British had let an Asiatic genie out of the bottle by signing the Anglo–Japanese Alliance in 1902; in Germany they observed critically, fearing always the spectre of the 'yellow peril', in Russia, the defeat by Japan sparked off the revolt of 1905 and encouraged the increasing unrest which finally resulted in the revolution of 1917.

Because of all these strong responses the Japanese humanitarian effort, powerful though it was, did not remain long in the collective memory, especially as the First World War was soon to eclipse the Russo–Japanese War both in horror and in casualties.

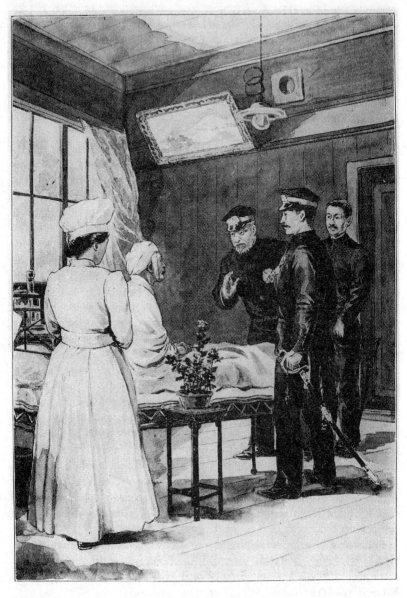

Ill. 7   Idealised picture of Admiral Togo visiting a wounded Russian naval officer in a Red Cross hospital in 1905

5 Russian Prisoners of War in Japan, 1904–5

ESTABLISHING GUIDELINES FOR PRISONERS OF WAR

There was no Geneva Convention[1] to protect war prisoners during the Russo–Japanese War. When the Japanese government, eager to demonstrate its humanitarianism to the world, looked around for a set of rules to apply to the treatment of prisoners, they had to rely on those adopted by the peace conference at The Hague in 1899. Within seven days of the outbreak of war, on 14 February 1904, the Japanese issued, under imperial ordinance, a series of regulations for the treatment of Russian War prisoners (see Appendix C) which were carefully worded, detailed and generous, including arrangements 'for the transfer of sick and wounded prisoners, or for their exchange, or for the discharge of prisoners on parole, on their agreeing not again to take part in the war'.[2]

As late as March 1899 the international Red Cross had declined any involvement with war prisoners. When the international committee had been approached by Spain (following the Spanish–American War in the Caribbean and the Philippines) asking for help to persuade the Philippine government to allow Spanish prisoners of war to be sent home, the reply to Spain from Geneva was unequivocal: 'We agree with you that the situation of the Spanish prisoners in the Philippines is worthy of interest and that humanity dictates sparing no effort to obtain their release, but we do not consider this act of philanthropy comes within the programme of the international relations of the Red Cross.'[3]

This discouraging response reflects the conservatism of a body which, despite being dedicated to humanitarianism, was unwilling to step beyond its brief, which had always been to help wounded soldiers.

RUSSIAN HUMILIATION

The Russo–Japanese War[4] was a major turning point in that it was the first occasion in modern times during which an Asiatic people proved

61

themselves on land and sea, in a full-scale war. Although the struggle was hard, and Japanese resources sorely stretched, on land in Manchuria and North China the highly motivated Japanese army fought to a standstill while, in May 1905, at sea, the Imperial Navy routed the Russian Baltic fleet at the battle of Tsushima (or Sea of Japan),[5] and effectively ended the war.

Some 70 000[6] of these Russians from both army and navy became prisoners of the Japanese and were transferred to Japan. Although many chafed at their confinement, there is no suggestion of ill-treatment. According to Russian figures produced after the war, there were nearly 60 000 Russians captured, of whom 18 Russian officers and 595 men died of their wounds in Japanese hands. Indeed the Japanese reputation for demonstrating their faith in high humanitarian principles rests on their behaviour at this time. Sick and wounded prisoners were nursed by the Relief Detachments of the JRC. As a token of their gratitude the Russian government sent a substantial donation to the JRC in recognition of the high standard of treatment accorded to their men. At the end of the war the Russians sent General Daniloff to Tokyo to supervise the repatriation of his fellow country-men. As Daniloff explained, 'he wished to express profound gratitude to the Japanese authorities for the treatment extended to the Russian prisoners throughout their detention in Japan and also for the arrangements made for their return to Russian territory'. As the first Russian officer to visit Japan after the war General Daniloff was received by the Emperor, who accorded him a gracious welcome.[7]

There is reference to a relatively small number of Japanese prisoners of war who were transferred to Russia after capture, including two Japanese surgeons who wrote of their experience.[8] After the ceasefire, some 1728 Japanese servicemen and 59 of their officers were being repatriated from Russia. They travelled via Germany by train and on arrival at Hamburg were warmly greeted by the German Red Cross which, on behalf of the Kaiser, presented them with oranges and cakes. The British steamers, *SS Vancouver* and *SS Camberman*, were waiting to carry them back to Japan.[9]

IN JAPAN

While Russian war prisoners were sent to 27 sites in Japan, usually to accommodation in infantry barracks, the sick and wounded, who came under the direct care of the Red Cross, were interned either at

Matsuyama, Fukuoka or Hamadera.[10] Several JRC Relief Detachments, which consisted of nurses (female), orderlies and pharmacists working under the authority of Red Cross doctors, looked after Russian prisoners at various hospital sites in Japan.

In Kanazawa there were 44 Russians in April 1905 but, because 'there was a want of harmony between them and the Army Medical Officers and attendants', these men were transferred to Red Cross care. The medical officers of detachment No.63 'took special pains to make the prisoners feel our kindness and succeeded in doing so'.[11]

The idea of properly trained Red Cross relief units available to look after sick and wounded prisoners was a new one and few Russian or Japanese soldiers would ever have experienced any medical care. It is not surprising that in the case of the Russians there was resistance to the 'rules of hygiene' which were expected in Japanese hospitals.

MATSUYAMA, EHIME, SHIKOKU ISLAND

At Ehime, Relief Detachment No.80 served with the Russians – 1382 patients in all – from 9 May 1904–28 October 1905. In addition the Red Cross Ladies of Ehime came in groups to the hospitals to assist with the relief until September 1905.

Detachment No.80 (Ehime) served 1 year 5.5 months. 9 May 1904–28 October 1905. Gave aid to 1382 prisoners of war.

Assisted in the equipment of the Place of Internment. After the arrival of 300 patients on the 15th May, half the Detachment served in Main hospital (portion of the Garrison Hospital) and another half in Section I (Buddhist Temple Kwanjensha). After the arrival of No.82 in the latter part of May, Section I was transferred to it, and the whole Detachment served in the Main Hospital, exclusively for officer-patients, till December.

From June 2, members of the Committee of Ladies of Ehime came by turns to the Place of Internment to assist in the work of relief, and this Detachment was charged with directing their labours till September, 1905. This Detachment was also charged with the work of procuring artificial arms, legs and eyes for the patients, and bestowed much labour on measurement, etc. One of the Medical officers was also placed in charge of ward for infectious diseases from June, 1904, till October, 1905.

Detachment No. 76 (Tokushima) Served 1 year 5.5 months. 14 May 1904–27 October 1905. Gave aid to 1315 prisoners of war.
Was put in charge of Section II (Buddhist Temple Dairinji) and received 167 patients on the first day. As the personnel of the Army Medical Service were few, this Detachment had to perform duties which properly belonged to them, such as book-keeping, care of private property belonging to patients, etc. From December, 1904, to March, 1905, in charge of officers' wards, afterwards of some wards for severe cases.

Detachment No.82 (Kochi) Served 1 year 6 months. 27 May 1904–6 December 1905. Gave aid to 1238 prisoners of war.
Served first in Section I; after removal to barrack, in ward for infectious cases and one for ordinary cases. On the arrival of No.42 in August, transferred to the ward for infectious cases. After the battle of Liauyang and the Shaho, charged with 5 wards; after the capitulation of Port Arthur, with 1 ward for officers and 2 for severe cases. Of 97 severe cases, 4 were insane patients.

Detachment No. 42 (Gifu) Served 1 year 3 months. 28 August 1904–6 December 1905. Gave aid to 1084 prisoners of war.
Served first in 1, then 2, then 3 wards. From March, 1905, in 1 ward for officers and 2 wards for severe cases. For some time also served in ward for invalids.

Detachment No. 81 (Ehime) Served 1 year 1 month. 2 November 1904–8 December 1905. Gave aid to 904 prisoners of war.
Charged with 3 wards. Severe surgical cases especially numerous from January to May, 1905. After March, 1905, charged with 4 wards containing at one time, 350 patients. From July of the same year, one medical officer put in charge of ward for nervous diseases.[12]

The wounded prisoners came from mainland China first to Ujina, the port of Hiroshima, the principal military base in western Japan, and thence by sea to Takahama and then by train to Matsuyama.
When one group of severely wounded men, who had earlier been held at a temporary hospital at Ninsen, Korea, arrived at Matsuyama, they were addressed by Mr Sugai, who was at one and the same time Governor of Ehime (in which Matsuyama is located) and head of the local Red Cross. Mr Sugai said,

I am the Governor of this Province, and congratulate you upon the fact that the voyage has not done you any injury. You all stand now under the power and protection of the Japanese Government, which I represent here, and in whose name I shall henceforth protect you. As several police officers are attached to this Nursing Place, you must obey their orders in all that concerns your retention here, and I am ready to allow you all the freedom and convenience permissible under the laws and regulations of the Government.

But I am at the same time the Chief of the Local Section of the Japanese Red Cross Society, with Headquarters in Tokyo. It is this Red Cross Society which has been entrusted by the Japanese Government with your treatment, and which has ordered me to open this Nursing Place for you. The medical officers and nurses that will take care of you have all been dispatched from the same society and you may safely confide yourself to their care. Be at ease and follow their directions, for surely they will do you good.

If there should be anything arising from a difference of manners and customs which does not satisfy you, speak freely to the English American or French missionaries of Matsuyama when they visit this place and I will do all in my power to satisfy you.

Notwithstanding these pious remarks it is necessary to look more closely at the reality of life for the Russians under Japanese care. Fortunately at least one Russian officer[13] kept a diary and this (published in Japanese in 1988) is more down to earth than the rhetoric of the governor.

Lieutenant Kaputinski noted that they (the officers) were courteously received when they arrived 'at an elegant two-storeyed wooden building which had been vacated for the use of our Russian military officers'. This hall in which they stayed was surrounded by a garden, containing a pond and green trees. The newly arrived officers were welcomed by a 'courteous interpreter' who told them, in poor Russian,

I believe this is a comfortable place. Russians are satisfied with the living conditions here. We can grant any of your wishes and you can buy from local merchants who are under government patronage. Japanese soldiers follow you if you go out but you can take an airing. You can visit the spa of Dogo to take baths, to drink beer and to rest. Japan and Russia have an agreement on the exchange of POWs and you will be set free in due time.

In general, Lieutenant Kaputinski did not quarrel with the inter-preter's remarks, noting that once a fortnight they could meet and converse with other prisoners and, at rare intervals, they did make journeys into the town. He also commented that 'I hear that we can visit the spa at Dogo where there are kind and sweet Japanese girls'.[14]

The establishment for prisoners at Matsuyama was a large one, the hospital Kaputinski believed accommodated 1000 soldiers and 30 officers. He lived in *Ichiban-cho*, No. 1 quarters, for 25 uninjured officers. He made a special point of emphasising the distinction which was made between officers and men, writing,

> Soldiers and officers were separated, the former being more closely watched. Not only that but their living conditions were worse and harder. Officers had private rooms, orderlies and furniture. They were allowed to go for walks and for shopping and they had money, plain clothes and personal interpreters. The soldiers lived in dim and damp temples and in chilly barracks where they were together in large groups. They were rarely allowed to go into town and they had no money and few clothes. While officers enjoyed a relatively free life soldiers were forced to live inconveniently.[15]

It should be stressed that at this time living conditions for ordinary Russians and indeed Japanese were very severe: peasants from either culture whether soldiers or civilians lived hard lives. The Russians complained of the 'incompleteness' of Japanese homes, and of the rice diet, the shortage of meat and vegetables and the poor quality of bread. The area was plagued with mosquitoes.

The Japanese noted that the Russians were segregated from 'Jews and Poles', were given the best medical treatment then available, that dead POWs were properly buried with solemnity and that other POWs attended the ceremony, while elementary and junior high-school students as well as the local population were encouraged to make contact.

The account of A. Novikoff-Priboy,[16] who served as paymaster's steward on the ironclad *Oryol*, was rescued and so captured by the Japanese after the battle of Tsushima in May 1905, is also notable. He made few comments about the conditions in camp near Kumamoto in Kyushu but he seemed to have been remarkably free to busy himself with a love affair in the neighbouring town. Novikoff's story relates to his relationship with a Japanese girl, Yoshiye, the sister of the prison camp interpreter, at whose home he spent a lot of time and where he told her brother that he wanted to marry her.

As Novikoff-Priboy writes, Sometimes carried away by my feelings, I addressed her passionately in Russian:

'Darling Yoshiye far north – within the Arctic Circle, the night lasts three months. When . . . the sun peeps above the horizon, . . . his heart is filled with rapture . . . producing in him the sensations that have been awakened in me by your crossing my path through life.'

I chose the most poetical images I could think of, and evidently she grasped my meaning. She smiled at me, showing her brilliantly white teeth. With her Mongolian eyes, slanting upward and outwards, she looked at me appealingly . . . She called me 'Aryosha' instead of 'Alyosha'. How delightful it sounds from her lips.

Notwithstanding his enchantment, Novikoff abandoned Yoshiye; his memories of her 'were those of an unfinished love song'.[17]

Sophia von Theil arrived in Matsuyama to visit her imprisoned officer husband on 31 July 1904 and left with him in December 1905. She was very impressed with the JRC nurses, writing 'their capabilities are splendid and worth praising'. She also wrote warmly of the work of the JRC and of the volunteer nurses.

She also commented favourably on the food provided, writing:

You cannot complain if you have, under the Hague Treaty, a diet of fish, rice, pickled plums and radish, and, in addition you have bread provided by the American missionaries, made from American flour. In addition you have meat, vegetables and tea. You are served three hot meals and have clean beds, linen and clothes as well as baths.[18]

During this war the Japanese, strongly supported as the underdog, received many offers of help through the Red Cross. All of these were refused because of 'the exclusion of all volunteer elements from such service'. Notwithstanding such a policy, offers of help were accepted from a few foreign nurses.

VISITING NURSES

Mrs Anita Newcomb McGee, MD, of Washington, planned to come to Japan with 600 nurses to assist in caring for sick and wounded men. This offer was accepted conditional upon Mrs McGee bringing nine nurses only. She arrived with her party on 22 April 1904 and the Japanese government made strenuous efforts to entertain and care for the ladies. They allocated Dr Baron Takaki, retired Inspector General of the Navy Medical Service, and Chief of the Benevolence Hospital of Tokyo, to take care of the arrangements. At the end of May the party were sent to Hiroshima to serve as a Relief Detachment in the Reserve Hospital; Dr McGee was given the status of Chief Nurse while the other ladies became Nurses. The ladies also visited the garrison hospital at Matsuyama (where some Russian officers were), the Naval hospital at Kure, and the hospital ships *Hakuai Maru* and *Kosai Maru*. They left on the American transport *Thomas* from Nagasaki on 21 October 1904 after they had 'expressed a wish to be relieved from service in October 1904 and the Japanese Government decorated them with orders and sent them presents'.[19]

It is not clear how long the Americans served in Hiroshima or indeed what Dr McGee thought on being designated 'Chief Nurse'. Certainly the McGee visit engendered a rich reward in terms of publicity for the Japanese in America and in Japan.

The British volunteer Mrs T. E. Richardson, the widow of a Colonel killed in the South African war, was also received by the Japanese. She had offered her services to the Japanese Minister in London on condition that she pay all her own expenses. She declined 'all receptions and sight-seeing out of regard for her deceased husband and she joined our Committee of Ladies and studied the art of nursing the sick and wounded'. As Dr Ariga explained, 'she made remarkable progress'. She served at the Red Cross Hospital in Shibuya, Tokyo, and later received permission to visit the Reserve Hospitals of Nagoya, Osaka, Hiroshima, Kokura, Kumamoto, the Prisoners' Hospital of Matsuyama and the Naval Hospital of Sasebo. In 1905 she was transferred to a hospital ship and so visited the Reserve hospital at Dalny and the Fortress of Port Arthur.

Mrs Richardson, not herself a young woman, was a mother and grandmother, who had lost not only a husband but also a son in South Africa. She spoke French and German, and seemed to find a strong rapport with the Japanese. She was certainly in no doubt as to the treatment given to the Russians by 'the courteous and chivalrous' Japanese. In her book she writes as follows of the Russian prisoners of war at Matsuyama:

> The Japanese treated them more as honoured guests than as prisoners and they seemed to appreciate the kindness shown them, although a few of the officers chafed under the unavoidable restraint of having to go out like schoolboys six at a time in charge of a

Japanese officer . . . Some of the elder men among the naval officers seemed sad and depressed; they had been in exile for many months – ever since they were rescued from the wreck of the *Rurik*.

The rations of the officers consisted of a daily allowance of 1 lb of meet or fish, 1.5 lb bread, about 1.25 lb of vegetables, butter, tea, sugar, pickles, etc. Privates had much the same but were supplied with the black rye-bread to which they were accustomed.[20]

The diet given by Mrs Richardson suggests that she must have been deceived because it was of course typically Russian, and there is no mention of rice. Mrs Richardson was in company with Miss Sato, the head and superintendent of the JRC nurses.

Later the same day she visited the hospital which was, she reported:

built on the same plan as other Japanese hospitals with the same comforts and conveniences. It contained 923 patients and another building to accommodate 1000 more was in process of erection. The offices were in large wards, divided into cubicles to hold two, with white hangings in front. They were mostly tall, fine-looking men, with fair hair, but some of them were very stout. Surgeon General Kikuchi was a marvel of tact and patience in his management of an officer whose mind was affected and who gave a great deal of trouble, as he was under the impression that he was still in command and also the head of the hospital . . . Several of the privates had a servile look . . . a good many of them could speak German and they crowded around eagerly craving for news . . . The men had comfortable mattresses on the floor, with plenty of blankets, white sheets and soft pillows instead of the hard little *makura* used by the Japanese and they all wore white wadded Kimonos.

A few of the wounds were serious but as a rule they were all healing rapidly under the skilful care of the surgeons. Nothing could exceed the attention of the Red Cross nurses who were evidently much attached to their patients.[21]

Mrs Richardson's account concludes as follows:

Many of these Russians had fine melodious voices and they treated me to some part-singing, but their songs were low and sad, often in a minor key, and sounded like the lament of captives in a strange land. No doubt some of them were contented with a life of enforced idleness, surrounded by comforts and consideration, but many were longing for their freedom and their homes . . . [A]t a later time the Japanese employed teachers to hold classes and to teach the prisoners who could not do so to read and write so that they might communicate with their friends. The Government was quite ready to send them back to their own country, if in accordance with international law, the Russians had been willing to make an exchange of prisoners.[22]

EXEMPLARY VICTORS

The Russo–Japanese war, a power struggle in the Far East, began in February 1904 and was brought to an end in August 1905 by the Treaty of Portsmouth, USA.[23] During the conflict on land the casualties on both sides had been very high, while at the naval battle of Tsushima (May 1905) the Russian Baltic Fleet was virtually annihilated and 8000 Russian sailors were taken prisoner. These, together with the captured Russian soldiers, may have given the Japanese some 70 000 Russian prisoners, most of whom were transferred to Japan. As the underdog Japan elicited much sympathy from Britain, and some from America. Britain indeed must take some responsibility for the war itself, for the signing of the Anglo–Japanese Alliance in 1902 was believed to have given a clear signal to Japan.

As a result of the pro-Japanese stance taken in the West the war in Manchuria proved to be a magnet for military attachés, journalists and nurses, almost all of whom wrote books praising Japan for her generous behaviour. During the course of the Russo–Japanese War, which strained the financial resources of Japan at all levels, the JRC spent over ¥5 000 000. The expenses included payment and maintenance of the Relief Detachments, chartering the two hospital ships and assisting the Russians. At this time the annual subscriptions from the membership brought in about ¥2 500 000.[24]

The war therefore was for Japan a challenge, closely watched by a curious world, and the generous treatment accorded to the imprisoned Russians was a way of demonstrating Japanese maturity. From the Emperor down to the lowliest stretcher bearer everyone knew the important humanitarian objectives of the Red Cross movement: during the Russo–Japanese War strenuous efforts were made to prove beyond doubt that Japan occupied the moral high ground.

6 German Prisoners of War, 1914–18

THE FIRST WORLD WAR

The years 1914–18 were 'good' ones in Japan for as an Ally, with Britain, France, Italy, Russia and later (from 1917) America, despite taking little part in the war, she shared in the triumph of victory.[1] Moreover her nascent industries received a welcome boost as demand for all Japanese products escalated following the withdrawal of the other warring nations from world markets. The humanitarian work for which Japan had gained much credit during the Russo–Japanese war of 1904–5 remained a high priority.

Japanese forces were not engaged in the European fighting, but in their own Pacific area there was much jockeying for position, as Japan took over the German toe-hold on the Shantung peninsula at Tsingtau, China. The only Japanese personnel who served in Europe were units of the Red Cross which were sent to Britain, France and Russia.[2]

GERMAN PRISONERS OF WAR

On behalf of the Allies the Japanese military authorities took over the care and management of over 4000 prisoners of war, mostly German, captured in China and elsewhere after the outbreak of hostilities. Because there were civilians as well as army personnel the Japanese referred to these men variously as internees or as POWs. Originally some 4600, there were deaths and a few were released, so that the number housed was about 4300.

The General Report of the Japanese Red Cross Society during the Last War 1914–1919 gives accounts of all that was achieved worldwide by the Red Cross in Japan and makes some reference to Japanese POW camps. The fullest report – 41 pages long – comes from Dr Paravicini of the ICRC who, between 30 June and 16 July 1918, visited all the camps in Japan.[3] Dr Fritz Paravicini, a tall and distinguished figure, was a Swiss doctor who had been resident in Japan since 1905 and was medical attendant to several embassies and legations. He was well-informed about Japan and was perhaps particularly sympathetic to the Japanese. He remained the representative of the ICRC until his death in February 1944 during the Pacific War.

The Germans were originally held in 12 camps at Tokyo, Shizuoka, Nagoya, Osaka, Himeji, Tokushima, Marugame, Matsuyama, Oita, Fukuoka, Kurume and Kumamoto but by the summer of 1918, according to Dr Paravicini, only eight camps at Narashino, Nagoya, Aonogahara, Bando, Niinoshima, Oita, Shizuoka and Kurume remained. Older camp buildings, often military barracks, were used in general but sometimes new buildings were required; the facilities provided came from military and Red Cross resources. The authorities believed that 'very great attention has been paid to the treatment of the prisoners. A canteen has never been wanting. There is besides a kitchen, bathroom, laundry, infirmary and recreation room. Gardens have been created for the cultivation of flowers and vegetables. Workshops have been fitted; recreation grounds and even land for cultivation provided outside the camps.'[4]

Dr Paravicini's reports in no way contradict the account which appears in the JRC Reports. In June 1918 he received permission to visit the camps following 'the best reception' from the JRC, the War Ministry and the Foreign Office, everyone, he reported was 'forthcoming and helpful, a very pleasant duty' and in conclusion he expressed his thanks for 'all kindness and good services'.[5]

Dr Paravicini's tour, between 30 June and 16 July 1918, was paid for by the JRC who also arranged 'for an administrator and an interpreter of the society' to accompany him; in addition 'the Ministry of War added an officer to the party for its guidance and information'. Dr Paravicini praised the excellent arrangement of the camps and the perfect state of health of the prisoners, all due to the assiduous care of a competent administration.[6] Unfortunately it has not proved possible to compare the reports of visits in 1918 with those the same Dr Paravicini paid to POW camps in Japan in 1942–43 none of which have been found.

Dr Paravicini's visits appear to have been thorough, examining the camp and talking to the occupants. He commented that he was provided with maps and notes so that he could familiarise himself with the terrain. As he reported:

> In the camps we established a more intimate picture of the situation, through the Camp Commander I received written answers to the questions I had already raised.

After this *we walked around for about two hours* [author's italics] and prisoners had the opportunity of raising their complaints, they did this in spite of the presence of translators in an uninhibited way and I hope that no-one took offence at their somewhat excited comments.

The Camp Commanders seemed understanding and well-meaning men and they all assured me that they tried to make the prisoners' position bearable giving them as much freedom as the War Ministry allowed.[7]

Dr Paravicini reported that 'the prisoners look healthy and well-fed, in general they have regular wages and they have put on weight'. He also listed the foods which were provided by the Japanese for the camps. Items included were beef, pork, beef bones, lard, fish, potatoes, peas, rice, beans, milk, pepper, salt, onions, barley and green beans and bread. It is not clear whether it was claimed that this food was actually delivered to the various camps or was a notional ideal diet for Western prisoners. Camps geographically located in various areas in Japan, mostly in the area from Kyushu in the West through Southern Honshu, could hardly have succeeded in delivering the same food to all camps. Taking only the provision of meat, of which 274 kilos of beef and 244 kilos of pork were listed for 200 men – the period over which these rations were used is not known – nevertheless, for the Japanese authorities to provide beef at all would have been remarkable in a country where beef is an expensive luxury product.

Paravicini gave other lists of foods, which he had collected from individual camps, but the calculations which he produced varied between 2050 and 2520 *Reinkalorien per diem*, which by calorific standards of today is very low. There were food parcels, mostly from German charities, and men who were working could buy extra food from the canteen with their wages; nevertheless it is not easy to make any judgment of the adequacy of the diet provided for the German prisoners of war by the Japanese in 1918.

The prisoners of war did complain of many things to the representative of the International Red Cross; 'Particular distress was', they said, 'caused by the length of their imprisonment especially as some of them were family men of over 50 years of age, they wished that prisoners could be exchanged, but this was not possible because the Germans held few Japanese. They felt forgotten, even if the food situation is better here (in Japan) they would prefer to starve in

Germany. Although they were treated fairly, small restraints made life unbearable. In any case Germans and Japanese are completely different, good interpreters are hard to find and this leads to confrontation, then restrictions and privileges withdrawn without notice. Because of censorship the distribution of mail is slow, the censors themselves have language difficulties, they look for secret writing in the letters. In Kurume there is a mood among the people hostile to the Germans,[8] elsewhere there is good communication, even though Japanese pride is countered by the attitudes of German officers who might not handle matters in the right way, especially as the Japanese are very sensitive about any suspected offence against them'.[9]

It may be helpful to have a summary of Dr Paravicini's report on one of the camps. Oita Camp, which was situated near Beppu in northeast Kyushu near the sea, with surrounding areas of forest and farm land, was opened on 4 December 1914, and was visited by the ICRC representative on 2 July 1918. The camp contained 250 German soldiers and 20 officers. The inmates could work and buy extra items from outside the camp. The men themselves did physical exercises, were allowed (under escort) to go for walks, visit the sea, and the 'latrines were excellent'. They had facilities for studying: some were preparing a dictionary of Asiatic languages, and others learning about Buddhism, while the orchestra was flourishing.

Dr Paravicini noted that the complaints included too little meat in the diet, the small site was crowded, misunderstandings sometimes curtailed the walks outside the camps, letters were not delivered promptly and so on.

Inevitably prisoners, after being incarcerated for four years, could never be satisfied and would always complain. It was noted that 'the greatest complaints were regarding the length of imprisonment'. Nevertheless the fact that Dr Paravicini's reports on each camp, in addition to his detailed general remarks, are full and precise and that he said he spent something like two hours in each camp going around and talking to the men, suggests co-operation and not confrontation on the part of the Japanese military authorities. It is of interest to note that Dr Paravicini was aware of 'the old-fashioned view that in war there should be no prisoners, but that now Japanese officers know only too well that these views are no longer tenable'. These of course were the old ideas on military behaviour which were to surface in Japan very strongly within twenty years.

The only Japanese in German hands were about 100 crew members of the *Hitachi Maru*, a postal packet boat of NYK, held since May

1917. The JRC brought news of these men to Japan and kept contact while they were in Germany.

An American, Miss Scidmore, praised the camps, as did American nurses (who visited Narashino) and who had been involved with the large numbers of Austro–Hungarian prisoners being held in Russia. The American nurses were sure that the Japanese camps were incomparably better than those in Russia. Had conditions in Russia deteriorated seriously following the upheaval of the Bolshevik Revolution of 1917, or had they never been good?

Indeed it was with the Austro–Hungarian POWs that the JRC Society indirectly became involved. In June 1919, a delegation from the International Red Cross, led by Dr Georges Montandon, arrived in Tokyo *en route* for the camps in Siberia. Montandon requested large quantities of dressings and medicines, all of which were provided by the JRC and taken on to Siberia. On his return Dr Montandon also carried back to Japan many requests for books, boots and clothes, all of which were met.

Even more remarkable were the verbal and written messages which Montandon collected in Siberia from prisoners interned at Nikolsk. These begged that the Japanese should take over some of the camps in Siberia,[10] for as the prisoners wrote, 'Not only do the Japanese treat prisoners infinitely better from the material point of view but instead of regarding them as slaves and dogs, as the Russians do, they regard them as men.'[11] Montandon himself seems to have thought this a practical request noting that 'at Nikolsk, which number 5,000, there are 3,500 officers. Now it is beyond doubt that, more even than of other prisoners whom you have in your hands, and who are thus acquainted with your good methods, you will win the gratitude of these prisoners if they are allowed to pass under Japanese administration.' Although action was taken following Montandon's request by the authorities in Japan, including the Red Cross and the military, the priority would then be to get the prisoners home, especially in view of the civil upheaval going on in many parts of Russia at the time.

Other than the involvement with these prisoners the Red Cross in Japan performed other ancillary jobs. The hospital ships *Hakuai Maru* and *Kosai Maru* worked between Japan and mainland China, carrying sick and wounded, including 31 prisoners, between September and December 1914. Two 'Sanitary' Detachments of the Red Cross, consisting of doctors and nurses and servants, were seconded between 28 October 1914 and 20 January 1915, and two further Relief Detachments were sent to Tsingtau, in China, when the German garrison capitulated, where the medical teams looked after over 300 imprisoned Germans between 26 November 1914 and 22 January 1915.

THE JAPANESE RED CROSS IN EUROPE

During the First World War the JRC did not have many calls on their services, and it was therefore decided at the end of 1914 to despatch JRC Relief Detachments to Russia, France and England.[12] These units of doctors and nurses served in Russia at the Nobles Club, Nevsky, Petrograd, throughout 1915 until 8 April 1916; in France at Hotel Astoria, Avenue de Champs Elysées, Paris, from February 1915 to 1 July 1916; and in England, from 1 February to the end of December 1915. In England the JRC Unit was put in the care of the BRC and was installed at Netley Military Hospital, near Southampton.

The JRC team of 22 nursing sisters and two doctors started work on 1 February 1915; Dr Suzuki and Dr Oshima and some of the Japanese nurses took responsibility for 'four huts of the Irish Hospital'. Other Japanese nurses were allocated to work with British staff. According to Dr Suzuki, 'In no circumstances did either the English medical officers or English sisters draw any line of demarcation between themselves and us. Nay, more; they treated us in the same kindly spirit as if we had been of their own kin.'[13]

By September 1915 the two Japanese doctors had in their care seven huts, or wards, each containing 20 beds. As Dr Suzuki explained 'Thus between 1 February and 31 December 1915 for 334 days two of us looked after 661 patients, mostly in the Irish section, while our sisters, under English medical officers in other huts, had the honour of taking care of 1,892 patients.'[14]

The JRC team had initially been sent for six months but this was subsequently extended to the end of 1915, after which the unit serving in England went home. The party did 'feel sad' at having to leave before the end of the war. Dr Suzuki had initially worried about the poor English of his party but, as he said, 'We are simply driven to the task, and we were justified by faith.'

The JRC party was given the 'Royal George' treatment, literally, as the King and Queen received them at Buckingham Palace, while Queen Alexandra, at Marlborough House, bade farewell and gave a gift to each member of the group. As a public relations exercise it was invaluable, and there can be no doubt as to the effect of such generous hospitality. Unfortunately there is no further information on the

Ill. 8 A group of twenty-two Japanese Red Cross nurses who, with two Japanese doctors, served at Netley Hospital, Southampton in 1915

success of the Japanese in the hospital wards. Dr Suzuki mentions that 'the patients themselves expressed their gratitude, and that their home-folk sent letters of thanks' but there is no insight as to how the medical teams co-operated, how much the Japanese or the British learned from working together, or whether Japanese treatment, based on German methods, varied from that of the English.

Were those Japanese units an embarrassment to the countries to which they were sent? Although Japanese humanitarian work was highly regarded in theory in International Red Cross circles, especially the achievement during the Russo–Japanese War of 1904–5, never-theless Japanese in general at that time were thought of as students rather than teachers. Do the arrangements in Paris and in Petrograd suggest either that French or Russian hospitals were unsuitable for the well trained Japanese units or that hospital staffs were unwilling to accept these Eastern strangers? Did the withdrawal of the JRC units – over two years before the end of the war – reflect the difficulties of the service?

In one sense the activities of the humanitarian movement in Japan between 1914 and 1918 came as an anti-climax to the furiously busy days which were associated with the Russo–Japanese War. It is true that the JRC were kept fully occupied, but they were thousands of miles from any battle zone and peripheral to the struggle going on in Europe. Was it an unkind fate which put over 4000 Germans who had previously been dismissive of the 'yellow race' into the hands of the Japanese? Were the Germans particularly fortunate in being cared for by Japanese, still during the First World War a humanitarian nation?

7 Humanitarianism Abandoned

THE XV INTERNATIONAL RED CROSS CONGRESS, TOKYO, 1934

The first large International Congress[1] ever held in Japan convened in Tokyo in October 1934, when 252 Red Cross delegates assembled to demonstrate a united front on humanitarianism to the world. That the 15th Congress should take place in Japan was felt to be a great compliment; apart from the Washington Congress of 1912, the four-yearly-gatherings, previously, had taken place in Europe. Tragically, by 1934 there was a frightening inconsistency between the humanitarian objectives of the Red Cross of Japan and those of the IJA, even then running loose in Manchuria and northern China. As events were to prove, time was running out for the pre-war Red Cross in Japan.

The JRC had attended international meetings regularly since Karlsruhe[2] in 1887, they had run an organisation notable for its thoroughness and efficiency, they had dealt honourably with war prisoners who had fallen into their hands in 1904 and 1914, and they had never been discriminated against in Red Cross circles. What more natural than that the movement should pay Japan so notable a compliment?

From the viewpoint of the ICRC Tokyo was a good location because it enabled the Red Cross 'to affirm its presence in every continent'. In addition,

> it enabled the Japanese Society, one of the oldest National Societies and one of the best established, with 2,700,000 adult members and 2,000,000 juniors to display its vitality. The 252 delegates attending represented almost all the recognised societies (57 out of a total of 61). The size of the American Red Cross delegation, with 67 members, showed the interest of the United States in their neighbours across the Pacific.[3]

At the inaugural meeting (20 October 1934) Prince Iyesato Tokugawa addressed the assembled delegates with the following words:

The opening of this Conference in Tokyo today is a source of deep gratification not only for the Red Cross Society of Japan but for the whole Japanese nation. Our people have long been desirous, because of their deep devotion to the ideal of relieving human suffering and to the ideal of service to others, of seeing a Red Cross Conference assemble on Japanese soil, and it is a genuine satisfaction to us all that the first World Conference entailing the participation of accredited Government representatives from all over the world which has ever been held in this country should meet here under the Red Cross emblem of neutrality and goodwill.[4]

As Judge John Barton Payne, the head of the American delegation, explained, the Conference consisted of those nations whose governments had signed 'the Treaty of Geneva – sixty-one nations were eligible for membership and fifty-seven nations were present'.[5] But the expense of the journey to Tokyo had posed problems: Albania, Bulgaria, Hungary and Luthuania had asked Judge Payne to represent them. Most governments detailed one of their Tokyo embassy staff to attend and many Red Cross Societies were also represented by a Tokyo-based government official.

The British Delegation consisted of Lieutenant General Sir Harold Fawcus (Director General of the BRC), Dame Rachel Crowdy, Lady Muriel Paget, Lady Glenconner, Mrs Rome, Miss Ida M.M. Simmons together with two government representatives seconded from the British Embassy in Tokyo.

The numbers of women as official delegates at the conference must have amazed the Japanese, all of whose 38 delegates were men. It is true that Miss Take Hagiwara was in attendance but she was there as President of the Nurses' Association of the Japanese Empire, and Superintendent of Nurses of the JRC. Forty-six of the Americans in Tokyo were women; clearly cultural and religious background determined attitudes.

The JRC prepared a full report of the cost of getting to Japan from many countries. They had negotiated discounts from various shipping companies, especially from Japanese lines.[6] There was some ill-feeling in the United States because the Red Cross Society could make no contribution to the expenses of any delegate, all of whom were therefore self-selected because of the amplitude of their means.[7] The delegates in Tokyo were not representative of Red Cross members of any country, rather they emphasised the elitist nature of the organisation.

There was an extraordinary range of banquets, receptions and visits provided by eager Japanese hosts. The tour of Tokyo, the Mayor of Tokyo's banquet, the trip to Kamakura and Yokohama, the Prime Minister's banquet and the expedition either to Nikko or Hakone were all wonderfully organised and enjoyed. The guests were invited to experience both Kabuki and No theatre and they received many wonderful gifts on all their visits. Both the Iwasaki family (Mitsubishi) and the Mitsui family held receptions, utilising their grand family homes and magnificent garden grounds. There is no doubt that it was a dazzling celebration.

The JRC held its Annual Meeting during the Congress and thus demonstrated to over 200 foreign delegates the extent of its membership. The National Convention was held in the attractive Constitution Memorial Hall in Gondahara on Tuesday, 16 October in the presence of 13 000 Japanese Red Cross members from all over Japan. Both the War Minister, General Senjuro Hayashi, and the Navy Minister, Admiral Mineo Osumi, were in attendance, as was Mr Fumio Goto, the Home Minister. The Empress, attended by a large complement of Imperial princes and princesses, read a brief message in a 'soft, clear voice' saying,

In attending the 42nd National Convention of the Japanese Red Cross Society today, we are grateful to notice the great progress which this institution has made in its enterprises and the improvements which have been made in its organisation. We are also grateful to note that the 15th International Red Cross Conference will be held in this country and that you are endeavouring still further to promote the enterprises of the Red Cross Society through international co-operation. We desire the president and the officers of the Society to unite their efforts in order that the Red Cross Society may meet the requirements of the time and contribute to the welfare of mankind.[8]

SERIOUS WORK: THE RED CROSS IN 1934

It is hard amongst the entertainments and the self-congratulation to discover the substance behind the froth. Judge John Barton Payne had been officially endorsed by President Roosevelt and before leaving home he had tried to discover in correspondence with Cordell Hull, the Secretary of State, the attitude of his government towards the Red

Cross. Cordell Hull in reply was verbose, but vague and non-committal, talking of the need 'for the further development of international law'. He commented, not unreasonably, that as he did not have detailed information on what the Red Cross Congress was to discuss in Tokyo, he could not express any opinion.

The Secretary of State did, however, make one general statement, writing: 'It is well-known that our Government has consistently advocated the total abolition of all chemical, bacteriological and incendiary warfare but failing this, any practical and effective measures for the protection of the civilian population from these types of warfare, as well as from air attack, warrant our entire support.'[9] The correspondence between Judge Payne of the American Red Cross and Cordell Hull, the Secretary of State, illustrates well the difficulty of defining national interest.

There was one incident which did cause a diplomatic flurry. Three nations were admitted during the Congress: the USSR, Iraq and Nicaragua. Judge Payne had introduced the subject of the membership of the USSR both at the international Conference at The Hague (1928) and Paris (1932). There had been opposition. But in 1934 in Tokyo, because of the change in personnel from various national delegations, Prince Tokugawa's resolution seconded by Judge Payne, to admit the USSR, was accepted.[10] Although Judge Payne had recommended the acceptance of the USSR into the fellowship of the Red Cross he was surprised when the leader of the six delegates, Mr Christian Rakowsky, made a passionate intervention, saying that:

> The Red Cross shows the will of the people to maintain peace. We are not diplomats. We cannot assure peace. But we have a duty to proclaim our desire for peace. We have a duty to state that war must be excluded from the methods that nations use to solve their differences. Former conferences of the Red Cross have adopted resolutions against war. To palliate suffering is laudable but to prevent such suffering is more laudable and more necessary.
>
> Between the technique of war and the technique of the work of the Red Cross, there is a formidable and increasing disproportion. New and infinite horrors have been added to the work of war. It has extended to non-combatants. The distinction between combatants and non-combatants is not much more than a fiction.[11]

The Russian delegation's resolution, which was not on the order of the day and had not been anticipated, read as follows:

Having regard to the resolutions of the earlier Red Cross Conferences and especially to the resolutions of the 11th (Geneva) and 14th (Brussels) Conferences declaring that the Red Cross, besides its usual war-time and peace-time activities must exert every effort in the struggle to prevent war.

And considering that the progress made in the technique of warfare places almost insurmountable obstacles in the way of the Red Cross in war-time.

The Red Cross delegation of the USSR expresses the hope that all peoples will draw the attention of their governments to the necessity of preserving the lives of tens of millions and saving tens of millions more from suffering and privations and preventing the worst catastrophes which threaten to destroy the material and intellectual wealth accumulated through the centuries by establishing throughout the world legal rules and international relationships of such a kind as will exclude the outbreak of war and guarantee the peaceful solution of international disputes.[12]

The Russian intervention with an unscheduled resolution caused some consternation. As Judge Payne reported to Cordell Hull:

The Soviet representative, however, introduced a resolution pledging the Red Cross Societies of the World to work for peace. The effect intended by the resolution was to commit them to a definite program against war and for peace. This brought on a very vigorous attack, participated in by Great Britain, France and a number of the lesser countries – Portugal and others. The debate took place in the Second Commission (I was a member of the first) and I did not debate the question, but stated to some of the delegates that if it became serious the United States would be in opposition. The resolution was referred to a special committee of three, of which the Portuguese was chairman. The objectionable features were eliminated and a resolution reported unanimously which was satisfactory to the British and other delegates who had been in active opposition.[13]

Unfortunately the text of the accepted resolution has not been found; nevertheless, the incident clearly reveals the powerlessness of the Red Cross, and the sensitivity of governments even to pious statements of intent. Within three years the Japanese were bombing thousands of civilians in China; later the Germans made regular bombing raids over Britain, which were then reciprocated, while in

1945 the Americans were 'saturating Japan' with fire bombs. Modern aerial warfare demonstrated repeatedly that for civilian populations there are no exceptions and no safe place. It was the use of two nuclear bombs which brought the Pacific War to an end.

The International Committee stressed the vulnerability of the Red Cross, despite the 500 000 Swiss francs contributed by the Swiss government, because of its precarious financial position. Although demands for its services were increasing the Committee was sorely hindered in its work, had to practise severe economy and keep staff to a minimum. It was the aim of the International Committee to bring the fund up to 3 000 000 Swiss francs.

There was a discussion of the work of the Junior Red Cross, some of whose Japanese members had welcomed the foreign visitors to Kamakura. The Junior Red Cross were humanitarians because, as Judge Payne remarked, they were involved in 'the exchange of international correspondence through portfolios containing letters, essays and pictures describing the school life, daily activities, history, culture and other interests of youth'.[14] There is no mention of the fact that governments could use the Junior Red Cross as a disciplined and semi-military organisation.

The XV ICRC Congress was an extraordinary publicity coup for the Japanese. As a propaganda exercise it had been superb. It had been used to convince the people of Japan that their country was indeed the centre of the world and that they, the Japanese, mingled with the best. For the delegates it had also been a special occasion, enlightening or puzzling them about Japanese culture, demonstrating Japanese efficiency, and convincing them of the Japanese commitment to humanitarianism.

Some 252 delegates from 57 out of 61 countries adopted 50 resolutions regarding 'Red Cross youth, the training of nurses, the Red Cross truce, international relief, medical flights, the protection of civilians against chemical warfare and aerial bombardment, the implementation of the Geneva conventions and the draft International Convention on the protection of civilians who were also of enemy nationality'.[15]

No-one mentioned the Japanese military aggression in Manchuria in September 1931, the occupation of northern China and the proclamation of the estabishment of the 'independent' State of Manchukuo on 1 March 1932. No-one mentioned the Lytton commission set up by the League of Nations to consider Japan's actions, which recommended rights for both China and Japan in Manchuria. No-one mentioned that the Lytton Report resulted in the withdrawal by Japan from the League of Nations on 27 March 1933, as a direct consequence of the criticism.

In fact, in 1934, Japan had no right to consider herself a member of the International Red Cross at all because her government had failed to adhere to the Geneva Convention of 27 July 1929. As the *Japan Advertiser* pointed out, in its celebratory issue, Red Cross Societies could only operate in countries in which the Geneva Convention was in force. Only on 18 December 1934 – perhaps as a result of pressure from embarrassed Red Cross officials? – did Japan become party to that part of the Convention which related to the 'Amelioration of the Condition of the Wounded and Sick of the Armed Forces'. And Japan never did accede to that part of the 1929 Geneva Convention which related to the treatment of POWs.

The confusion over Japan's adherence to the Geneva conventions on war was a symbol of a profound malaise within the nation. By October 1934, when the Red Cross organisation met in Tokyo (in one sense to honour Japan's humanitarian stance), the option of military aggression had already been taken. For many years some had been working with fervour to establish Japan as a formidable military power.

CREATING THE 'NEW MODEL' JAPANESE ARMY

The restoration of the Emperor in 1868 had been achieved by a group of *samurai* from the clans of the south west, including Choshu and Satsuma, determined to modernise Japan. Many of these men were of lower ranking *samurai* families who had much to gain from a re-organised society. They were much concerned with the status of Japan in the world and were generally conservative and illiberal in their outlook. It was Aritomo Yamagata[16] (1838–1922), a Choshu man, whose objectives, following those of his mentor, Masujiro Omura (1824–69), were a mixture of old and new Japanese values, who dedicated himself to the creation of a modern Japanese army. He was determined to achieve a powerful conscripted force, as distinct from the old divisive *samurai* units, but he was also anxious to reverse Japanese weakness abroad. He died in 1922 but it was in part his *persona* which continued to inspire the military expansion of Japan that succeeded, by the early 1940s, in temporarily driving the West out of East Asia.

In his youth Yamagata was active in the *Sonno Joi* movement –
Revere the Emperor and expel the barbarians – but following the
allied bombardment of Choshu positions at Shimonoseki in 1863 he
became an active participant in the campaigns to remove the
Tokugawa regime. It was because of his success as a military
commander that in 1870 he was made Vice-Minister for military
affairs. He soon, despite toying earlier with liberal views, came to
believe that the open-mindedness encouraged in the West was
inappropriate for Japan. His conservative tendency was further
strengthened when, in Europe[17] during the course of the Franco–
German War (1870–1), the highly structured Prussian army of the
newly united Germany routed the French and entered Paris. He also
noted with disapproval the many noisy opposition groups in Europe
which in his view fomented socialistic and other radical views. During
the 1870s Yamagata achieved and consolidated military power by
taking three steps, two of which were directly related – in the long term
– to the 1941–5 war.

In 1873 he succeeded in putting through the Conscription Ordinance
which required all young males to serve for three years in the army or
the navy, while in 1878 he re-organised the Japanese army along
Prussian lines and established an independent general staff system.
In the interval he was responsible for the crushing of Takamori Saigo's
Satsuma Rebellion of 1877 and with it the last army ever put in the
field by the old *samurai* élite. The success of the imperial army – of
three-year conscripts – against the rebels was an important signal
heralding the new era. In this way the powerful myth of the *samurai* as
triumphant warriors was effectively destroyed although, as will be
seen, the old *samurai* code of honour in some senses was transferred to
the new army.

Perhaps even more crucial – and a decision which would have a
direct bearing on the 1941–5 war – was the establishment of the general
staff of the army and the navy as a group from which Ministers of the
Army and Navy were chosen, with direct access to the Emperor,
independent of the civilian cabinet. This system of active duty officers
as service ministers (*gumbu daijin gen'eki bukan sei*) originated in 1871
when the Ministry of Military Affairs (*Hyobusho*) insisted that it
should have at its head a man of major-general or rear-admiral rank
or above. In 1900 the rule was amended to ensure that the head of the
armed forces (there were separate Army and Navy ministries from
1872) should be either a full general or an admiral on active duty. The
use of serving officers in these crucial positions created for the military

an unassailable power base. Although the cabinet of Gonnohyoe Yamamoto abolished the 1900 provision, the men at the head of the military continued to be active officers and the original rule was formally reintroduced in 1936 during the build-up to the war. Inevitably, with direct access to the Emperor, the military resisted any civilian control and quietly made themselves the ultimate authority in Japan. These arrangements, by the 1930s, made civilian government difficult, for by either declining to nominate or opposing a service minister, they could, and did, prevent the formation of a cabinet not to their liking.

Yamagata set out to create in Japan 'the Army; an Army sprung from the farming villages'[18] which was highly trained but which also followed the adapted *samurai* values of *bushido*. Thanks to Yamagata's unrivalled position and his survival to the age of 84, the Choshu army faction was able to maintain its grip on the power structure.

Four of his followers (all Choshu men), Taro Katsura, Gentaro Kodama, Masatake Terauchi and Giichi Tanaka, served as war ministers between 1898 and 1924. Three of these four (Katsura, Terauchi and Tanaka) served as Prime Minister between 1901 and 1928. It is Giichi Tanaka who is of particular interest and who ensured that the Choshu influence on army affairs continued into the 1930s and 1940s. These army men may well have supported the JRC, but their interest was primarily in the service which the Red Cross could render to the armed services of Japan, not in its role as a humanitarian society.

MARSHALLING A PEOPLE FOR WAR

From 1906, immediately after the end of the Russo–Japanese War, the Choshu faction of the Japanese army resolved to organise the men and women in every village to support the army.

The Imperial Military Reserve Association was established, on 3 November 1910, the fifty-eighth birthday of the Meiji Emperor. On that occasion, Yamagata (who had already retired, but was eager to give his blessing) spoke, saying:

> We soldiers . . . must humbly master our warrior code, assiduously polish our military technique, and become the pillars of the national army.

When we return home, we must influence the younger generation with our virtue, become model citizens, and not hesitate to take on the task of the Emperor's strong right hand.

We reservists, reverently receiving our president's princely message, must carry out our organisation's primary aims and fulfil the ideal that all citizens are soldiers. Not only must we repay our obligation to the Emperor, but we must also make our nation prosper.[19]

This reservists' organisation was the opening of a thorough and continuous campaign to bind the elements of the Japanese population together, to make Japan strong and powerful. Local branches of reservists were set up all over the country and from 1914 there were also factory branches, at which military education was taught to those men who were physically fit and especially to those who had already completed their army service.

Important though this was, very many remained outside the net. During the 1914–15 period Giichi Tanaka, with the co-operation of senior officials from the Home and Education Ministries, launched a careful and well rehearsed plan to create the National Youth Association, which would incorporate the thousands of small youth clubs scattered throughout Japan into a larger body. The local branch was intended to 'popularise patriotic values and serve national goals through local acceptance and mutual co-operation with other community groups and leaders'.[20] Many new groups were set up and they, together with societies already established, had to include patriotic and ethical education, physical training and military drill under reservist leadership in their programme.[21] All these efforts reinforced peasant frugality and hard work. Army reservists often arranged to hold their calisthenics and military drill at daybreak and this particularly pleased Tanaka, who noted that 'early risers' clubs', before the working day, effectively 'helped to prevent frivolity in the evenings' as weary youths were glad to go early to bed.

There had been a Patriotic Women's Association (*Aikoku Fujin Kai*) in Japan from 24 September 1901, when it was established under the presidency of the widow of Tomomi Iwakura. This and the Red Cross Women's Associations were much praised by the army during the Russo–Japanese War. In 1905 the membership of the *Aikoku Fujin Kai* topped 450 000. These women's groups were élitist organisations which attracted better-off fashionable ladies and they hardly answered the purpose which the army officers had in mind. Earlier Tanaka, Ugaki and other officers had not felt the need to organise women separately, because Japanese society, being family-oriented and male-dominated, automatically involved women of the family in subservient roles. Women, although not members, had always aided military reservists in their work in the villages. When the work involved, for example, active farm work, the women were there, especially as rice transplanting was traditionally a woman's task.

However, at the beginning of the 1930s Japan was living in what many believed to be an increasingly hostile world and there were army officers who looked forward to a period when total mobilisation of the population in Japan would be necessary. To this end the National Defence Women's Association[22] (*Kokubo Fujin Kai*) was launched in March 1932. Always under the strict supervision of army officers, it was claimed that the Society had 500 000 members and that it had grass roots support because many of the founders were the wives of army officers and military police. It spread like wildfire, having some 8 000 000 members by 1838 and 10 000 000 in 1941.[23] The Women's Organisations were amalgamated on 2 February 1942 into the Great Japan Women's Association (*Dai Nihon Fujin Kai*). At this time all women, aged twenty or over, married or unmarried, 'and even women under this age who were married' were required to become members. Neighbourhood Associations (*Tonarigumi*) which ensured neighbourly conformity were also active.

The earlier Patriotic Women's Association, which claimed 3 000 000 members, was out-manoeuvred by the Women's Defence Association in the range of services provided. In the branches of the latter they

> provided labour for the families of men on active duty, helped prepare and perform the funerals of war dead, sponsored lectures and films to disseminate military ideas, conducted all manner of savings, frugality and anti-luxury campaigns, helped at the army's annual draft examinations and inspection of youth and reservists, sent off and greeted soldiers to and from barracks, and performed war relief.[24]

Indeed the strong relationship of small hamlet Defence Association societies with their own village men, overseas on active service, meant that personal contact was, where possible, maintained with the men at the front. Colonel Akihito Nakamura, the Army Minister responsible for the Defence Women's Association, believed that his members were fulfilling their 'military obligation as a citizen, serving as "home front soldiers" and that every woman so enrolled was performing "a spiritual mission for her people" '.[25]

As the preparations for marshalling the nation went ahead, the JRC was increasingly brought under military control; its activities were dominated by support of the armed forces. As the official history of the Society notes, 'our service to the military increased and our peace-time activities either decreased or ceased altogether'.[26] In this way, as part of the build-up to war, the humanitarian traditions which Japan had painstakingly established over sixty years of international endea-vour were cast aside. The ease with which the military authorities subverted the JRC reflects the dangers when humanitarian efforts are closely associated with the armed forces. As the members of the Red Cross in Japan were never volunteers at this time but rather those who were drafted into the movement, they willingly acceded to the change of role. Indeed it is not hard to believe that in Japanese eyes the Red Cross was, despite its international reputation, *always* an army support group.

In fact the JRC, with its huge membership, was no different from the other super-patriotic associations discussed here. All the members were regimented into pro-Japanese activities. There was no place for the internationalism for which the JRC had hitherto been famous.

THOUGHT-CONTROL

Notwithstanding the success of the various patriotic leagues in rural Japan, men and women in the larger urban areas remained largely unaffected until the invasion of China in 1937, which was, and still is, known in Japan as 'The China Incident'. In August 1937 the government initiated 'The National Spiritual Mobilisation Cam-paign', which involved the whole population including school chil-dren. Women made up 'comfort-bags' for men fighting in China, children in school did patriotic marches every morning and were lectured by their teachers on 'The Holy War in Asia' and 'The War to establish the new order under Japan's leadership'.

As one Japanese commentator noted:

Education in national schools was not a part of the educational system running from elementary to higher education . . . It was a separate curriculum based on strong ideological and nationalistic lines. Ethics, language (Japanese), history and geography were nothing but the imperialistic and nationalistic views of Japan. Great emphasis was placed on group activity and behaviour, ceremonies, school events, and especially physical training. Children had to march to and from school in a group with a leader, as an integrated body. Morning gatherings in the playground, bowing to the miniature shrine where photographs of the Emperor and Empress were kept etc. became very important activities at school. Children's lives were controlled, regulated and restricted.[27]

The National General Mobilisation Law in 1938 placed everyone and all resources, such as textiles and metals, under strict government control requiring that substitutes be used wherever possible. In 1939 the pace and the pressure were stepped up; the first day of every month was designated 'Service Day for the Development of Asia'. All sorts of luxuries, including hair-perming, were banned, while women were encouraged to spy upon their neighbours. Given the closeness of the scrutiny few could escape. It was the kind of intrusive supervision[28] which it is hard for Westerners to comprehend.

Rice rationing was introduced in Japan in 1940, long before the war began; earlier, in 1939, rice polishing had been forbidden. These measures in 'the land of abundant rice'[29] were greeted with consternation and foreboding. Although the population survived on rationed rice, in after years some dated their appreciation of the peril in which Japan found herself from the limitation of supplies of rice in 1940.

Readers of Yukio Mishima's *Sea of Fertility* will find in the second of his great tetralogy the story of the *Runaway Horses*. This novel is a vivid expression of the frustrations which the Japanese felt towards the world society of nations to which they had recently adhered. The brilliance of Mishima's story-telling emphasises the bitterness which the Japanese felt, as he recounts the tale of a secret society, 'The League of the Divine Wind' (a group of fanatical students), as they plot to assassinate those Japanese 'capitalists' who have, they believe, betrayed Japan to the West.

Mishima's fiction was, at the time of the war, real to many Japanese soldiers. As he wrote,

> Purging away the evils of the West
> Let us be faithful to our land
> Stalwart; giving no ear to traitor's pleas
> We shall hand down our great cause
> Without the least fear of death.[30]

If the fanaticism, as expressed in *Runaway Horses*, reflects in any way the feelings of the Japanese armed forces, devoid of any trace of humanitarianism as they took command of thousands of Allied prisoners of war, then the outlook was bleak indeed.

Part III
Old Clothes for the New Emperor

8 Shame and the War Prisoner

THE YAMATO RACE AND 'THE BITTERNESS OF GALL'

The training of a nation for war, initiated by the military faction in the aftermath of the Russo–Japanese War, depended ultimately on the discipline of the Japanese army. It became the duty of army officers to ensure effective conditioning and so convince their men that they must never surrender. The Japanese have always believed that they were a chosen people, their Emperor descended from the Gods and, that they, isolated in their islands, were racially pure. For many it was predetermined that Japan would free East Asia from the domination of the Western powers.

Japanese schoolboys of the late 1920s and 1930s were taught about the 'Unequal' Treaties imposed by the Western powers on Japan in the 1850s, the Richardson incident which resulted in the attack on Kagoshima, and the bombardment of the Choshu batteries in the 1860s. As one wrote:

> Our history course also planted certain resentments deep in our hearts. We learned that after our successful war with China in 1894–5 our territorial gains in Manchuria were taken from Japan by threats from France, Germany and Russia . . . When you remember the Three Power Intervention remember too that 'the bitterness of gall' was a common saying which our teacher quoted, and the bitter flavour clung to the names of France, Germany and Russia.[1]

In Japanese eyes further humiliation followed, when, at the time of the founding of the League of Nations, in 1919, Japan, one of the victorious Allies, was refused a simple declaration of 'racial equality'. As the idealistic, peace-loving President Woodrow Wilson[2] was then calling for the espousal of democratic values this, for the Japanese, smacked of hypocrisy. Worse was to follow when Australia and the United States passed strict laws on immigration, specifically designed to keep the Japanese out.

It was Tokutomi Soho who wrote (of the American Immigration Act) that this law was the 'most unprecedented humiliation in the

recent fifty years of Japanese history'. 'What', Tokutumi asked, 'can
we do', and answering his own rhetorical question, 'Persevere, foster
power, know thy shame and endure it, and think how thou can cleanse
thy shame.'[3]

For the men of the IJA, who had had it drilled into them that they
must never surrender, the status as war prisoner could hardly be
tolerated. As one Japanese commented:

> The shame of capture was just about unbearable, our conventions,
> our histories are different. We were shocked when we learned that
> Americans and Australian prisoners actually *asked* to have their
> names sent home, so that their families would know they were alive.
> We could never have inflicted that upon our families. We received
> no mail as prisoners, and we wanted none. We were dead men. We
> had been dishonoured, and we felt our lives as Japanese were over.
> Frankly I felt I could never face my family again.[4]

SHAME AND THE PRISONER

The destiny of the defeated was death: for the Japanese there was no
other way. The final blazing climax must come as a fitting end to all
that has gone before. As Ivan Morris has explained, 'Nobility in the
face of certain defeat proclaims the magnificent tragedy of life, and the
ultimate criterion of heroic sincerity is the way in which a man
confronts his end.'[5] The death of the defeated soldier was ensured
by the victorious army, for prisoners were rarely if ever, taken.
Brutality was inevitable. Remaining alive – as a prisoner – was a
disaster.

When the Japanese Military Field Code, also known as the 'Field
Service Code', was issued on 8 January 1941, it commanded that, 'On
the battlefield, soldiers who have received an Imperial Command must
exhibit the spirit of the Imperial army. They must always gain in attack
and win in battle. Thus they must propagate the Imperial rule
universally and make the enemy impressed with the Imperial Majes-
ty.' Item 8 of the code said, 'Never be taken alive; never accept the
humiliation of becoming a prisoner of war.'[6]

During the 1941–5 war the Japanese themselves carried this policy of
'no surrender' to the utmost limits.[7] Men out-manoeuvred and out-
gunned saved their last grenade for themselves. Facing certain defeat,
groups of men, even without adequate weapons, would charge the

Ill. 9 *Samurai* warrior, dressed in armour designed to terrify the enemy. The characteristics of the *Samurai*, modified for modern use, were incorporated into the Japanese soldiers' offensive behaviour between 1941 and 1945

enemy in a final mass suicide attack. During the retreat from North Burma, towards the end of the war in 1945, there were 17 166 Japanese killed, while 142 'surrendered'. Most of those who were captured were wounded or unconscious at the time.

The Western warrior is equally heroic, but if, after battle, surrender is the only option, there is no dishonour. To the Japanese the status of prisoner was disastrous, bringing dishonour not only to the man himself but also to his ancestors and to future generations of the family. For the Japanese there could be no greater disgrace than to be labelled *Ryoshu* or *Horyo*, prisoner.

Joseph C. Grew, in the early 1930s the minister for the United States in Tokyo at the time of the 'Manchurian incident', who submitted a message to the Japanese government advising them that a certain Japanese soldier had been taken prisoner, received a reply saying 'the Japanese government was not interested in receiving such information. So far as they, the Government was concerned, that man was officially dead. Were he to be recognised as a prisoner of war, shame would be brought not only upon his own family but also his Government and his nation.'[8]

The Japanese did not expect to be made prisoner. As one POW (responding to Australian interrogation) said,

> The POW expected to be killed on capture and would have preferred that to the disgrace of being a POW. Although as a human being he would naturally like to see his people again, he felt at present that, like all Japanese soldiers under similar circumstances, he would not return. In any case, it had always been the case to execute men on their return and he doubted whether any allowance would be made for the fact that he was young. Although parents would be glad to see their sons again they would nevertheless not expect them to remain alive after disgrace and capture.[9]

In the case of Western prisoners, the Red Cross initiative in collecting information about them so that families could know that they were alive was warmly welcomed. For the Japanese it could not have been more different, for the last thing the Japanese wanted was his family to know that he had disgraced them. Japanese prisoners did not use the Red Cross facilities to write home: as far as he, a prisoner, was concerned, 'he could not hold up his head in Japan', as far as his former life is concerned he was 'dead'.[10]

It was often the case that Japanese when captured refused to give their name and rank. They frequently gave assumed names, often those of 'famous warriors or culture heroes'[11] to deceive their captors. They had no idea of how to respond as captives, and they were ignorant of the role of the Red Cross as an intermediary during time of war. As the International Red Cross reported after 1945, 'In the official bureaux at Tokyo, nominal rolls of Japanese prisoners and prisoner mail were left untouched . . . the information bureaux would have acted more cruelly had they sent next of kin news that would have brought them far more sorrow than relief.'[12] It is a curious reflection that the Red Cross, created as an organisation capable of crossing political frontiers, should have so failed in that Japanese soldiers could not conceive of its international dimension.

If death in battle were itself a victory then there was no place for wounded or sick men, who were, through no fault of their own, incapacitated. They were 'damaged' and so were, in a military sense, useless. In theatres of war remote from Japan, such as New Guinea, Borneo and Celebes, during the final Japanese withdrawal no forward planning was undertaken to save the casualties. They were abandoned; they either killed themselves – hand grenades were often used – or the departing medical officer shot them on leaving.[13] This policy continued during the Japanese retreat in the Pacific War Zone in 1944 and 1945.

JAPANESE WAR PRISONERS IN NEW ZEALAND AND AUSTRALIA

The behaviour of Japanese war prisoners demonstrates the way in which these matters had penetrated the Japanese psyche. In both New Zealand[14] and Australia there were unprecedented massive violent breakouts from prison camps, resulting in many deaths. Although there were 'grievances' which supposedly sparked off the riots, it is clear that the men were obsessed with the need to purge their dishonoured state as prisoners. As one Japanese wrote, 'The government prescribed all the courses and text books . . . this resulted in "mass production of boys with a standardized mentality, possessing uniform, government-selected information and regimented habits of thought".'[15] In the prison camps the soldiers and sailors remained strongly influenced by fanatical officers and non-commissioned officers.

In the New Zealand case some 800 Japanese POWs, captured on land or picked up at sea, were incarcerated at Featherston sometime after September 1942. By March 1943 the men were established in a 60 acre wooden hutted encampment which included mess and shower huts and covered latrines, all of which were described by a neutral Red Cross observer as 'airy and well-lit'. Clothes and blankets were plentiful and food generous. Daily rations were 'as much as six ounces of meat or fish, four ounces (later ten) of rice and twelve ounces of bread as well as fresh milk, butter and fresh fruit'.[16] Many Japanese arrived suffering from tropical or deficiency diseases, but after a few months almost all were in better health. Some 500 of the prisoners 'were members of work units of the Imperial Japanese Army' and these men accepted New Zealand discipline without any difficulty. The remainder, including eight naval officers and some naval ratings, as well as regulars of the Japanese Army and Air Force, were awkward, challenged orders, refused to do cleaning up and other menial duties and generally presented an air of truculence and disobedience. This behaviour occasioned no special alarm, for the New Zealanders believed that this lack of co-operation was similar to that displayed by Allied prisoners in German hands in Europe. None of the Japanese at Featherston availed themselves of the opportunity to write home.

Notwithstanding the quality of the Featherston Camp there was a wall of misunderstanding between the Japanese and their guards. At this stage in the war, early in 1943, New Zealanders were tense and nervous following the the fall of Singapore in 1942 and the loss of two Royal Navy vessels, the *Prince of Wales* and the *Repulse*, in Malayan waters. The Japanese prisoners were equally dispirited for they knew nothing of the Red Cross Convention on Prisoners of War and they were, in addition, guilt-ridden for having failed to live up to imperial standards.

At Featherston, where the New Zealanders operated strictly in accordance with the Geneva Convention of 1929, there were serious misunderstandings about the liability of the Japanese prisoners for work. Prisoners were required, without pay, to clean their camps and generally maintain good order in their living quarters. Although officers were not involved in these tasks there was confusion and resentment in the camp over this. Another matter which provoked hostility among the Japanese was the order for naval ratings to work alongside members of the Imperial Work Force who held a lowly rank. Thus, orders to do a kind of domestic work around the camp were judged by the Japanese as a deliberate attempt to humiliate them.

Matters came to a head on 25 February 1943 when a working party, from the group containing naval and regular army prisoners, refused to parade. After two hours of parleying, threats by New Zealand officers were greeted by open amusement by the prisoners. They refused to co-operate in any way. One protesting Japanese officer was removed. Another continued to advance on the New Zealand adjutant, who finally fired and shot him in the shoulder. There were by this time 34 armed New Zealand guards facing about 240 Japanese prisoners. As the prisoners advanced the guard fired, a burst which lasted for '15 to 20 seconds'[17] and which killed 48 and wounded 61 Japanese while one New Zealander died and 17 others were injured.[18] A wide variety of domestic implements – which could have been used as weapons – were found in the Japanese quarters after the incident.

News of the incident was sent to the Japanese authorities who protested. The New Zealand government was particularly concerned lest the deaths at Featherston spark off reprisals against New Zealand prisoners already subject to deplorable treatment in Japanese hands. At the Jaarmarkt camp on Java, a notice was posted stating that there had been 111 Japanese casualties in a New Zealand camp and threatening reprisals if there were no satisfactory explanation.

In Australia,[19] at 1.40 a.m. on 5 August 1944, Japanese prisoners staged a massive breakout from Cowra Camp, New South Wales, during which 234 Japanese died and 108 were wounded, while 4 Australians died and 4 were wounded. Although at the time, and subsequently, the Australian authorities were obsessive about secrecy, there are accounts by Japanese and Australian eye witnesses published after the war as well as more recent interpretations of what took place. Kenneth Seaforth Mackenzie, was, at the time, one of the guards at the Cowra Camp who subsequently wrote a novel, *Dead Men Rising*. This tale, while primarily about the lives of the military guarding the camp, is revealing about Australian attitudes. One soldier commented, 'More Japs, ugly little animals, not human'; another wanted to parachute all the POWs into Japan, with 'Japanese prisoner – not wanted by enemy' branded on their foreheads.[20]

By August 1944 Japanese morale was entirely different from that in February 1943 when the Featherston breakout took place. The Japanese still could not believe that they would be defeated but they knew that the war was, for them, going badly, while the Australians were increasingly optimistic as both Germany and Japan were forced to give ground.

The ostensible reason for the revolt at Cowra was the decision of the Australian authorities to separate enlisted men from their officers because of the ever increasing numbers of Japanese being brought into the camp. In March 1944 there were 439 Japanese in 'B' camp; by the time of the attempted escape there were 1104. The Australians knew that this section of the Cowra Camp was overcrowded and they were warned of forthcoming trouble by a Japanese prisoner of Korean descent who arrived at Cowra on 3 June 1944. Steps were taken to introduce modern automatic weapons for the guards, to keep a closer watch, and to dispose of some prisoners to a camp at Hay.

On 4 August the Camp Commandant informed the Japanese camp leaders that prisoners below the rank of lance-corporal would be transferred on Monday 7 August. The Japanese protested: they were told that the decision could not be discussed. On returning to their quarters the Japanese hut leaders decided unanimously 'to oppose this separation of other ranks from non-commissioned officers even at the cost of death'.[21] Both the Australian guards and those Japanese they guarded were tense. Suddenly one Japanese rushed out, frantically giving a warning which was turned into a challenge as a trumpet blared out amid cries of 'Banzai', and prisoners dashed from their huts towards the perimeter fences.

The prisoners hurled themselves at the fences in huge groups of 200–300 men. They held a variety of improvised weapons, and they carried blankets to cover the various strands of barbed wire of the restraining fences. Prisoners' huts were aflame – the Japanese had started diversionary fires – and as it happened these provided the only light, for earlier shots from the Australian guns had, unluckily, cut the electricity cable.

Over 300 Japanese escaped through the perimeter fence; others who had tried to break out at other places were killed or wounded. Some 50 Japanese, who had broken into the Japanese officers' D compound, remained there until daybreak. The officers themselves did not mutiny although one was killed and one wounded.

In the case of the Cowra Breakout in New South Wales, Australia, in August 1944, it was the introduction of some extra prisoners, and the obsession of an implacable sergeant-major which galvanised the prisoners into action. The breakout cost the lives of 234 Japanese and 4 Australians; 108 Japanese were wounded.[22]

It took the Australians nine days to recover 334 Japanese, and 25 of these were dead, in various ways, having committed suicide. One unarmed Australian officer searching for prisoners with a patrol was

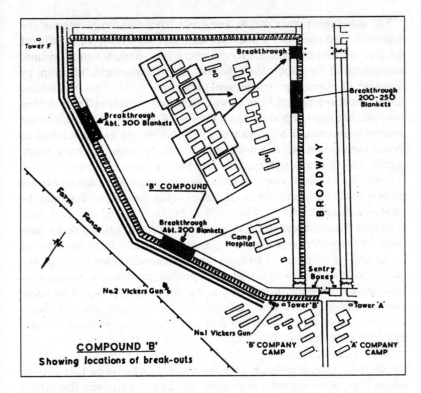

Ill. 10 Plan showing Japanese Section of prisoner of war camp at Cowra, New South Wales, Australia, from which over 300 Japanese prisoners of war broke out in August 1944

set upon and killed. No Australian civilians were harmed, although several Japanese appeared at isolated farms where there were only women and children.

The breakouts at Featherston, New Zealand, and Cowra, Australia, were rather different. At Featherston it was a revolt of some 240 naval ratings commanded by Japanese naval officers who resisted the New Zealand authorities' command that they work with, or do the same work as, the Imperial work force (men who had no comparable status to men of the IJN). At Cowra the prisoners were drawn from all the services and the merchant marine and were led by non-commissioned officers, perhaps because the officers at Cowra had no special 'familial' links with any of the other ranks.

All the rioters appear to have been 'purging their shame' as prisoners. The Military Field Service Code of 1941 which adopted words and phrases different from those of earlier codes ensured that, as one former Cowra inmate reported, 'Every Japanese Soldier was so educated to believe in the old *samurai* virtues.'[23]

The Japanese prisoners remained apprehensive about being forced to return to Japan because, 'in the Imperial Forces there existed a strict principle that anyone who became a prisoner of war had to receive the death penalty. Many of us thought we could never go back home again.' Another commented, 'We had become dis-honourable prisoners and did not want to return to Japan. If we had been able to remain in New Zealand most of us would have stayed there. They forced us to return to Japan.'[24]

But the Japan to which the ex-prisoners returned was not that which they had left. As one former prisoner noted, 'Unfortunately or fortunately our country had an unconditional surrender unprecedented in history. I heard that all Japan was under occupation and all Japanese were captured now, so we made up our minds to come home inevitably.' Another ex-prisoner wrote, 'The unconditional surrender of Japan and the fall down of the old Empire had for the first time broken down that traditional principle towards a prisoner of war completely.'[25]

The ex-Cowra men did return home and, as far as is known, did rejoin their families but never spoke of their experiences thereafter, while the Featherston men, conscious of the cameraderie which membership of the Imperial Navy had given them, created a Featherston Association to which they invited New Zealanders.

It is many years since the events at Featherston, New Zealand, and Cowra, Australia, and Japan is now an economic giant secure in her position in the world. The ideas of *ryoshu*, shame and the war prisoner may today seem dated, but as one watches the steady stream of Japanese citizens at Sengakuji Temple, Shinagawa, in Tokyo, lighting candles and paying respect to the forty-seven *ronin*, who, in 1703, all died by their own hands to satisfy a concept of honour, one wonders.

9 Prisoners in Travail

THE JAPANESE ADVANCE

In September 1941 the Japanese, taking advantage of the defeat and occupation of France, landed in French Indo–China[1] with 60 000 troops. On 7 December 1941 they attacked the Americans at Pearl Harbor and the British at Hong Kong; the latter capitulated on 25 December 1941. The Japanese then advanced south with impressive speed through the Malayan peninsula, investing Singapore[2] at the end of January. In Hong Kong and Singapore there were Australians, Canadians and New Zealanders in addition to the British. On 15 February 1942 General Percival,[3] Governor of Singapore, was forced to sign an unconditional surrender by which he and up to 70 000[4] of his men became prisoners of the Japanese. On 20 February 1942 the Japanese went ashore at Timor in the Dutch East Indies and over the next two weeks quickly overcame Dutch resistance in Sumatra and finally Java. By 9 March General Starkenborgh and nearly 90 000 Dutchmen were also in Japanese hands. On 6 May, after five months, the defence of the Philippines at Corregidor was finally broken and General Wainwright surrendered himself and 50 000 Americans. In this way the Japanese effectively ended the great colonial empires of the East, asserted the supremacy of the Yellow race, and became responsible for perhaps as many as 200 000[5] Allied citizens.

There can be no doubt that the Japanese were astonished, and dismayed, to find that they had, beause of the unprecedented speed of their advance, so many enemy armed forces on their hands in South-East Asia, early in 1942. It was therefore an immediate necessity to find ways of accommodating such large numbers. In general clothing was easily dealt with; in the tropics, garments or footwear were rarely issued, and prisoners were expected to rely on their own ever-diminishing resources. The basic food provided was rice, supplemented sometimes by vegetables. In some areas, notably Java, supplies should have been abundant and prisoners should not have starved, but elsewhere in the Japanese Great East Asia Prosperity Sphere there were genuine shortages. At the site of some prisoner camps, at mines

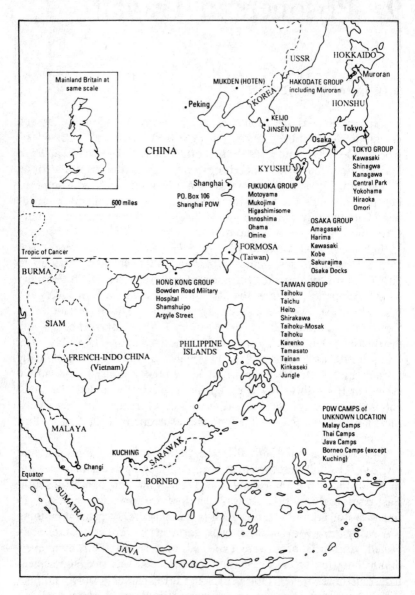

Map 2 Location of prisoner of war camps, 1941–5

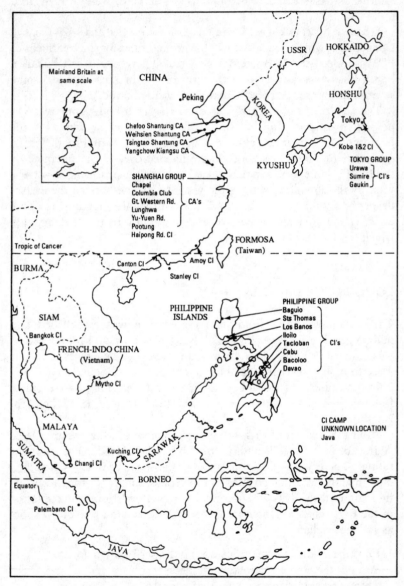

Map 3   Location of civilian internment camps and assembly points, 1941–5

and quarries, for example, there was primitive housing, typical of South-East Asia. Large scale buildings of all kinds were brought into use.

Japanese officers knew that Japan had not ratified the 1929 Geneva Convention, which had laid down the ground rules for the treatment of POWs. Indeed the Japanese denied virtually any role to the ICRC in South-East Asia, although farther north, and in Japan proper, some severely circumscribed Red Cross visits were allowed.

The *idea* of the Red Cross as an international body, committed to helping people in time of war (well understood in Japan at the beginning of the century), was in the 1940s repudiated. Large quantities of Red Cross goods[6] were handed over to the Japanese by the ICRC. Some of this material was issued to the prisoners; much was used by the Japanese who, as the war progressed, became themselves desperately short of supplies. All these difficulties, relating to food, clothing and housing, were however compounded by the brutality with which discipline was imposed.

LONG IS THE IMPERIAL WAY

The Japanese army's hold on its own men was established and maintained by the imposition of a strict hierarchy at all levels which was backed by brutal physical punishment. The newest recruits undertook the servicing of those more senior, bringing meals, and doing cleaning and polishing. Each roll-call, morning and evening, followed the same pattern and established the routine of Emperor worship.

After the soldiers of each squad had counted off, they were ordered 'Turn to the East' 'Worship the Imperial Palace!', 'The supreme salute'. There was absolute silence as the men, bent low from their hips, maintained that position for several seconds. 'Return to attention, about face'. This was followed by the order 'Respectful recitation of the Five Imperial Doctrines'. These followed a loud, soldierly shout as the men yelled

First the soldier makes it his destiny to perform patriotism,
Second, the soldier maintains etiquette,
Third, the soldier respects martial courage,
Fourth, the soldier values truthfulness,
Fifth, the soldier remains austere.

These were part of an imperial rescript which, known by heart by all Japanese soldiers, took fifteen minutes in total to recite.

After the rendering of the Rescript, or its principal points, the order came again: 'Face the East, Worship the Imperial Palace. The Supreme Salute, Return to Attention. About Face.' For practical purposes the Emperor was always judged to be in the East. In any case the East was where the sun rose, and as the Emperor was descended from Amaterasu, the sun goddess, the East was the right direction in which to bow.[7]

When the inspections took place during this roll-call the slightest thing was noticed. An unfastened button could lead to violent button pulling, as the inspecting officer tore off, and put in his pocket, all those he could remove. If the offending soldier was lucky, all he had to do was to find replacement buttons and sew them on by morning. If he was unlucky he might be subjected to a severe face-slapping. This punishment produced severe blows to the side of the face and was designed to humiliate, to shock and to hurt.

There was a joke in the Japanese army which ran as follows,

The Lieutenant slapped the Sub-Lieutenant; the Sub-Lieutenant slapped the Sergeant; the Sergeant slapped the Corporal; the Corporal slapped the Private First Class; the Private First Class slapped the Private; the Private slapped the Private Second Grade; the Private Second Grade, who had no-one to slap went into the stable and kicked the horse.[8]

During the months and years, between 1942 and 1945 it was the Allied POWs who found themselves in the position of the horse.

The brief accounts which follow are culled from the huge mass of literature published in the years after the war by men from Australia, Britain, Canada, New Zealand and the United States. The torrent of books which appeared are some indication of the anger of men subjected to unpredictable and violent treatment for three and a half long years.

THE BURMA–SIAM RAILWAY

The building of the railway to link the Singapore–Bangkok line with that of Rangoon–Ye was undertaken by the Japanese Southern Army Railway Corps, to facilitate the movement of men and supplies in the area. Because the Japanese were very anxious to complete its

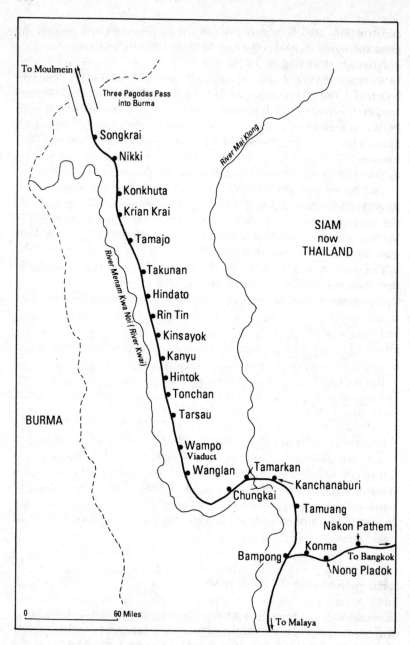

Map 4 Principal prisoner of war camps on the Burma–Siam Railway,
from October 1942

construction, they ruthlessly exploited their prisoners and created the most infamous death camps for the Allied POWs and other 'coolies' dragooned into building it.

Work started simultaneously at both northern and southern ends on 2 October 1942;[9] the gap was 263 miles. It is believed that 330 000 workers (coolies, or local people) were involved, of whom 61 000 were POWs. It was a huge earth and rock moving operation carried out by hand with the most primitive of tools, picks, axes, shovels and hammers. The task was undertaken by men half-starved, stricken by disease and ravaged by the misery of the wet season.

The casualties were horrifying. In 1946 the Allied War Graves Registration calculated that nearly 12 500 prisoners of war died on the railway, while the numbers of Burmese, Tamils, Javanese, Malayans and Chinese who died were over 70 000. It is likely that these figures are underestimates.

This account is based on the experience of many, but particularly that recorded by one Australian[10] who, on leaving the jungle for transshipment to Japan, entrusted his diaries, which recorded his time as a prisoner in Java and Thailand, to Colonel 'Weary' Dunlop who had been medical officer to the Australians on the Burma railroad. (Sir Edward Dunlop's own account of his management of his men's health is reprinted from the *British Medical Journal* in Appendix D.)

The railway work was essentially a labouring and man-handling job. The men started by clearing the forest and bamboo, felling the timber and dragging it away from the proposed track. One day,

Fifty of us with forty Japs, shouldered machetes, axes and theodolite and went over the scarpment to the railway clearing. We kept on through the dry, unshaded monotony of parched, dead bamboo leaves and bare trees. After five miles we struck north, until we came to a mountain-side of massed shelving rock – split and upturned. We spent a hot afternoon here surveying and hacking down bamboos and trees in the line of sight.[11]

Tree felling in the jungle was a dangerous chore as the climbers and lianas entangled all the larger trees. Later the men tackled the ground itself. As one man wrote, 'We have been clearing rock after blasting our section. It was picks, shovels, chunkels and baskets as we struggled with the broken rock spoil between the new, raw white limestone walls of the cutting. They reflected the heat and the glare, almost cooking and blinding us.'

Week after week the gruelling work continued:

> at the moment our lives are centred upon the Embankment. It is a long curving affair secured by a high knoll at one end reaching out towards a bridge at the other. It will be about twenty-three feet high and is known as the seven-metre bank. Basket by basket, *tanka* by *tanka* [bag stretcher], we carry the earth which has to be scratched from between the rocks in the jungle, tramping it out to the slowly forming bank. It is real coolie work and the monotony can only be offset by private thoughts and observations.[12]

The prisoners also prepared the way for the blasting of the limestone. They were required to hammer in a steel drill, a long exhausting process:

> every now and again, we lift out the drill and scrape the powder from the hole with a wire scoop. Then we pour a little water and let the drill drop back . . . The water as we clink, clink, clink away with the hammer, turns to milk and then to paste . . . slowly the hole sinks – twenty centimetres, fifty centimetres, or a metre, depending on how they want to blow the rock. About dinner-time the charges are put in; we take shelter; and the rock is blown up.[13]

Quite often the men were struck by rock which flew around after the explosion. These accidents were inevitable in such surroundings, but they were another sudden hazard facing these already disheartened prisoners.

The railway was completed in October 1943 after terrible suffering, exacerbated by the pace of the work, *Speedo*, with very few *Yasume*, or rest days.

VOYAGES

Many Allied prisoners of war were moved by sea from one part of the short-lived Japanese empire to another, so that the men could supply labour where their captors thought it would be most needed. Towards the end of the war (after the Burma railroad was built, for example) men were sent north to Japan and elsewhere. This movement in 1944 also coincided with increasing Allied attacks which were driving Japan from the more remote southern areas of Japanese-held territory. In some cases the men suffered greatly from being moved north from the tropics to the cold of Hokkaido and Manchuria.

The voyages themselves were miserable, for the ships were old and worn out, and the men were crammed into spaces between decks and into holds designed to carry cargo. Hatches were often battened down and visits to the latrines, usually hung over the side of the vessels, were an agony for men suffering from diarrhoea and dysentery. Allowing men on deck for exercise was sometimes permitted but during bad weather, or on coming into port, or when anywhere near land, men were kept below decks.

There are several accounts[14] of these infamous voyages; the one referred to here was of 1250 prisoners from Singapore to Moji in Japan which took from 1 July to 8 September 1944. The partly burned ship, of 3000–4000 tons and in terrible condition, was armed with an ancient muzzle-loaded brass cannon with iron cannon balls at the stern of the ship. Some 1250 men (1000 Australian and 250 Dutchmen) were loaded into the holds where they were to live for nine weeks. As was reported 'The ship was like a wreck; ragged, rusted gear, broken castings, bits of plating and junk, winch cylinders almost rusted through, great cankers of rust as if the ship had leprosy, the lagging of the steam lines rotted and gapped like ulcered limbs.'[15]

In the bow, under the forecastle there was an open space. It was here after much dispute that the prisoners' own doctor was allowed to set up his hospital. The ship had no hatch-covers and so in the event of a torpedo hit she could be expected to sink very quickly. The Australian officers negotiated with the Japanese to allow the men on deck so that they could be trained in emergency procedures. These exercises, useless had the ship been attacked, were splendid for morale.

There were brutal scenes from time to time when some incident angered the Japanese guards. When, during an attack on the convoy by Allied submarines with depth charges, one vessel was hit, two Australian prisoners cried out 'You beaut' which, together with the fear of a direct hit, so angered the already nervous and jittery Japanese guards that 'They rushed among the prisoners with drawn bayonets, flailing them dangerously. There were a number of cuts and bruises as the men scrambled helter-skelter over the coamings and down the lines and ladders to the deck below.'[16]

While the ship struggled through storms for her life, the men:

fell into helpless paroxysms of sickness. Stomachs contracted, rock-hard. On all fours with misery, men's backs arched: their shoulders rounded up and they collapsed onto their elbows, barely able to keep their faces clear of the decks as they retched. Chests tightening, squeezing the last gasp of breath out of them. Uncontrollably heaving, they were stricken with a horror that they would disembowel themselves through their throats. Their heads felt as if they were being pulled off like a fly's by some invisible giant's extending fingers . . . and born of all this agony . . . only a thin string of slime.

This ship survived and gained the shelter of some islands somewhere to the south of Taiwan. After thirty hours of no food or drink, the galley fires had again been lit and rice was prepared. For the first time in months, the few who could still eat had more than enough but they had been semi-starved for so long that were they to eat greedily their shrunken stomachs would revolt and they would suffer resultant agony.

The men struggled hard to keep themselves clean. After the storm the hold leaked wonderfully, enabling the men to wash in clean sea water. They even made one hole in the hull bigger, guaranteeing a supply of sea water for washing. In time the Japanese found the hole which had been called Village Spring; the ship's carpenter made a huge plug and rammed it fast into the ship's hull.

On 30 August they made land fall at Naha, the main port of Okinawa. The men felt only relief at having almost reached Japan. As they moved on again, passing Loo Choo (the sleeping dragon) islands as they approached the mainlands of Japan, the men were curious about this enemy country whose small ungainly soldiers had brought them here. They anchored off Kagoshima before moving on northwards towards Nagasaki, hugging the coast and then around the point of the Moji signal station through the Straits of Shimonoseki, to land on Kyushu.

It was, however, the case that Japanese soldiers were also moved around the seas of South-East Asia during the war years in similar vessels. There is a vivid account of a miserable voyage undertaken by Japanese soldiers in an overcrowded ship where the divided hold accommodated the horses and the men, in lower and upper sections.[17] The stench from the horses' manure, and rotting hay, was for the men overwhelming.

THE MINE

Allied prisoners of war undertook heavy and gruelling work in mines throughout the extended empire of the Japanese, particularly South-

West Honshu and Kyushu and in Hokkaido and Manchuria. Tunnelling and underground passageways, designed for the small Japanese miner, caused Caucasian men grievous difficulties.

Despite the rough, harsh conditions of the mine work, prisoners were not, in general, badly treated by mining personnel. In fact the mining companies did their best, under war-time conditions, for their prisoner workmen; their regime was rarely deliberately brutal. For one group, allocated to the Ohama[18] Mining Company, a change of employer was welcome especially as, on arrival, they were each given a small bread roll baked by British prisoners. The interpreter at this camp, a man named Tanaka, was a Japanese American whose bilingual skills made life easier for all.

At the mine itself the POWs were greeted by mine officials – older men with a mildness that surprised[19] – as well as by mine guards. There were also the women and children of the village nearby, whose presence reminded the prisoners not only of their own homes and families, but that even their enemies were part of the human family. The mine officials told them that their help would be welcome, and they would be taken to their quarters and would rest and recuperate from their long sea journey before they started their work in the mine.

The men found that they were billeted in rooms with twelve *tatami* mats, that is twelve places, six feet by three feet, on each of which there was a thin padded mattress and a cotton-filled top cover, all new; after inspecting their sleeping places they were able to bathe, with soap and hot water. They could not believe their good fortune. In the case of this particular group of men, who had lived in the open for two years, to live indoors seemed the ultimate luxury.

The contrast between the POWs who had just arrived from the south and the men – some 150 British Royal Air Force (RAF) personnel – who were already miners was quite startling. The British 'miners' were silky white in appearance and their muscles could be readily seen. The newly arrived Australians were brown, tanned and healthy looking; some were even fat, but it was the fat of oedema, indicating starvation.

The brutal element at this mine was the Japanese army sergeant who had absolute control despite the presence of a Japanese officer; the latter, a former school-master, seemed to stand in awe of the sergeant. One of the more tiresome duties which the Australians had to learn was the ritual of the evening parade when with true military precision the Japanese sergeant, escorted by the prisoners' commanding officer, the adjutant and the sergeant major, inspected the men and received, in Japanese, the report.

During the two weeks before they started working on the mine they were escorted on long walks, which revealed their poor physical condition. They undertook jobs on the surface, preparing old mine timbers for firewood for the cook-house. They increasingly found the routine of saluting and bowing, together with many other petty regulations, burdensome. Then came their initiation. They were split off into three groups to make up three shifts, *Ichi Shotai, Ni Shotai* and *San Shotai*, morning, afternoon and evening, that is from 6 a.m. to 2 p.m., 2 p.m. to 10 p.m. and 10 p.m. to 6 a.m. They started down the mine. The entrance was through a large bricked archway which led down a very wet stairway, the steps of which were made of logs. They came to another tunnel through which ran the tracks for the mine railway which carried the coal trucks.

As one Australian explained conditions in the mine,

At long intervals were small yellow globes giving a weak jaundiced glim to the dark, dank timbers which carved thick slices of jet black shadow out of the air. Water seeped and flowed over everything. The lighting wires were patched and joined so that no piece was more than twenty feet long. Many of the joins were bare, some were wrapped around with yellow insulating tape the ends of which hung down at varying lengths, dripping water. Often they were up to their ankles in mud and their knees in water. Water flowed in streams in drains . . . into sumps where the electric pumps worked continuously to keep the mine workable. They learned the value of split-toed boots in this slippery place.[20]

The Japanese workmen who were also attached to the mine worked well with the POWs; they were fatalistic but not unfriendly. Some of the Australians felt that it was this quality of acceptance which represented the real strength of the Japanese people. Perhaps the men in the mine were also antagonistic towards the army which had at this time such a dominating role in Japanese society.

It was frightening as they dug out an area rich in coal only to have the Japanese insist they work on despite the sharp snapping of pit props as the area above them, between the mine and the sea, adjusted itself. Eventually the whole area did collapse but fortunately when the area was empty. All the foreign miners felt anxious because there seemed to be no safety margins.

UNIVERSITY OF KUCHING, SARAWAK, BORNEO

There were some camps in which officers only were imprisoned and in these, despite Japanese discouragement, educational experiments were carried out by different groups at several locations. From the experience of one British officer[21] it is clear that the author and his fellow students maintained a spirit of hope by the discipline imposed by studying and by the making up, from various unlikely sources, of 'text books' which were the underpinning of the lecture courses. This officer was based in five camps, two in Java, one in Singapore and two in Borneo, and it was in the Kuching Camp, Sarawak, that the 'University' operated.

The 'Undercover University', with the motto *artes in arduis*, (learning through work) and organised in the officers' wing of Kuching Camp (which also contained separate units for civilian Internees, Dutch Officers, British other ranks and women and children), was not immediately banned by the Japanese; but when they discovered the variety of classes offered they began to be suspicious. They decided to strengthen their regulations against such collective endeavour. Regulation No.21 stated that POWs are not allowed to teach or lecture to others on any subject. As the prisoners decided to carry on with their classes they had the added incentive of doing so clandestinely.

Kuching University was launched with an enquiry to every member of the British Officers' Camp, 'What would you like to learn?' 'What would you be prepared to teach?' As a result of this initial survey almost everyone in the camp expressed an interest in something.[22]

Most of the work was done during the first year[23] when officers in this camp were reasonably well fed and had a routine into which studies could be fitted. The second year was much more problematic, partly because of a severe shortage of food which resulted in serious ill-health, partly because of the exhaustion of teaching material, and partly because of the general uncertainty as the Japanese faced defeat.

The classes in the general subjects relied entirely on the expert knowledge of those officers responsible for the courses. Studying business methods attracted many students and encouraged those prisoners who were optimistic enough to think of the future. Courses in pig farming and poultry keeping aroused keen interest in hungry men, some of whom kept chickens and occasionally pigs in the camp.

The modern language teaching depended not only on the knowledge of the teacher but also on the availability of a text book. Kuching University had about twelve text books in all, owned by different officers. But otherwise students and staff of the University copied out language material from books which they had borrowed in earlier POW camps. Much of the learning was done from miniature books which camp members had prepared on carefully-hoarded small scraps of paper available.[24] In some camps these little books – made up with so much care and trouble – were the most remarkable part of the University.

Dutch was well taught; there was a text book, Hugo's Dutch Grammar, and students made good progress. French was successfully taught in small groups and students enjoyed evenings telling stories in French to which everyone in the circle contributed some words or phrases. Otto's German Grammar had been temporarily available in one POW camp and this was copied out by the Kuching men before it and its owner were moved on. The German classes continued until the end. By good fortune a copy of Hugo's German Grammar came into the possession of the class from a Japanese clerk in exchange for a small dictionary, the pages of which – made of fine Indian paper – were very good for made up cigarettes. To teach Italian and Russian they borrowed (from the civilian internees' camp) grammar books in those languages and then feverishly copied out the text for their own use. A Spanish grammar book had also been copied out and on this was based the language course. Urdu was taught by a former jute planter in India.

As a result of the efforts made by these men to spend their imprisonment profitably and to improve their education during times of difficulty and danger, twenty-two Kuching University Diplomas[25] were awarded.

FOOD, LACK OF

Prisoners were of course obsessed by food or, rather, by the lack of it. Diaries kept by some men became a catalogue of the food provided and the weight of each man. One such diary[26] reveals the information given in Table 9.1.

The Australian author of this diary comments as follows:

This was the ration scale laid down by the POW Camp authorities in Taiwan. Officers were always classified as camp workers whether

Table 9.1: Notional Diet for POWs in Taiwan, 1943:
Food at Camp No. 3, Heito, Taiwan, 19 September 1943

	Rice and barley (grams)	Brown rice (grams)	Cleaned barley (grams)
Working Party	570	430	140
Camp Workers	420	315	105
Diligent Workers	680–708	453–472	227–236

Other items

Flour	90	per day per man
Fish	13	
Meat	12	(mostly pork)
Fats	20	
Saké	500	
Spices		pepper, curry powder
Salt	40	
Sugar	20	
Tea		Green tea and Black tea
Vegetables		Potatoes, green onions, carrots, *daikon* (Japanese radish), other roots, sweet potatoes
Fruit		Bananas, oranges, tomatoes, papaya, water melon, pineapples (100 a day)

Source: 'Spud' Spurgeon's Diary, handwritten.

they worked or not. After the first two months I do not remember
seeing any barley at all, and there was no compensating rise in the
rice ration.[27]

Meat and fish were limited to a token ration on days which were
for some reason significant to the Japanese.

Saké, spices and tasty additives were a myth!

Vegetables were in the main limited to Daikon (a large tasteless
radish), crude greens, mainly sweet potato tops, carrots which were
rare and other greens were a form of swamp garlic.

Fruit when available was almost always 'stolen' by the Japanese
camp staff for their and their families' use or for sale to the local
town folk.

Although we grew up to five acres of sweet potatoes at one stage,
we very rarely saw any other than the greens. The potatoes
themselves were spirited away.[28]

The single-minded involvement with food was inevitable given the sorry lack of it. There were Red Cross parcels from time to time but quite often there would be 100 parcels to be distributed between, say, 500 men. One diarist[29] notes that tins of food were always opened (by the Japanese) so that they had to be eaten at once and could not be kept in store.

However, on a happier note (18 May 1943): 'Amazing R.C. issue, ¼ lb chocolates, 1 tin biscuits, 1 tin creamed rice, 1 tin sugar, 1 tin fishpaste, 1 tin tomatoes, ½ tin margarine, ½ tin jam, 1 pudding, ½ tin golden syrup, and 1 pair boots, from South Africa.'[30]

The disturbing message which comes through in this diary and others was the skill of the Japanese in making everything seem rosier than it actually was. For example, on 4 June 1944 the Red Cross Representative (Harry Angst) visited Camp No.3, Heito, on Taiwan and 1 tin Prem, 1 tin coffee were issued; but the roast pork, which presumably Mr Angst had seen cooking, or at least smelt, was cancelled and the increased rice allowance vanished after he had left. There was occasionally a canteen open at the camp and men could buy fruit, perhaps water melon and bananas, but there was often difficulty over the currency which was accepted. Inevitably there were severe cases of diarrhoea and many men died. From time to time, injections – the vaccine being of Japanese manufacture – were given against dysentery and typhoid. Those who survived, despite the hardship, weighed about 8 stone (or 55 kilos), which must have been about 3 stone less than their normal weight.

BITTERNESS AND BRUTALITY

The anger still felt by those prisoners of war held by the Japanese over forty years ago has been much discussed. Feelings of hostility are inevitable in such a relationship and are always present when victor is dealing with vanquished, but it would seem that the hatred felt by Western prisoners for the Japanese has never eased. There is one account of a British officer, captured in Malaya, who had been born and reared in Japan and who therefore spoke Japanese. His experience as a POW makes particularly interesting reading. He commented on how Japanese arrogance flourished as their armies pushed successfully south through East Asia. But he also knew how important he himself was as a Japanese-speaking Scotsman in calming passions and reducing excessive violence by the Japanese towards his fellow prisoners. As he noted:

> I was useful because there was communication in the camps where I lived. This meant that the death rates in those camps was less because crises, which would otherwise have developed could be diffused. We had some vicious guards but, whether it was an official instruction or not, they never liked me to see any beatings-up.
>
> I was in Hokkaido for two years. We had an arrangement whereby I lived, isolated, with the doctor. There was one of our guards who was a tertiary syphilis case and an absolute lunatic, and his idea of fun was to beat the prisoners. He used to post his pal at the other end of the barracks so the prisoners could not get out and had no way of getting messages to me. But the moment I arrived it stopped.
>
> Time and time again, the situations were just getting nasty . . . They could not get over the business that I knew their country and spoke their language.
>
> My *Edo-ben* (Tokyo dialect) also helped. We tended to get a peasant-boy-type for guards, so you did your slightly 'BBC' Japanese and this went down rather well. In fact, they were slightly intimidated by it. We used all kinds of psychological tricks to survive.[31]

The systematic brutality of the Japanese towards the Allied POWs was, as has been explained, caused by many factors. Side by side with this should go an appreciation of the equally harsh treatment meted out to those Japanese who did not display, while in the armed forces, the *Yamato damashii*, or Japanese spirit. By cultivating *Yamato damashii* the Japanese soldier gained something spiritual by which 'one felt ennobled, confident, resolute as an iron bar, secure in the knowledge that . . . he followed the path that had made the Japanese the noblest and most powerful of men'.[32]

One young soldier in Manchuria, of artistic temperament, university educated, interested in poetry, drama and the theatre, drew down the wrath of the conventional Japanese officer. He was from Tokyo; they and his fellow recruits were from the country. They feared his education and his culture; they despised his inability to be a good soldier. This man was subject to constant physical abuse and was punished almost daily.

As the account explains:

The kinder men merely hit him in the face or on the side of the head with fist or open palm. Either way, slap or blow, the objective was to knock him down. This he learned quickly, and even a moderate blow could knock him two metres. He then sprang quickly to his feet and stood rigidly to attention to receive a sulphurous dressing down. Sometimes the whole procedure was repeated twice, or even three times.[33]

Others made him take off his belt and, using it as a whip, would beat his face and head, leaving red welts and occasionally open cuts. Worst of all was the corporal from Yamaguchi who, bawling insults at luckless recruits, gave the most severe punishment without inflicting any physical pain. As punctuation for his verbal abuse, 'he pulled off buttons one by one from tunic, from fly, private's stripes and all other detachable parts of the uniform. These he placed in his own pocket, never to be returned. Before inspection the following day every missing button and insignia had to be replaced.'[34] The men in this soldier's unit believed that because he was so inept he attracted punishment, but as this deflected attention and so protected them they made a point of helping him.

The most serious incident involving this same soldier followed his careless use of the word *watashi* as the personal pronoun, instead of *jibun*, the correct and manly form, in referring to himself. On hearing this the corporal, beside himself with rage,

knocked him down three times, in a calculating manner . . . Then rage seized him and he struck with all his might. When he failed to rise he kicked his inert body and grasping his tunic pulled him upright. He then tried to remove 'Makoto's' belt but found it impossible to support the unconscious body at the same time. Holding the soldier with one hand he struck again and again with the other, indiscriminately striking eyes, nose, mouth, skull, wherever uncontrolled blows happened to fall. Finally, knowing he had gone too far, he dropped the bloody bundle and glaring about him, entered the nearest barracks.

The soldier was in hospital for four months; no comment is made about any punishment of the officer.[35]

These examples underline the everyday nature of punishment in the Japanese army. That similar behaviour should be the norm in POW camps may shock but should not surprise.

10 Ultimate Weapons, Drugs and Disease

A SHAMEFUL SECRECY

During the 1930s permission was granted to allow some Japanese to undertake, mostly in Manchuria, medical research which could have led to the large-scale destruction of enemy peoples either by drugs or disease.[1] Despite what seems to have been large-scale investment of men and resources, the results were marginal. The work of infecting, with deadly diseases, enemy populations and prisoners of war remained experimental, although it is claimed that 3000 POWs were experimented on, and bombs packed with infected fleas may have been dropped on areas of China. In addition to the attempted 'germ warfare', opium was used to debilitate and destabilise society in those areas of China overrun by the Japanese after 1937.[2]

During the 1930s, elements of the Army Medical Corps undertook experiments which were designed to enable Japan to wage biological war. The leader of Unit 731, near Harbin, Manchuria, and the original instigator of the programme, was Lieutenant General Shiro Ishii,[3] whose work was supported by other higher military authorities. Ishii, as a young scientist, had done pioneering work on a 'ceramic water filter' which bore his name; subsequently, his biological warfare work was euphemistically known as the 'water purification unit'.

It was all highly secret. The principal work was done at a camp outside Harbin in Manchuria, although some experiments were done at Unit 100 in occupied China at Changchum and at the TAMA detachment at Sanjing as well as some in Japan. Very few Japanese would have had any knowledge of this work.

These secret matters surfaced at the Tokyo War Crimes Trial in 1945 only to disappear quickly.[4] Critics of the US government claim that information about Unit 731, and its leader Shiro Ishii, was deliberately suppressed by the Americans because Ishii traded immunity from prosecution as a war criminal on condition that his scientific data was transferred to Fort Detrick, Maryland, in the USA. The temptation, at the end of the war to obtain the Japanese knowledge of 'germ' warfare without having to undertake the necessary but unacceptable experiments, which the Japanese had done, was, it is argued, more than the Americans could resist.

The matter has been brought to public attention in both Japan and America. In Japan the existence of the TAMA unit was confirmed in a programme for the Tokyo Broadcasting system in 1976 when a Japanese reporter found five surviving Japanese, who agreed that they had worked at Unit 731, and that they had escaped being tried as war criminals because their research papers had been sent on to the United States. The sensation which followed these revelations resulted in a book, *The Devil's Insatiability*, by Seiichi Morimura, which sold over one million copies in Japan. In addition in 1984, a post-graduate student of Keio University browsing in one of the many second-hand bookshops in the Kanda district of Tokyo came upon a dusty box of papers. Curious as to its contents, he poked about, lifting out what seemed to be tables detailing numbered patients and their disease. When he got the box home the implications of the papers became clearer. The case notes and tables recorded the progress of a fatal disease, anthrax, in a group of numbered patients all of whom had apparently been deliberately injected, on given dates, with the bacillus. The papers belonged to a Lieutenant Colonel Naeo Ikeda. The Keio student had stumbled on reports relating to Unit 731 and the experiments directed towards biological warfare, perhaps discarded by an elderly widow, and the only such papers ever to be found in this casual way.[5]

On the American side the information came originally from one man, John W. Powell,[6] whose father, John B. Powell, was a well-known American journalist in China during the 1930s. John B. Powell, who had lost the use of his legs in a Japanese civilian interment camp in China during the war, gave evidence during the Tokyo trials to the Military Tribunal on the rape of Nanking by the Japanese in 1937.

The son, John W. Powell, remained in China after the war, apparently as a friend of the Communist regime there. He was believed by the Americans to have committed treason during the Korean War, and for this he was later tried, although the Grand Jury failed 'to vote an indictment'.[7] Following the US Freedom of Information Act, Powell had access to files previously closed. Powell's arguments, those of the political left, were that the United States had been willing to cause devastation in Asian countries, first by using atomic bombs in Japan and second by using chemical poisons to devastate large areas in Vietnam and that American irresponsibility should be exposed.

The Russians were also eager to know more of the Japanese biological warfare programme. It was they who, having declared war on Japan on 8 August 1945, plunged into Japanese-held Manchuria and, in addition to capturing hundreds and thousands of Japanese soldiers, discovered the wreckage of what had been Unit 731. In 1949 at the Khabarovsk trials, at which the Russians indicted those Japanese who had served at Harbin, it was revealed that American, Australian and British POWs had been used 'to study the immunity of Anglo-Saxons to infectious disease'.[8] Otherwise it was apparently Chinese who were the victims of the biological warfare experiments.

In Britain, the researches of two men then working for the commercial southern region TV station led to the making of a programme entitled 'Unit 731 – Did the Emperor Know?' They subsequently wrote a book which is called *Unit 731*. This chapter is based on the articles published by John W. Powell and on Williams' and Wallace's book, *Unit 731*, as well as by material published in *Mita Gakkai Zasshi* by Professor Matsumura.

The British position was that although chemical weapons were given up unilaterally in the 1950s, work to protect the population from chemical attack must continue. The Ministry of Defence's Chemical Defence Establishment, at Porton Down, remains one of the most secret places in the country.

SHIRO ISHII, THE INSTIGATOR OF THE BIOLOGICAL WARFARE PROGRAMME

The story starts in the early 1930s when, after Japan had occupied Manchuria and China's north-eastern provinces, Shiro Ishii persuaded his superiors of the potential of biological warfare. He appears to have succeeded in setting up 'a large, self-contained installation with sophisticated germ and insect breeding facilities, a prison for the human experimentation testing grounds, an arsenal for making germ bombs, an airfield, its own special planes and a crematorium for the final disposal of its human victims'.[9]

Shiro Ishii was born on 25 June 1892, the fourth son of a wealthy landowning family. He proved a good student at school and in course of time succeeded in gaining a place at Kyoto Imperial University where he studied medicine and graduated before joining the Imperial Guards as an Army Surgeon. He spent some time (1922–4) at the First

Army Hospital in Tokyo before returning to Kyoto to do post-graduate work in 'bacteriology, serology, preventive medicine and pathology'.[10]

His research was interrupted when he was seconded to the island of Shikoku, where at Kagawa a virulent form of encephalitis had broken out. This epidemic, the first known appearance of 'Japanese B' encephalitis, was to kill over 3500. Ishii's task was to isolate the virus believed to be causing the disease; whether he succeeded in doing this is not known, but the work in Shikoku established a life-long interest in the prevention of epidemics and in water filtration. Back in Kyoto, Ishii married the daughter of the President of Kyoto University, Torasaburo Araki. Throughout his life he was unusually successful in making contact with influential men who furthered his career.

At this time, say 1925, public hostility to chemical warfare was very high. During the First World War the Germans had used gas, to devastating effect, on the Western front and there was a strong feeling among the military as well as the general public that the use of such methods disgraced those who used them. On 17 June 1925 the Geneva protocol, which 'prohibited the use in war of asphyxiating, poisonous or other gases and of bacteriological methods', was adopted.[11] Neither Japan nor the United States of America ratified this.

Ishii had already begun to advocate experimentation into biological methods of waging warfare but his pleas initially fell upon deaf ears. In 1928 Ishii left Japan for a study trip which would take him to many countries, and allow him to visit many foreign laboratories. He was well-provided with introductions to Japanese military attachés and during his two-year sabbatical is supposed to have seen experimental work in nearly thirty countries, of which the most important were in Russia, France, Germany and the United States.

To his superiors on his return, he argued (probably wrongly) that despite the Geneva protocol the most powerful Western powers were researching into these 'forbidden' matters. He illustrated this by demonstrating how Germany, despite the Hague Declarations of 1899 and 1907 which banned poison gas, had used chlorine, phosgene and mustard gas on the Allies. He noted also the devastating effect of the plague in Europe in earlier centuries.

He explained that medical researchers in Europe, steeped as they were in their mission to save life, could never push their work forward by using humans for experiments in defiance of the Hippocratic Oath[12] in which Western doctors vowed 'to do the sick no harm'. It would seem that some Japanese doctors' scruples were deadened by their patriotism which allowed them to use any means to make Japan great.

Given the serious inhibitions relating to the Hippocratic oath which impeded Western researchers, Ishii argued for a speeding-up of Japanese work on germ warfare and hoped that if human experiments could be sanctioned Japan would have an unassailable lead. He was supported by three powerful men; Colonel Chikahiko Koizumi, who was about to be appointed as the Army's Surgeon General, and was later a Japanese Health Minister; Colonel Tetsuzan Nagata, who was later to be chief of the War Ministry's Military Affairs Bureau; and War Minister Sadao Araki[13] to whom Ishii was distantly related through his wife. Of these only Sadao Araki was arraigned in 1946 by the Military Tribunal of the Far East in Tokyo (although not on any charges relating to biological warfare). He was convicted on Counts 1 and 27 of the Indictment relating to charges regarding the Japanese 'common plan' or conspiracy to wage aggressive war so as to dominate East Asia and was sentenced to life imprisonment, but released in 1955.

OPIUM AND DISEASE

The Japanese policy in occupied China was to encourage trade in opium, heroin and morphine through the Japanese Army's special services branch, which would produce profits sufficient to sustain the Japanese military government. Evidence emerged at the Tokyo War Crimes trial that Japanese drug experts, whose job it was to ensure that Japanese did not take opium, recognised that in China 'There is no hope for anything better because no other good source of revenue has been found for the puppet government.'[14] In this respect the Japanese, as imperialists, were following the classic path, using opium as a tool to manipulate and manage a subject people.

Japanese opium monopolies were created as early as 1932 after the Kwantung army's occupation of Manchuria, and continued under the guise of organisations to suppress the trade throughout Japanese-held territory. There were harsh penalties for any Japanese, whether soldiers or civilians, caught using opium; but by 1940 one American observer calculated that 'there were 600 licensed opium emporia in Peking, 460 in Hankow, and 852 in Canton'.[15]

Farmers were encouraged to borrow capital at low interest to open up more land for opium, but the anticipated profits rarely materialised because of the low fixed price at which the opium was bought by the Japanese. More than 150 000 acres in Manchuria were turned over to poppy cultivation which ensured that the Chinese peasant farmers remained permanently tied, by their indebtedness, to the Japanese.

The whole operation was apparently financed by bonds issued by the Industrial Bank of Japan, which had the backing of several *zaibatsu* including Mitsubishi, Yasuda, Kawasaki, Sumitomo and Mitsui. Article 4 of the document drawn up when the bonds were issued reads: 'These bonds to be secured by the profits of the opium monopoly . . . the principal and interest shall be paid preferentially from the monopoly of profits.'[16]

The evidence for germ warfare comes from the material collected in the course of preparing the prosecution for the Tokyo War Trials in 1945. It would appear that the large-scale experiments took the form of dropping 'plague' bombs.[17] The Chinese press reported (27 October 1940) that a bomb carrying plague-ridden fleas had been dropped on Ninpo, a city in East China, near Shanghai. There was a heavy infestation of fleas and 99 people contracted plague, of whom 98 died. The Chinese health authorities denied that the rats in the city had plague, which is the usual preliminary for such an epidemic. On 4 November 1941 grains of wheat and rice, pieces of paper and cotton wadding rained down from Japanese aircraft on two streets near the East Gate of Changde, Hunan Province, China. Six people died, although there was believed to be no plague amongst the rat population. These incidents in time of war, when there is much confusion, may be suggestive but can hardly be called conclusive evidence of Japan trying to create epidemics.

The experimentation unit set up under Shiro Ishii's command had operated at a camp near Harbin for some years before 1941, when the attack on Pearl Harbor brought the United States into the Pacific War. There would be no compunction about using Chinese criminals and other outcasts as subjects for this work but, once Anglo-Saxon POWs became available, it was tempting to test the reaction of these men to various diseases. Americans, Australians and British prisoners who lived in a POW camp at Mukden[18] were apparently subjected to experimentation. The camp, similar to others then scattered all over South-East Asia, had long low primitive wooden huts with earth piled onto the roofs because of the bitter cold winters of Manchuria.

There was something unusual about this camp for, far from having little or no medical attention from the Japanese, which was the complaint from most POW camps, the Mukden camp was the centre of much attention. Visits by members of the Japanese Propaganda Corps were routine and POWs were expected to play games, take part in quizzes and spelling bees, join the camp orchestra and sing in the choir for the benefit of the Japanese cameras and film units.

More seriously, these men seem to have been under constant medical surveillance: white-coated Japanese were in frequent attendance; injections, reputedly against cholera, dysentery, diarrhoea and tetanus and much else, were frequently administered. The diary of one British officer, only preserved because of the skill with which it was hidden in the beds of very sick men, reveals an extraordinary series of injections and tests on the prisoners. It would appear that the prisoners in Mukden were given injections, which determined whether they would live or die. Was it also the case that it was only Americans who died: were the British and Commonwealth prisoners used as a control group?

Recent researchers in Japan have contacted surviving Japanese who worked in Unit 731 at Pingfan. From these conversations it is clear that the main work was to carry out dissections on dead prisoners. One Japanese worker at Pingfan believed the Americans were given 'infected materials' to drink and then, when the men died, in the bitter winters, further research was done on the cadavers.

In terms of experiments against individuals there was the 'freezing project' where limbs were 'frozen' by draughts of very cold air. This led to terrible injuries with rotting hands and arms. Gas gangrene was also induced by exposing men's buttocks (the rest of the body was protected) to nearby bomb explosions.[19] All ten men involved in this experiment died. Chinese women used as prostitutes for Japanese soldiers were infected with syphilis.[20] After the war these matters were publicised by the Russians and the Chinese but stories from such Communist sources were readily dismissed, especially by the Americans, as propaganda. The Russians put some Japanese on trial for these crimes but, at the same time, were holding as forced labour thousands of Japanese captured in Manchuria.

On 25 November 1969 President Nixon, speaking on behalf of the United States, repudiated the use of 'germ warfare', announcing that 'Biological weapons have massive unpredictable and potentially uncontrollable consequences. They may produce global epidemics and impair the health of future generations. I have therefore decided that the US shall renounce the lethal biological agents and weapons and all other methods of biological warfare.'[21]

President Nixon's announcement helped to re-establish the United States' position as a humanitarian nation and did something to counteract the earlier impression of lack of scruple shown during the immediate post-war period when Shiro Ishii was apparently able to trade immunity from prosecution for the passing of his war secrets to his former enemies.

11 Keeping the Humanitarian Flame Alight

FOR MEN ARE NOT CAST IN ONE MOULD . . .

It was Dr (later Sir) Selwyn Selwyn-Clarke, Medical Officer of Health of Hong Kong, who having himself suffered badly during the Japanese occupation of the colony, wrote that "No one can deny that man's potential for cruelty was exhibited on an appalling scale by the Japanese in the stress of war".[1] Nevertheless his book:

> is dedicated to Rev Kiyoshi Watanabe, formerly officer interpreter of the Imperial Japanese Army, who helped to save the lives of many British prisoners of war and British and Allied civilian men and women and children interned in Hong Kong during the Japanese occupation of 1941–1945 at the risk of losing his own. His wife and daughter were killed during the Allied bombing of Hiroshima on 6 August 1945.

Most of the people whose actions are reported here were Swiss representatives of the ICRC who, as citizens of a neutral country, operated as effectively as they could in a Japan unsympathetic to their work. There were other foreigners, including Jews, who in co-operation with local officials in Japan effected the salvation of thousands of European Jews. Others were Japanese at various levels of society and in various circumstances, who voluntarily performed kindly acts.

JAPANESE GENEROSITY

On 26 August 1946, from the Malacanan Palace in Manila, the President, Manuel Roxas, wrote to General Chiang Kai Shek at Nanking in China a personal letter asking the Chinese General, if it

131

were possible, to intercede on behalf of a Japanese Lieutenant General, Nobuhiko Jimbo, then being held in prison in China for war crimes. President Roxas wrote,

> I should like to submit that Col. Jimbo is responsible for my being alive today. He was known in the Philippines as one of the few Japanese officers with a genuine sympathy for our plight, and as one of those who did what he could, within the limits of his official station, to alleviate the brutal savagery of his superiors and subordinates. On one occasion he risked his life by disobeying an order issued for my execution, and made a successful appeal at a later time for the rescinding of the execution order. This action was not based especially on a personal esteem for me, although he had that too, but on a repugnance for the senseless cruelty and murder madness which possessed his commanders and associates. He was, of my acquaintance, the most humane of the Japanese invaders.[2]

Colonel Jimbo was subsequently released by the Chinese and returned home to Yamagata. President Manuel Roxas died suddenly on 15 April 1948.

Another war-time Japanese hero was Rev. Ryoichi Kato, who was sent, as a civilian employee of the IJN, to Ambon Island in what was then the Dutch East Indies. There seems to be no doubt that Rev. Kato put his own life at risk by remonstrating with the Japanese authorities, as they rounded up people in Ambon, thinking they were spies. Kato succeeded in saving several lives. He also intervened successfully when the Japanese threatened to use local women as 'Comfort women': that is, as prostitutes for Japanese troops.[3] After the war, back home in Japan, Rev. Kato established the South-East Asia Cultural Friendship Society to bring Indonesian students to Japan for further education. He may have succeeded in funding over 600 people.

These are but two examples of those Japanese who refused to accept the mores of the time. Yet another Japanese became involved with the Jews, another persecuted group.

JEWISH REFUGEES

It was a young Dutch Jewish student, Nathan Gutwirth,[4] trapped in Lithuania in the autumn of 1939, who discovered the beginnings of a loophole in official regulations and therefore a means of escape from the Germans. Anti-Jewish feeling had already reached fever point in Nazi Germany and pogroms were well advanced so that German conquest elsewhere in Europe could be expected to jeopardise the life of any Jew. Gutwirth asked the nearest Dutch official, L. P. J. de Dekker in Riga, Latvia, if he could have a visa for the Dutch colony of Curaçao in South America. The reply was that neither Gutwirth nor anyone else required a visa to *go* to Curaçao, although in fact on arrival only the Governor could provide a landing permit. This being the case, the honorary Dutch Consul in Kovno, a Mr Zwartendyk, stamped Gutwirth's passport 'No visa for Curaçao is required'. Once this was known in Kovno, Jewish refugees (mostly from Poland) crowded in to the Dutch authorities to obtain 'Curaçao Visas'.

The Japanese Consul in Kovno between September 1939 and September 1940 was a young diplomat, Senpo Sugihara.[5] Once the 'Curaçao Visas' had been stamped on the papers of the Jews, they quietly besieged the home and office of the Japanese consul. Sugihara issued up to 6000 Japanese transit visas for Jewish refugees in Kovno giving them permission to stay in Japan, as transit passengers, for up to 21 days. Did Sugihara act in the name of an humane Emperor? It could not be his concern to know whether the Russian authorities would issue transit visas to the Jews to travel through Russia or whether the Japanese authorities would permit the refugees into Japan; nevertheless, like other consular officials in the Baltic states, he acted in good faith, as a humanitarian, in a world where such commitment was increasingly rare. Recently, in Japan, Sugihara's humanitarianism has been acclaimed and his reputation restored.

The curious Japanese–Jewish relationship which developed during the Second World War had its origins in the Russo–Japanese War when a German–American Jewish financier, Jacob H. Schiff,[6] made friends with Korekiyo Takahashi[7] from the Bank of Japan. Takahashi was in London in 1904 hoping to organise large credits on a reluctant London money market, in order to ensure Japan's ability to continue to finance her war against Russia. It was believed in Japan that Schiff's agreement to be a party to the loans was crucial in persuading others, and accordingly Schiff became a national hero in Japan.

With the take-over of Manchuria during the 1930s some Japanese conceived the idea of making Manchukuo the refuge for large numbers of Jews displaced from elsewhere. Known as the Fugu plan,[8] it was intended to encourage the Jews to start businesses and new lives in this enclave of northern China. This, it was believed, would bring money,

Ill. 11 Senpo Sugihara, Japanese Consul, who, in 1940, in Kovno, Lithuania, against orders, issued up to 6000 Japanese transit visas to Jews who fled from the Germans across the USSR

development and, even more important, a weakening of American hostility, as Japan offered a haven in Manchukuo to displaced European Jews.

The essence of this plan, which was discussed in the 'highest councils of the Japanese Government',[9] was to enrol 'the talents and skills of European Jewry, plus the capital, influence and sympathy of American Jewry, in the building of Japan's twentieth century empire, the Greater Asia Co-prosperity Sphere'.[10] The Japanese involved included naval Captain Koreshige Inuzuka, Mitsuzo Tamura, industrialist, and Colonel Norihiro Yasue of the Japanese army. These men were not necessarily pro-Jewish, but they did believe that Japanese and Jews might be involved to their mutual benefit.

On the strength of their temporary Japanese visas, thousands of Jews applied for, and received, transit visas to cross the USSR *en route* for Vladivostok. There they boarded a boat for Tsuruga on the north-west coast of Honshu, the main island of Japan. The refugees were welcomed onto Japanese soil by emissaries from the tiny Jewish community in Kobe, where some 50 Jews were engaged in the import and export trade. Although the transit visas were for less than 21 days the Japanese authorities could often be persuaded to extend these for as long as eight months. Between July 1940 and November 1941 'out of 10,000 Jews stranded in Lithuania, 4,608 refugees escaped by this route'.[11]

At the beginning of the Second World War Kobe was the second largest open port which, following the outbreak of the Sino–Japanese War in 1937, had become a great military depot. Out of a population of 1 000 000 there were some 3000 foreigners. The Jewish population made themselves responsible for the Jewish refugees from Lithuania although expenses were partly met by funds sent by the United States Joint Distribution Committee and by the Hebrew Immigrant Aid Society. American aid stopped in July 1941 when, as relations between America and Japan worsened, both countries imposed trade embargoes. Secretly the Japanese authorities allocated extra bread and flour for the refugees although there was fear concerning the reaction of the local population, which was already, before the war had started, suffering from food shortages and rationing. Japanese doctors treated, some without fee, nearly 800 refugee patients, and many received vaccinations. The Japanese in Kobe are said to have responded to these foreigners using the word *Kawaiso* ('we feel sorry for them').[12]

On 22 June 1941 the Germans invaded Russia, but by then the flow of refugees via the Trans-Siberian railway had already come to a halt.

In Kobe the Japanese secret police, who kept a close eye on any foreigner and were terrified of communist infiltrators, were getting increasingly anxious about the refugees. As a result of Japanese nervousness most of the Jews travelled on to Shanghai where, in the Japanese controlled Hongkew district, they set up a Jewish settlement which ultimately housed 18 000 refugees. Life was very difficult, especially after February 1943 when, following German pressure, 'a mild ghetto was imposed' on the Jewish community.

In addition to Senpo Sugihara there was at least one other Japanese who espoused the cause of the Jews. A. Kotsuji,[13] perhaps the only Japanese Hebrew scholar, was active on behalf of the refugees. As a friend and former colleague of Yosuke Matsuoka,[14] the then Foreign Minister, Kotsuji was able to seek an interview in Tokyo. When the two men discussed the position of the Jews in Kobe, the Foreign Minister suggested that central government in Tokyo could turn a blind eye if Kobe officials extended, temporarily, the Jewish transit visas. Kotsuji therefore used his influence to persuade the police in Kobe to extend the short term transit visas, sometimes for several months, while individual Jews sought to obtain asylum anywhere in the world.

SWISS DELEGATES, INTERNATIONAL REPRESENTATIVES IN JAPAN

The ICRC's first task was to discover from the Japanese how they proposed to deal with matters relating to the POWs and civilian internees. It was encouraging that the Japanese legation at Berne reported as follows:

> Since the Japanese government has not ratified the Convention relative to the treatment of prisoners of war, signed in Geneva on 27 July 1929, it is therefore not bound by the said Convention. Nevertheless in so far as possible, it intends to apply this Convention *mutatis mutandis*, to all prisoners of war who may fall into its hands, at the same time taking into consideration the customs of each nation and each race in respect of feeding and clothing of prisoners.

With regard to civilian internees, the Japanese Legation at Berne stated on 14 February 1942: 'During the whole of the present war the Japanese Government will apply *mutatis mutandis*, and subject to reciprocity, the articles of the Convention concerning prisoners of war to non-combatant internees of enemy countries, on condition that the belligerent states do not subject them against their will to manual labour'.[15]

These pronouncements by the Japanese government gave reason to hope that the activities of the ICRC might be carried out in a spirit of co-operation and mutual help. This proved too optimistic a view. The Japanese POW Information Bureau (*Horyojoho Kyoku*) was a government service, entirely subordinate to the Ministry of War, and its members, (retired army officers who distrusted foreigners) were unwilling to co-operate.

In practical terms the work of the International Red Cross was severely limited because of Japanese hostility. Their extended empire was divided into three sections. In Japan, Korea, Manchuria and Formosa delegates were permitted, to operate under restrictions; in Shanghai, Hong Kong and elsewhere in mainland China, which was in Japanese hands, humanitarian work might be possible from time to time; but in the occupied territories of South-East Asia, which was regarded by the Japanese as a war zone, the ICRC was forbidden.[16] As a result even the location of POW camps in parts of South-East Asia was unknown and there were no visits from any neutral official.[17]

In Japan the accredited Swiss delegates were led by Dr Fritz Paravicini[18] (1874–1944) who had operated on behalf of the ICRC since the First World War (see Chapter 5 above). He was assisted by Mr Max Pestalozzi[19] and later by Mr Harry Angst[20] (appointed 22 July 1943). No personal papers appear to have survived, although from war-time reports both from the JRC and the ICRC it is possible to know something of the work done in Japan.

In March 1943 the ICRC, in the persons of Dr Paravicini, assisted by Mr Max Pestalozzi, did succeed in visiting POW camps in Osaka, Hyogo, Hiroshima and Fukuoka prefectures. In May Mr Paravicini visited POW camps in Taiwan, but this appears to have been his last excursion. Mr Pestalozzi was at the third branch of the Tokyo POW camp, at Kiraoka (Nagano Prefecture) in June; in August he visited the northern army headquarters and camps at Hakodate on Hokkaido, and Ishinomaki near Sendai; in November he was in Korea and Manchuria at Mukden, while in December he visited Zentsuji.[21]

One can only guess at the frustrations of ICRC work during the war years of 1942 and 1943. The Red Cross authorities in Geneva early in 1944, wrote with sorrow of the death of Dr Paravicini 'who had served the ideal of the Red Cross with a rare distinction'.[22] The Japanese

Foreign Minister, Mamoru Shigemitsu, wrote of his 'accomplishment of the high humanitarian mission of the Red Cross in greater Asia'.[23] The funeral was attended by two vice-presidents of the JRC, the head of the official Japanese Bureau for POWs, and a representative of the Japanese Foreign Office as well as by many diplomats and members of the Swiss community. The loss of Dr Paravicini, who spoke Japanese and was known and trusted by the xenophobic Japanese, was a severe blow to the ICRC. One can only speculate as to whether anxiety over his war work shortened his life.

The representatives of the ICRC have received a bad press from the former POWs in support of whom visits to prison camps were made.[24] The Far Eastern prisoners cannot accept that the ICRC did anything positive to aid the Allied soldiers, sailors and airmen during their hour of need. The Swiss representative, working in Japan, believed that they had, at whatever cost, to maintain their links with the Japanese, and as a result they were unable to exert any pressure. Comment is difficult; is it possible that the dedicated Swiss Red Cross delegates allowed themselves to be intimidated by the Japanese military? It is certainly the case, no doubt due to censorship, that the Swiss wrote anodyne reports of their camp visits, which could be, and doubtless were, read with satisfaction by anyone, including the Japanese. But after the war these reports, which were sent to the ICRC in Geneva, infuriated POWs who took the trouble to read them. It is shocking to report that early in 1944 on hearing of the death of Dr Paravicini 'some 400 POWs in Omori Camp, Tokyo, cheered and cheered'.[25]

RED CROSS PARCELS

It should have been possible for the Japanese military authorities to distribute Red Cross parcels, collected from contributing societies from all over the world, to the POWs in the many camps scattered throughout the Japanese empire in eastern Asia. That those parcels were not regularly distributed reflected the power of the commanding officers of the prisoner camps who used the parcels as a form of coercion. Accounts of POW experience repeatedly assert that the issue of Red Cross parcels was arbitrary and reflected the unpredictability of the camp authorities. Almost all prisoners also believe that the contents of many of the Red Cross parcels were enjoyed by the Japanese themselves, who were desperately short of supplies of all kinds.

In the ARC bulletins, which occasionally reached the POWs, there were references to the 'weekly food packages' which were intended to supplement rations supplied by the Japanese. According to one senior officer no Red Cross parcels were received by American prisoners for one year after capture. Thereafter, from April 1943 to the end of the war in August 1945, they had been given '15 packets in 3 years and 3 months' which was 'a collapsible suitcase containing about 50 items of immediate need to the newly captured prisoners'.[26]

Later, a prisoner held in Manchuria in the spring of 1945 reported that 'the Red Cross depots in Vladivostok, overflowing with food and mail and clothing and we go hungry, wear rags, and have had no mail since coming to Manchuria (last mail received 9 months ago)'. Not only were food parcels withheld from prisoners, but mail was also denied. The usual Japanese excuse was that the letters had to be censored; this was a particularly cruel deceit, because letters for the prisoners were usually up to two years old, and had come, after interminable delays, from Australia or Britain or wherever.

Perhaps more frequently towards the end of the war, when supplies were short, the Japanese themselves made free use of the Red Cross supplies intended for their prisoners. There are many accounts of these transfers. One Australian officer noted that "Guards were frequently seen smoking cigarettes from Red Cross cigarette tins" and, in one jungle camp near Aperon in the middle of 1944, the Japanese guards lived for a period of five months on the Red Cross tins and foodstuffs which should have gone to their prisoners.

Indeed some Australian prisoners, having seen 'three goods vans packed with American Red Cross boots' on a train going north to the Japanese army, prayed that the Red Cross would not send further supplies which could be taken over and used by the enemy. The extent of the failure to distribute Red Cross parcels was only known after the POWs were freed (see Table 11.1).

DR MARCEL JUNOD

After Dr Paravicini's death early in 1944 a replacement was sought in Europe, and Dr Marcel Junod,[27] with his interpreter Mlle Margherita Strachler, was appointed to Japan. At the insistence of the unco-operative Japanese they left Geneva in June and reached Manchuria on 28 July 1945. They travelled via Paris, Naples, Athens, Cairo, Teheran, Moscow, Siberia, Chita and Otpor to Manchuria because

Table 11.1 Money and supplies dispersed by the International Red Cross in the Far East, 1941–5

	Funds supplied by Governments and Red Cross Societies	Funds collected on the spot	Total
Drugs, surgical apparatus, dental treatment	953 032.46	38 568.25	991 600.71
Soap, washing and toilet, disinfectants	289 894.03	6 859.10	296 753.13
Food	8 784 470.04	547 737.33	9 332 207.37
Clothing, footwear, thread, buttons	601 196.26	89 197.07	690 393.33
Toilet articles; tooth brushes, tooth powder, razors, blades, combs, brushes, etc.	134 809.15	2 440.35	137 249.50
Books, games, sports equipment, musical instruments	44 060.30	28 354.40	72 414.70
Beds, mattresses, blankets, sheets, towels	126 899.67	37 359.60	164 259.27
Household utensils, brooms, toilet paper	104 476.50	5 024.42	109 500.92
Office fittings, stationery, pencils, etc.	37 213.47	74.40	37 287.87
Allowances (for civilians)	831 644.73		831 644.73
Pocket money (POWs and civilians)	1 518 161.47	50 080.14	1 568 241.61
Relief packages	371 161.70		371 161.70
Tobacco, cigarettes, articles for smokers	486 265.89	177 307.13	663 573.02
Officers' mess (Shanghai)	18 281.15		18 281.15
Rent, telephone, electricity, heating, repairs to building, furniture, kitchen fittings, wages (800 000 fr, of which was for the 'Rosary Hill Red Cross Home' Hong Kong)	899 099.86	44 891.95	943 991.81
Miscellaneous, including carriage of goods, transports, cable charges	913 338.40	155 512.74	1 068 851.14
Total (Swiss Francs)	16 114 005.08	1 183 406.88	17 297 411.96

Source: Report of the ICRC, Second World War, Vol.1, p. 463.

the Japanese authorities would only sanction a route which did not pass through 'enemy territory'. Dr Junod and Miss Strachler did not in fact reach Japan until August 1945, at the time of the atomic bombs and the Japanese surrender. It is to Dr Junod that we owe the first-hand accounts which we have of his visits to Japanese prisoner of war camps in Manchuria, as he made his way laboriously, and with many delays, to Japan in the late summer of 1945.

During the hiatus between Paravicini's death at the beginning of 1944 and Junod's arrival 20 months later, Max Pestalozzi and Harry Angst undertook the anxious work of organising visits to the POW camps. Prisoners-of-war diaries, some of which were subsequently published, did refer to the visits of the ICRC representatives, although invariably in dismissive terms.[28] Individual prisoners were lucky if they saw the Red Cross representatives even at a distance, for the routine enforced by the military guards was to keep the prisoners and their Red Cross visitor apart, thus effectively defeating the purpose of the visit. At no time during the Second World War is there any report of a visit involving any meaningful exchange between prisoners of the Japanese and ICRC representatives. Contrast the two-minute conversation allowed in August 1945, in Manchuria, between prisoner General Wainwright and visitor Dr Marcel Junod, with the two-hour visits which Dr Paravicini reported on his POW camp tour of 1918.

The efforts of the delegates of the ICRC to visit the prisoner of war camps, in the period when Pestalozzi and Angst were the representatives, were not entirely unsuccessful. As Dr Junod writes:

> On three occasions in as many years they were allowed to pay a short visit to POW camps in Korea. Twice they were allowed to go to Formosa. But it was not until November 1943, after a year of complete silence, that they were allowed to go to Manchuria, and even then they were permitted to visit only one camp, that in Mukden. They never succeeded in getting permission to visit any of the camps in Burma.[29]

In the official account it is reported that 'In spite of obstacles the delegation succeeded in visiting 63 camps, 42 for POW and 21 for civilian internees.'[30]

Accounts of these visits were made to the ICRC, and they were published in the *Revue International de la Croix Rouge*,[31] but these dry factual acounts, subject to strict censorship, bear little or no relationship to those angry accounts from prisoners' own personal journals.

There are also Dr Junod's own accounts, which are worth recording, of his and Miss Strachler's visits to camps in Manchuria in August 1945.

After innumerable delays they paid two visits to POWs in Manchuria, each memorable in its own way. At a camp in the suburbs of Mukden, Junod visited the camp hospital, as he wrote:

> We were taken along a corridor with sick-rooms on either side. Standing by the wall near each door were three or four sick prisoners all of whom bowed low as we approached. Those prisoners who were unable to rise were seated tailor-fashion on their beds, their arms crossed on their chests, and they too bowed as low as their bandages, wounds or mutilations would permit. When the last Japanese officer had passed they resumed the upright position, their eyes raised to the ceiling. Never once did their eyes meet ours.[32]

Dr Junod was horrified by the fear with which the POWs regarded Colonel Matsuda, the commandant of the camp. He tried to talk, asking 'Is there a doctor amongst you?' Not a muscle moved. Eventually Colonel Matsuda indicated an Australian doctor who found it almost impossible to converse with the Swiss, looking constantly to the camp commandant for permission. The implications of this behaviour shocked Dr Junod.

The following day, Junod succeeded in visiting the camp at Seihan where 15 senior officers were held. These included Generals Wainwright (United States) and Percival (British) and Governor Starkenborgh (Netherlands). On reaching the camp, the Red Cross delegation was obliged to listen to the one-and-a-half hour lecture on the excellence of the camp. At the end of this it was announced that,

> You are authorised to visit the camp provided that you give me your word of honour that you will make no gesture of sympathy whatever to the prisoners and that you will not say a word even 'Good Morning'.
>
> On your attitude today will depend the whole future of the International Red Cross Delegation in Japan.[33]

Junod agreed not to speak to fourteen of the prisoners but insisted that he must address one prisoner to tell him that the delegation was from the ICRC!

In the grey house where the senior officers were kept, which had previously housed European mine managers, Junod was startled to find the fifteen prisoners 'upright and motionless in the middle of the room'. As soon as the officer's sabre 'rapped on the floor' all bowed low, their arms close to their bodies.[34]

The Red Cross delegate addressed a few simple stock questions to Wainwright (to whom he had chosen to speak) but when Junod asked him if he had any request, there was a sharp intervention: 'Any request will have to be put in writing and sent to Tokyo', he declared. The longed-for interview had been less than two minutes.

As Junod walked away there were angry voices:

> a thin, nervous-looking man broke through the barriers of Japanese sentries and ran towards me. He was very pale but determined. Out of breath he reached us and addressed me 'Excuse me, I am General Percival, I protest against the fact that you have been authorised to talk to General Wainwright although I am the senior officer here. There is a lot I would like to tell you. Things take place here that you ought to know'.[35]

Junod (having promised to speak to no one but Wainwright) then turned to the interpreter:

> This is an impossible situation. Please ask the Colonel to give me permission to make the necessary explanations to General Percival. When I asked permission to speak to General Wainwright I did not know that General Percival was the senior officer in the camp and he is perfectly entitled to feel astonished that I did not speak to him. The nature of the visit I have been compelled to make here today must truly astonish him.[36]

Colonel Matsuda allowed a one minute conversation. Dr Junod explained to General Percival the circumstances, the conditions which had been imposed. 'When will you come again?' asked General Percival. 'As soon as I possibly can' replied Junod. 'Promise me to come back, promise me to come back.' General Percival was hurried away by the Japanese guards.

It was 6 August 1945, over 1000 miles to the south-east; the first atomic bomb exploded over Hiroshima. Within three weeks Dr Junod was visited at the New Grand Hotel, Yokohama, by Generals Wainwright[37] and Percival, resplendent in new uniforms. 'This time we will be able to talk in peace', said General Percival.

Junod left Manchuria for Japan in a Japanese military plane on 9 August 1945, the day on which the second atomic bomb was dropped on Nagasaki. He arrived safely in Tokyo and was greeted by his Swiss friends, but as he was travelling in Tokyo he became aware of the terrible devastation from the American bombing campaign. Junod listened to the Emperor's speech on 15 August 1945 which announced an armistice. Would the Japanese comply? There was great anxiety amongst the foreigners in Tokyo, for it was widely believed that the prisoners of war would be murdered if the war ended in defeat.

Dr Junod's reaction to the uncertainty was to think of the prisoners of war, 'cut off and stranded in camps in metropolitan Japan'. He accordingly organised groups of neutral Europeans, Swiss and Swedes, who would go to act as observers at the seven main prisoners' camps in mainland Japan. The, now co-operative, Japanese authorities quickly gave their approval and the neutral delegates, acting for the ICRC, left for the camps on 27 August. On arrival at each camp they were able to use the Japanese radio to advise General MacArthur that they were in position to oversee the evacuation of the prisoners from the camps. When Dr Junod despatched his temporary teams of ICRC delegates to the POW camps,[38] he asked the group going to the Hiroshima[39] area to pay a visit into the city and to report on the effects of the bomb.

THE JAPANESE RED CROSS SOCIETY, 1941–5

For the international division of the JRC the years from 1941 to 1945 were a time of shame, for the Society had great difficulty in keeping its international links open. Money for relief, medicines and goods were sent for the use of prisoners in their camps. Did the prisoners benefit from this? Vice-President Shimazu[40] of the Red Cross travelled widely, and on several occasions visited POW camps with the ICRC delegate. Thousands of items were handled for POWs and other Allied internees: in 1944 the Japanese Red Cross dealt with 100 000 letters from POWs and other detainees.[41] Nevertheless the inability of the JRC to ensure that its humanitarian ideals were adhered to must have been a matter of shame to those who headed its International Relations Section.

As the ICRC reported:

The Foreign Department (of the Japanese Red Cross) was unable to carry out the rapidly increasing duties which were connected with the war. The burden of work fell on a Director and a Secretary assisted by three voluntary workers, who were not well acquainted with foreign languages. Custom demanded that a representative of the Society should accompany the ICRC delegate in their camp visits, but the Secretary who was the only person available, was soon exhausted by the onerous task. In view of staff shortages, the Red Cross of Japan had renewed difficulties in co-operating usefully with the Committee delegation in Tokyo.

It was a depressing time for the foreign desk of the JRC, for all their efforts were nullified by the attitudes of their own military authorities. Nevertheless, as the ICRC notes, 'On several occasions the intermediary of the Japanese Red Cross proved of great help to the Swiss delegates', who additionally recorded that the JRC also 'always met the expenses entailed by the visits of delegates to the camps'.[42]

In fact the JRC reverted to being a narrow nationalistic Society, almost all of its efforts being geared to servicing the Japanese army and navy. Relief Detachments were recruited solely to help in military and naval hospitals; for, willingly or not, the JRC had emerged as a subsidiary arm of the military authorities. JRC nursing staff served on all the fronts during the war, suffering as the Japanese soldiers did, especially during the latter phase of the war when the Japanese were in disarray and forced to retreat. One of the most poignant references comes from a Japanese soldier in Burma who saw the dead 'Japanese Red Cross nurses floating downstream with their hair spread out on the water. I can never forget the sight of their bodies drifting towards our raft as if drawn towards it.'[43] After the war the Society recruited at least one soldier who, wounded in China, was so impressed with the standard of care of the Red Cross nurses there that he joined the organisation as an administrative officer in 1946.[44]

During the Pacific War the JRC reverted to its role as patriotic society. Perhaps the Society was coerced by the military authorities, certainly military behaviour made any humanitarian effort dangerous and problematic.

It was Dr Selwyn Selwyn-Clarke, the former Medical Officer of the colony of Hong Kong who, after the war was over, wrote 'men are not cast in one mould, even by war, even by a code or an ideology'.[45] And so it was possible to find many, including some Japanese, who kept the humanitarian flame alight.

Part IV
1945, and After

12 'The Face of War is the Face of Death'

DEFEAT

In the first eight months of 1945 the Japanese themselves found to their cost that, in the words of the American Secretary of State for War, Henry L. Stimson,[1] 'War is death.' As American forces closed in on the Japanese mainland, ferocious bombing raids were launched onto the sprawling conurbations of Japan. As fire bombs rained down, thousands died as acres of land, covered by small flimsy wood and paper houses, were engulfed in flames. These terrible raids did not produce any plea for peace from the Japanese government. At 5 a.m. on 6 August 1945, President Truman gave permission for the first atomic bomb to be dropped at Hiroshima.

It was Laurens van der Post, a British officer who was then a prisoner in Japanese hands, who wrote that when the bomb fell on Hiroshima 'it must have looked as if the sun goddess Amaterasu herself had hurled fragments of her sun at Japan to shatter it out of its suicidal course'.[2] There was still no word from Japan.

On 9 August 1945 the second atomic bomb was dropped on Nagasaki; thereafter, on 15 August, the Emperor made his historic radio broadcast – speaking in an ancient courtly Japanese, not readily understood – to announce that Japan would accept the articles of the Potsdam agreement. This, issued by the United States, Britain and China, demanded 'the unconditional surrender of the Japanese armed forces'. Surrender was an unprecedented and, to many, a shocking response for the Japanese military authorities, many of whom took their own lives rather than face submission and occupation. Because there was doubt in Tokyo as to whether the generals overseas would accept the surrender, imperial princes were sent from Tokyo to China, South-East Asia and Manchuria to ensure compliance.

Throughout the Japanese Greater Asia Co-Prosperity Sphere thousands of Japanese, many of whom would never see Japan again, fell into the hands of their former enemies. When the Allies arrived, the Americans concerned themselves primarily with planning the occupation of Japan proper; the British, French and Dutch with re-occupying their old empires. The Russians, previously not at war with Japan, who had been relieved of the terrible war on their western front by the surrender of Germany in the spring of 1945, with large forces poised on the northern borders of Manchuria, on 8 August 1945 declared war on Japan and marched into Manchuria.

During the course of the hostilities, from the war against China in 1937 to the end of the struggle in August 1945, the Japanese had lost not far short of 2 000 000 men (see Table 12.1). In Japan, almost all civilian casualties – totalling nearly 400 000 – were incurred after March 1945, when the US Air Force began its campaign of saturation bombing.

Table 12.1 Approximate Japanese losses during the Pacific War, 1941–5

China War, 1937–41		185 647
Imperial Army, 1941–5		1 140 429
Against US Forces	485 717	
Against British and Dutch Forces	208 026	
China	202 958	
Australian Combat Zones	199 511	
French Indo–China	2 803	
Manchuria and USSR	7 483	
Other, overseas	23 388	
Japan proper	10 543	
Imperial Navy		414 879
Total		1 740 955
Civilian deaths from air raids were given as follows:		
Tokyo	97 031	
Hiroshima	140 000	
Nagasaki	70 000	
63 other cities	86 336	

Source: J. W. Dower, *War Without Mercy* . . ., p. 297.

In addition to the 2 million Japanese fatal casualties there were over 300 000 men who were so severely wounded that long-term government pensions were agreed. Of those repatriated in 1945, immediately after the war, nearly 4.5 million – almost all the fighting men – were judged to be in poor health.[3]

The surrender document was signed at an impressive ceremony on the aircraft carrier *USS Missouri* on 2 September 1945 in Tokyo Bay. General Douglas MacArthur,[4] the Supreme Allied Commander, had already landed at Atsugi Air Base near Tokyo on 28 August 1945. The occupation of Japan went forward without incident, as the Japanese bowed their heads and accepted their fate with quiet dignity, even though conditions in the towns and cities were very bad, food in short supply, and living conditions deplorable.

WAR CRIME TRIALS

The first task the Allies set themselves was to bring to justice those who were believed to be 'war criminals'; this included those thought to have disgraced the good name of Japan by brutal behaviour towards countless peoples, including Allied servicemen, other native forces, serving the colonial powers, and local peoples throughout the region.

All over the former Japanese empire, Allied forces began the task of arresting those Japanese who were thought to have been implicated in war crimes, either against local civilians or against POWs. It proved difficult to prosecute in many cases partly because, during the interlude between 16 August when the Allies accepted the Japanese plea for peace, and 8 September when MacArthur's occupation administration was set up, the Japanese authorities had cabled their offices all over South-East Asia to destroy all incriminating evidence.

From the War Ministry Office on Ichigaya Hill in Tokyo to remote Pacific islands, bonfires raged as conscientious officers burnt masses of paper before the Allied occupation could take place. It would appear that transcripts 'of *all* imperial conferences, *all* the records of the Supreme Council for the Direction of the War, *all* the deliberations of the Cabinet and Privy Council, *all* files on prisoners of war, *all* orders and plans relating to the attack on the Philippines and South East Asia and *all* the documents relating to the Manchurian and Chinese campaigns' were destroyed.[5]

Further, a top secret cable urged Japanese field commanders to see that 'those documents which would be unfavourable to us in the hands of the enemy are to be treated in the same way as secret documents and destroyed'. The same cable advised that 'personnel who mistreated prisoners of war and (civilian) internees . . . are permitted to take care of it by immediately transferring or by fleeing without a trace'.[6]

Such action left those Allied lawyers who were trying to gather evidence for the prosecution of Japanese for war crimes woefully short of material. Notwithstanding, serving officers were determined to

bring those Japanese officers to justice who were known to have
behaved brutally to POWs and to civilians.

The principal involvement of all the Allies, including the late
arrivals, the Russians, was with the Tokyo War Crimes Trial held
in Tokyo between 3 May 1946 and 12 November 1948. Although
American lawyers dominated, it was an Allied tribunal to which
eleven nations each contributed one judge. The judges were Radha-
binod Pal (India), B. V. A. Röling (Netherlands), Edward Stuart
McDougall (Canada), Lord Patrick (Britain), Myron C. Cramer
(United States), Sir William Webb (Australia) who was President,
Ju-ao Mei (China), I. M. Zarayanov (USSR), Henri Bernard (France),
Harvey Northcroft (New Zealand) and Delfin Jaranilla (Philippines).
The prosecutors and defenders were from all the nations, while
several Japanese and American lawyers distinguished themselves
defending the Japanese. The chief prosecutor was the American
Joseph Keenan. There were 25 defendants of whom seven, six of
them army generals, were convicted on several serious charges and
sentenced to death. The remaining defendants were sentenced to
detention in prison.

The trial was controversial from the beginning and several judges
disagreed with some of the decisions. Judge Pal[7] from India did not
attend much of the trial and dissented from all the verdicts, while the
President, Judge Webb from Australia, disapproved of the death
sentence in principle, while Judge Röling,[8] from the Netherlands,
was also critical. It was probably the case that retribution rather than
reason determined the sentences. Certainly, former Allied POWs
would have felt even greater outrage had no punishment been meted
out to those who had some responsibility for their misery over the war
years.

In addition to General Hideki Tojo (1884–1948), who took full
responsibility for the actions of the Japanese government and insisted
upon exonerating the Emperor from liability in the conduct of the war,
and who was regarded by the Allies as the chief war criminal, those
sentenced to death[9] were General Kenji Doihara, Baron Koki Hirota,
who was the only civilian executed, General Seishiro Itagaki, General
Heitaro Kimura, General Iwane Matsui and General Akira Muto (see
Appendix B).

Apart from the trials in Tokyo there were hundreds of others
including that of General Tomoyuki Yamashita, the 'Tiger of
Malaya', who had later been the commander of the Japanese troops
in the Philippines, and who was brought to trial in Manila on

25 October 1945 and on 7 December was convicted and sentenced to death. Yamashita's trial has been severely criticised. It was held in the Philippines before 'a military commission of five American generals, none of whom had either combat or legal experience'.[10] The charge was that Yamashita had 'unlawfully disregarded and failed to discharge his duty as commander to control the operations of the members of his command, permitting them to commit brutal atrocities and other high crimes'. On appeal, the case went eventually to the US Supreme Court where it was upheld by a vote of 5–2, Justices Frank Murphy and Wiley B. Rutledge being the two dissentients. Murphy wrote:

> This petitioner was rushed to trial under an improper charge, given insufficient time to prepare an adequate defense, deprived of the benefits of some of the most elementary rules of evidence and summarily sentenced to be hanged. In all this needless and unseemly haste there was no serious attempts to prove that he had committed a recognized violation of the laws of war.[11]

Nevertheless it would have been very difficult to find a single ex POW who would have accepted Justice Frank Murphy's impeccable reasoning.

Like the other Allies, the British were determined to bring to justice those who had been involved with brutal incidents and long-term cruelty against British and Commonwealth POWs. It was an extremely difficult matter requiring patience and tenacity. The enquiries discussed here will be confined to the work of Cyril Wild (1908–1946),[12] a captain and senior intelligence officer, who had carried the white flag of surrender, and who had been taken prisoner with General Percival at Singapore on 15 February 1942.[13] After the war, as Colonel Wild, he became the British War Crimes Liaison Officer (Malaya and Singapore), which involved him in interviewing Lieutenant General Yamashita, 'the Tiger of Malaya' in Manila, prior to his trial there and also in attending as a witness and giving evidence at the Tokyo War Crimes trial. Sadly Wild died in an RAF Dakota plane which crashed on leaving Hong Kong airport on 25 September 1946.

On 28 October 1945 Major C. H. D. Wild, in his interview with General Tomoyuki Yamashita, repeated allegations of Japanese brutality to Yamashita. Most of the atrocities, about which Wild knew at first hand, concerned events in Malaya at the beginning of 1942. The conversation started with Wild referring to the letter which

Yamashita had had dropped from the air demanding the surrender of
General Percival in which reference was made to the bravery of the
British. Yamashita agreed, saying 'Your troops in Malaya did fight
extremely bravely.' Nevertheless, as Wild pointed out, the surrender
resulted in Japanese officers refusing any rights to the British as POWs
because they had surrendered unconditionally.[14]

Wild instanced five occasions on which atrocities were perpetrated
by the Japanese, as follows:

1. two massacres of Australian and Indian wounded after the battle
   of Muar;
2. presumed shooting of L'Sgt Keiller, Australian Imperial Force
   (AIF);
3. Alexandra Hospital massacre;
4. shooting of fourteen Australian prisoners 19 February 1942;
5. massacre of Chinese in Singapore.

In this last case Yamashita denied that it was anything to do with the
army but agreed that the Japanese secret police often acted against
those whom they called 'thieves and robbers'. Wild believed that
hundreds and possibly thousands of Chinese civilians were murdered
in an act of terror.[15]

Notwithstanding the retribution meted out to these tried and
convicted Japanese, they were but a few and the tip of an iceberg.
Many of those who might have been brought to trial quietly
disappeared, and in time resumed their normal lives. Yet the
execution of a few was in some ways an attempt to atone for the
horrors of the Rape of Nanking in 1937, the Rape of Manila in 1945
and the countless other acts of barbarity perpetrated between 1931
and 1945 wherever the Japanese had established themselves as colonial
rulers.

ALLIES VICTORIOUS

In addition to the grim state of the country the Japanese were
exhausted and many were relieved that the war was over. As a people
the Japanese were subdued and their sense of shame at their defeat
profound; somewhat to their surprise the Americans, who with
representatives of all the Allies occupied Japan, did not behave
oppressively. The ordinary citizen found that the anticipation of

occupation proved to be more frightening than the reality, and most Japanese social controls fell into disuse.

The Allies other than the Americans (that is, the Dutch, French as well as the British) believed that the end of the war would enable them to re-establish their colonial empires. In fact the short-lived Japanese empire – which lasted some three-and-a-half years – had itself created a revolution in expectations, for the subject peoples resolved that the foreign imperialists would never return. After 1945 colonial administrations found it difficult to accept the fact that the temporary Japanese take-over had destroyed their colonial empires, making independence the only acceptable outcome.

As the Dutch, French and British moved in to re-occupy South-East Asia, they in their turn became responsible for thousands of Japanese who had been fighting in these areas when the cease-fire came. Few accounts of the feelings of 'surrendered enemy personnel' remain, but one response to the British must be quoted.

Yuji Aida was one of those who were held by the British to supply menial labour in Burma until 1947, when they were returned to Japan. From November 1945 to May 1947 Aida was, as he wrote, a *Prisoner of the British*.[16] His book seemed a catalogue of cruelty; camps for Japanese were, he believed, established in deliberately foul places near swamps and rubbish dumps, and British arrogance was demonstrated by the contempt with which they treated the Japanese. One of Aida's friends was urinated on by a British soldier because he, the Japanese, had, while cleaning the latrines, dared to urinate in the same place as the British.[17] Reburying British corpses neatly to make decent cemeteries was an unpleasant forced labour; cleaning out women's quarters, while the women paraded shamelessly naked, to show their contempt for Japanese, was a terrible affront to a Japanese male. Aida argued that he would have preferred physical cruelty.

As Aida concluded,

> It is true that the British did not beat prisoners up or kick them or butcher them alive. They committed almost none of what are usually termed atrocities. But this does not mean that they behaved according to humanitarian principles. On the contrary they often behaved with childish vindictiveness. And yet even the most vindictive act had a facade of reasonableness, and was carried out in such a way as to avoid any accusation being made against them. And British troops were always cool and collected and carried out these actions calmly, with great indifference. From one point of view

they were certainly not cruel, but from another point of view I felt that their treatment reflected the cruellest attitude a man can have towards his fellow men.[18]

Certainly the British were responding to Japanese war-time behaviour; everyone knew of the suffering of the Allied POWs. Was Aida exceptional? Many Japanese military men were relieved to surrender and profoundly glad that the war was over. Was Aida, later professor of History at Kyoto University, as deeply scarred by his experiences as a 'surrendered enemy personnel' as the former Allied POWs?

In Russia, an enormous build-up had been taking place, on the northern Manchurian border, as Russian troops were transferred to the Far East from the western front in the Spring of 1945. By the summer of 1945 the Soviets were thought to have as many as 1 500 000 troops with about 5000 tanks and nearly 5000 combat aircraft facing the Japanese Kwantung army in Manchuria.[19] There were perhaps over 1 000 000 troops in Manchuria fighting for Japan, made up of 650 000 Japanese and 350 000 Mongolians, Chinese and others.

In Manchuria there was utter dismay and disbelief in the Kwantung Army headquarters where Japanese officers in considerable numbers, who could not face the reality of defeat and imprisonment, took their own lives. Before the cease-fire was agreed the Russians swooped as far south as they could, dropping paratroop units into the cities of Mukden, Hsinking, Harbin, Kirin and Port Arthur and seizing airfields and communications centres. It must have given senior Russian officers considerable satisfaction to take over areas from which they had been driven by the Japanese in the earlier war of 1904–5.

All over Manchuria Japanese army units surrendered, and terrified Japanese settlers, imposed on the country and maintained there by the Kwantung Army, were abandoned to the mercy of the local Mongolian people and the Russian soldiery. Almost all 600 000 Japanese armed men were captured and were transported to the Soviet Union, where they became forced labourers. Repatriation began in 1947, some two years later. From then until 1949 513 139 Japanese – out of 594 000 originally taken – were returned to Japan.

The position of the Japanese settlers in Manchuria was even more pitiable for large groups of Japanese, including considerable numbers from religious groups who had allowed themselves to be persuaded to take up residence in Manchuria and who had lived in their own settlements, were abandoned. One such village was Halahei, on the railway line between Halon-Arshan and Hsingan in the north-west of Manchuria. The massacre of the people of Halahei, who had left their village and tried to walk south-east towards Japan, by units of the Russian army is well documented, but is only one of many such incidents which took place during the confused days of late summer 1945.[20]

Marcel Junod remained in Japan as the ICRC representative. When he was asked by the Japanese, eager to have his help to recover their citizens lost on the Asian mainland, to intervene with the Russian authorities, he explained that the ICRC 'relations with the Soviet Union were far from harmonious and it was not likely that they would listen to him'.[21] Eventually the Soviet reply to General MacArthur, the Supreme Commander, came: 'We do not recognise the need for official visits of this kind.'[22] In this way the Japanese – post 1945 – eager to work with humanitarian groups in an attempt to save their own citizens, were rebuffed in the way that they had earlier acted when they themselves were powerful and successful.

Notwithstanding the common view of the Russians as oppressive guardians of former prisoners, a rare account of one man's experiences does not bear this out. 'Makoto', the nickname of a young Japanese soldier, with 13 officers and 250 men from anti-aircraft companies, had been captured in Manchuria by the Russians in August 1945. In mid-November they were entrained and they travelled north then west into Russia. On the train 'the food was Russian and it was adequate, cereals cooked with oil from sunflower seeds, brown bread, cabbage, potatoes, onions and stews with unidentified pieces of meat'.[23] Their treatment from the guards was kindly, they were given opportunities to get rid of lice, and their clothes were fumigated while they themselves had hot showers. After 24 days they left the train and marched to their quarters, 'a group of five large buildings surrounded by a high board fence.'

The men had arrived at Karaganda in Kazakhstan and, of course, although the war was over, they like many others (including Germans and Rumanians) were, if not POWs, forced labour. The chief industry was coal-mining but the Japanese group, including Makoto, were to build houses. Food was similar to that provided on the train and the Japanese, eating meat and sunflower oil regularly, were astonished at the generosity of the diet. In this sense the diet, although less to Japanese taste, was more nutritious than that of the average Japanese. Communication was possible because a German prisoner translated the Russian into English and Makoto, who had reasonable English, then changed it into Japanese. The Russians 'had been fiercely eager to have their watches and they also coveted fountain pens, pencils, writing paper and pocket knives', but apart from this pilfering the Japanese were not maltreated.

Discontent showed itself through political awakening, as one disgruntled Japanese soldier began to criticise the Emperor system, with its strict military control. He mentioned the rights of the common people in 'England and America'. The Russians were not apparently a party to these developing factions, as the Japanese chose to be 'militarists' or 'democrats', but when Japanese interrivalry threatened to become more serious, members of the so-called 'fascist' group were removed leaving the 'democrats' in charge. The anti-fascist group slowly became more pro-Russian, and were offered special training, openly becoming 'Communists'. With the arrival of more Japanese, civilians from Manchuria who had been cotton-picking, the camp became more crowded and there was a good deal of hostility. Finally the Russians began to plan to send the Japanese home, first in a trickle, then in larger groups. Eventually they were entrained again and travelled eastwards to Vladivostok, from which they embarked on a Japanese ship. Immediately there was a riot as the 'pro-Communist' activists were beaten; many of the men being repatriated realised that, back in Japan, it would never do to be associated with 'Communists'. The men, including Makoto, landed at Maizuru, from which few men wanted to send telegrams. They had been held for 26 months in Russia and they now knew that their fellow countrymen feared them, as Communists.

Makoto himself, shocked by the devastation in Tokyo, was also coolly welcomed at home although his brothers and sisters slowly warmed to him. He was ashamed to tell them that his imprisonment had been enjoyable, that they had suffered but not he. He described only the 'magnificent scenery he had seen from the train in Siberia'.[24]

NUCLEAR BOMBS, HIROSHIMA AND NAGASAKI

Few can doubt that the use by the Americans, on behalf of the Allies, of two nuclear bombs, which brought the war to an end, was the worst retribution which could have been devised against Japan. The Americans argued[25] that the bombs had to be used because Japan had amassed half a million of her best remaining troops on the island of Kyushu ready to withstand the planned Allied invasion, and that the

casualties – had an invasion been launched – would have far out-
weighed those of Hiroshima and Nagasaki. In addition it is widely
believed, not least in Japan, that the lives of the POWs held in Japan,
and probably those held elsewhere in South-East Asia, would have
been sacrificed had invasion taken place. Those who denounce the use
of the bombs do not accept this reasoning.

What were the implications of this new type of bomb for defenceless
civilian populations?

It is worth recording the report of those immediately on the scene,
including neutral citizens representing the ICRC, like Dr Marcel
Junod. On 2 September 1945 he received the following telegram from
his representative in Hiroshima.

> Visited Hiroshima 30th. Situation horrifying. 80 per cent of town
> razed. All hospitals destroyed and severely damaged. Have visited 2
> provisional hospitals; conditions indescribable. Full stop. Bomb
> effects surprisingly severe. Many victims, apparently recovering,
> suddenly experience fatal relapse owing to degeneration of white
> corpuscles and other internal injuries. Deaths occurring now in large
> numbers. More than 100,000 injured still in provisional hospitals in
> neighbourhood. Grave shortage material, bandages, medicaments.
> Stop. Appeal allied high command asking supplies be parachuted
> immediately into centre of town. Urgently need large supplies
> bandages, cotton wool, ointment for burns, sulphamides, blood
> plasma and transfusion kits. Stop. Immediate action necessary.
> Also send medical investigation commission. Report follows. Please
> acknowledge.[26]

On 3 September 1945 Dr Junod sent on the Hiroshima report to the
Supreme Commander of Allied Forces and requested, in the name of
the ICRC, 'immediate aid in food and medical supplies for the
Hiroshima victims. I offered to go there myself to organize relief
operations, as I was the only doctor among the ICRC delegation in
Japan.'[27]

On 8 September Dr Junod, together with a hastily assembled
commission of American physicists and doctors, one photographer
and two Japanese doctors, flew west to Hiroshima. The Americans had
allocated twelve tons of medicines and medical supplies, all of which
were given into the care of the ICRC delegation.

There was some nervousness as to how they would be received, but
fears were groundless. As Junod remarked,

We soon arrived at the headquarters of the Japanese Army in the prefecture of Hiroshima . . . The duty officer yelled 'present arms' as we went by . . . and we were taken to a Japanese colonel and several officers. Introductions were made and everyone behaved impeccably and shook hands . . . Never at any time was there a feeling of hostility . . . these officers were obeying their Emperor's orders.[28]

By an extraordinary circumstance, when they reached Hiroshima itself (because of the devastation they had to stay overnight many miles from the town) they found that the Red Cross Hospital 'had miraculously escaped the holocaust'.[29]

As Junod wrote,

It was a magnificent stone building, well constructed, standing squarely on its foundations. Indeed the front door and the hall were completely intact and, from the outside, the building looked almost normal; however as soon as I arrived on the upper floors, I noticed that not only all the window panes but also the frames were missing, shattered by the blast of the explosion. All the laboratory equipment had been put out of action. Part of the roof had caved in and the hospital was opened to the wind and the rain. One of the Japanese doctors told me that a thousand patients had been taken in on the day of the disaster; six hundred had died almost immediately and had been buried elsewhere, in the immediate vicinity of the hospital. At present, only two hundred remained. There were no blood transfusions because there was no equipment to carry out examinations and the donors had either died or disappeared.[30]

The terrible devastation was added to by the shortage of skilled personnel. In Hiroshima

Out of 300 doctors 270 were killed or injured
Out of 1780 nurses 1654 were killed or injured
Out of 162 dentists 132 were killed or injured
Out of 140 pharmacists 112 were killed or injured

With the devastation throughout the urban areas of Japan plain to see, the Americans made haste to bring in large quantities of aid. Prompt help was sent to Hiroshima and Nagasaki. Whole teams of American advisers arrived to work with the Japanese themselves. As will be discussed later, the JRC was one of the bodies which was to benefit from American expertise.

Not surprisingly the JRC, internationally, took an active part in urging 'the restriction of the use of nuclear weapons and the prevention of damages caused by their experiments'.[31] Japan, already limited to Self-Defence Forces, herself refused to have anything to do with nuclear weapons.

Later calculations suggest that 80 000 people died immediately with the initial blast, and that some further 100 000 were injured and died subsequently, either of wounds or lack of medical care, or of damage caused by x-rays and gamma rays. It would appear that the area remained radioactive for at least five days.

Dr Junod's report concluded with a section on future defence in a world with atomic weapons. He expressed his horror that civilian populations were as vulnerable to war as the armed forces. He took an optimistic view in one sense, that after the use of poison gas at Ypres in the First World War, it was not thereafter used again during the Second World War. He begged that world powers would ban the further use of atomic weapons.

13 Phoenix Resurgent

RE-INCORPORATION

The old JRC, so closely identified with the defeated military regime, found itself abandoned and cast aside following the military defeat of 1945. The huge Japanese membership, originally recruited as super-patriots and imperialists, but now impoverished and exhausted, could argue that 'the Red Cross had become useless in Japan, as the Army and the Navy were abolished by the new constitution'.[1]

The new body which arose like phoenix from the ashes remained essentially Japanese, but additionally had a strong injection of those democratic procedures which came directly from the United States of America. American influences will be discussed later.

In 1945 the JRC was virtually bankrupt; its funds had been exhausted not only by the expense of sending medical relief teams to support the Japanese armed forces all over the East Asian Co-prosperity Sphere, but also with the heavy bills incurred by the purchase of large quantities of relief and medical supplies. The Society's reserves, which took the form of 'Securities amounting to 100,000,000 U.S. dollars . . . turned to valueless paper'[2] as Japan struggled through a period of galloping inflation.

Physically, in 1945, almost all JRC hospitals and other buildings were either extensively damaged or in ruins. Two large Red Cross hospitals, each of 1000 beds, had been requisitioned by the Allied forces, and Japanese patients had been evacuated. As one Red Cross report noted, 'Eighty-eight cities were destroyed by air raids, 2,500,000 houses were burnt down and 10,000,000 people lost their homes. Eight million were unemployed, vagrants and war orphans were crowding every street.'[3]

AMERICAN INTERVENTION

It was in these circumstances that the Americans offered their help. They did so not only to aid the revival of the Society but also because, additionally in Japan, the Red Cross had an important post-war role

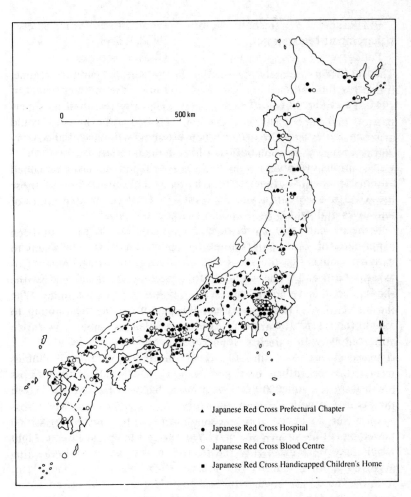

Japanese Red Cross Prefectural Chapter

Japanese Red Cross Hospital

Japanese Red Cross Blood Centre

Japanese Red Cross Handicapped Children's Home

Map 5 The Japanese Red Cross Society, 1976

'of administering to the needs of the Japanese people through its hospitals and other health programs and services'.

By mid-1946 Tom Metsker had been assigned as director of an ARC unit in Japan with six advisers with special duties. These were:

Bill Raney	responsible for	First Aid and Water Safety
Ferdinand Micklantz	" "	Fund Raising
Paul Hyer	" "	Disaster Services
Edith Olson	" "	Nursing Services
Audrey Bassett	" "	Junior Red Cross in Schools
Margaret Gooch (Duffy)	" "	Volunteer Services[4]

When the Americans arrived they brought with them the idea of 'volunteering' as an essential basis for a humanitarian organisation. It was a curious twinning, for the Red Cross in Japan had always been an authoritarian elitist organisation, headed by the Empress herself, while the ARC, in accordance with the spirit of the nation, encouraged local initiatives and prided itself upon its democratic procedures.

Some indication of the change of emphasis can be seen from the experience of Sachiko Hashimoto, herself recruited (as a young married woman) to the service of the Red Cross after 1945. When asked by a friend if she would go to a meeting about the Red Cross, she replied: 'I have never been sick in my life so I am not suitable for the Red Cross.'[5] During the discussion one of the Japanese commented, to the assembled women, 'You are now all too busy to work for your family with rationed food, busy fanning a fire in your clay charcoal stoves. At a time like this, you are the ones who want to receive service rather than give service to others.'[6] This lack of enthusiasm for voluntary service inspired Sachiko Hashimoto to join the discussion with the following story.

With her husband, a businessman working for the North China Development Company, she had lived during the war in Peking, from which they were eventually repatriated in the spring of 1946. This involved a long tedious rail journey from Peking to Tien-Tsin, followed by a sea voyage to Sasebo in Japan. At the Red Cross meeting Mrs Hashimoto used the story of the train journey to illustrate the need for service to others. As she explained,

The trains running from Peking to Tien-Tsin were not really for people's use. They were open coal wagons. Forty people making a platoon, rode in the same wagon, each taking along a two metre square tablecloth. One piece of tablecloth alone would have been of little use. But by sewing all the tablecloths together, we made a roof over our heads to shelter from the rain and wind. As for a toilet, we did not have a proper one but an oil can put in a corner. Nobody would have used it if it had not been for the tablecloths sewn together to make walls to screen the women and children. My concept of service is to offer what little time, money, power or wisdom each one of us owns for the sake of others as well as himself.[7]

Later she attended a further meeting at which she was invited to repeat her story for the benefit of representatives of the forty-six prefectures. This was the beginning of Sachiko Hashimoto's long service with the JRC and her special involvement with the Junior Red Cross.[8]

The Japanese Junior Red Cross, originally established in 1923, had been encouraged before the war as a rather narrow form of patriotic youth service. After the war, with the advice of Audrey Bassett of the ARC, the Junior Red Cross work was re-established. It was Sachiko Hashimoto who became leader and advisor of the Juniors, and today there are over 2 000 000 young Japanese members from over 8000 schools.

In the post-war world Japanese Junior Red Cross young people worked very hard; as 'language volunteers' during the Tokyo Olympics of 1964, and also at the 'paralympics' which followed immediately. In 1970 'Konnichiwa '70' was launched by the Japanese Juniors, inviting youth delegates to Japan from eighteen nations, including the then USSR and the USA, from around the Pacific Ocean.[9]

As one American consultant wrote:

The American Red Cross consultants perceived their role with the Japanese Red Cross as that of advisors and helpers. Our job was to assist the Japanese staff in rebuilding the Society's programs in ways that would best meet the needs of the Japanese people and their communities. There were no directives or orders issued, just long discussions held through interpreters, followed by written material that required translation and further discussion. Differing philosophies – those of East and West – were involved, and we all had to learn to understand each other's ideas and the fine meanings and shadings involved in the translation of words. It was a slow learning and understanding process for both the Japanese staff and the American consultants.[10]

HOSHIDAN, 'VOLUNTEERING'

It was Margaret Duffy who was responsible for suggesting ways of recruiting volunteers who would undertake the thousand and one jobs needed in post-war Japan. When she came to have her personal cards printed with her title, 'Consultant on Volunteers', this was printed by the Japanese as 'Drafter of Volunteers'. This revealing interpretation illustrated a powerful belief, which had to be re-examined, that in Japan you did not volunteer but were 'drafted'.

Given the devastation of much of the urban landscape of Japan it was vital to harness volunteers to 'keep the cities, towns and villages clear of debris and garbage'.[11] Mrs Duffy also recalls several hundred blind boarding students at the National College for the Blind in Tokyo with too few carers in attendance. She notes that the Tokyo Chapter of the JRC called on volunteers – mostly mothers – from the immediate neighbourhood to give time to assist in the running of the College for the Blind.

The American consultants were very busy travelling all over Japan, from Hokkaido in the north to Kyushu in the south. The disaster consultant was primarily concerned in assisting the Japanese to get their pure water and sanitation systems working efficiently. New training guides were produced to be used for training nurses, while the Junior Red Cross consultant was keen to show how young people could volunteer to do valuable jobs for the local community.

The Japanese were enthusiastic, and from the President, Prince Tadatsugu Shimazu, to eager young Japanese Red Crossers, all worked hard to understand the principles behind the work of the American advisers. Conditions of life were poor: as Mrs Duffy reported, 'they warmed themselves over the pale glimmer of weak electric heaters or *hibachis* and drank gallons of hot tea while exchanging ideas through interpreters'.[12] According to Mrs Hashimoto, who was herself being trained during these years, the Japanese learned from the Americans the meaning of words like 'volunteer, community, freedom, democracy, individual dignity' as well as 'coexistence, independence, and interdependence beyond one's own family bond'.[13]

The introduction of new ideas, other than the para-military ones prevalent before the War, was undertaken by a variety of officials from the United States as part of the post-war democratisation process. *Fujinkai*, women's clubs and societies, but invariably headed by men, were the object of some American intervention.[14]

THE NEW RED CROSS SOCIETY OF JAPAN

The San Francisco Peace Treaty between the Allies and Japan came into force in 1952 and the Japanese Red Cross Hospitals were finally handed back to the Society in 1956. JRC Law was re-stated, following Japan's acceptance of the Geneva Conventions on 12 August 1949, defining Japan's position in relation to relief and aid work both in Japan and overseas.

Article 7 of the new law stated, 'There is no task [for the Society] as the auxiliary organ of the armed forces.' It was made clear that, in its relations with the Japanese government, 'the independence of the JRC should be respected'.[15] This ensured – for the first time – that the JRC could pursue without interference its objectives as an humanitarian organisation.

Prior to 1940 the Society had maintained 160 hospitals with 20 000 beds, which catered in peace-time for civilian patients, as well as other clinics. It had also trained, over a long period of time, 43 000 nurses. In the post-war world it was to Social Welfare that the Society turned, aiming to bring medical services to the Japanese people.

The Red Cross resolved to re-construct its war-damaged hospitals as the first stage of its programme of rehabilitation. With no other alternative, the Red Cross borrowed (at high interest rates) large sums of money from the commercial banks, which were then used to re-build, repair and re-equip their hospitals in Tokyo and elsewhere in the provinces. In this way the Society re-established itself at home, and by so doing encouraged the Japanese to contribute once again to the Red Cross.

THE JAPANESE RED CROSS RE-ADMITTED INTERNATIONALLY

Japan's position in the post-war world community of Red Cross societies was controversial. Many, perhaps not appreciating the grip which the Japanese military regime had exerted, believed that Japan's Red Cross had, during the war, betrayed their humanitarian purpose. As a result between 1945 and 1950 the JRC were forbidden from attending, in their own right, any international gathering. At the XVII International Conference in Stockholm in 1948 the Japanese were present as 'technical advisers to the representatives of the Occupation

Forces'.[16] It was a severe blow to a nation which had itself played host to the XV International Conference in Tokyo in 1934.

The Japanese protested at their treatment, for they believed that they should have had the right to attend as a member of the ICRC, unless 'excommunicated'. They claimed, curiously in view of their impotence in time of war, that 'the national Red Cross Societies enjoy their full independence and are there to help the enemy in wartime'.[17] The work which the JRC did with refugees transported earlier to Japan against their will, before and during the war, earned them much praise.

THE REPATRIATION OF NORTH KOREANS

The stand taken by the JRC in the post-war world in the matter of the repatriation of 100 000 North Koreans who had been forcibly removed to Japan to work before and during the 1941–5 war did much to re-establish their position as an independent humanitarian organisation.

Following the Korean War of the early 1950s, the country had been divided, North Korea remaining under Communist control and South Korea becoming a capitalist country with strong American backing. During the late 1950s North Koreans in Japan began to complain that while South Koreans could leave Japan and be re-established at home, repatriation had proved to be impossible for them.

When the North Koreans in Japan started hunger strikes,[18] settling themselves at the gates of the old Red Cross headquarters in Shibuya, the matter became public, embarrassing and urgent. It landed on the desk of Masutaro Inoue, a former diplomat who headed the JRC international desk, and who had joined the Red Cross in June 1955 and served there until January 1965. After visiting some of the North Koreans at home in Tokyo he convinced himself that the matter of their repatriation was a humanitarian problem to which political considerations should not apply.

Mr Inoue's interpretation was accepted by the President of the JRC, Shimazu, and this became the Society's official position. The Japanese government, anxious not to offend the all-powerful Americans and their anti-Communist allies, were nervous; could the JRC postpone the proposed repatriation indefinitely? After much discussion, despite the furious protests[19] of the government of the Republic of South Korea, the Japanese government conceded that humanitarian values should prevail and that the North Koreans should be allowed to return home.

A delegation was sent from the JRC[20] to meet representatives of the North Korean Red Cross in Geneva. Meetings were held from April to August 1959, and from these came an accord by which the repatriation could take place. Once back in Japan and ready to organise the journey home there was much confusion, for South Koreans, living in Japan, vehemently opposed the proposed return and their government (of the Republic of South Korea) threatened to attack any repatriation ship. It was the Soviet government which agreed to escort any vessel carrying North Koreans back home.

The North Koreans were assembled in the north-western port of Niigata and from there, under the watchful eye of an ICRC delegate, boarded the ships which would carry them home. The first ship left Niigata in December 1959, but thereafter some 100 000 North Koreans were able to return home under this scheme (see Table 13.1).

Table 13.1 Repatriation of Japanese through the Red Cross in the 1950s

	1953	1954	1955	1956	Total
China	26 127	1 096	2 043	1 301	30 567
Soviet Union	811	420	167	1 291	2 689
North Korea	-	-	-	36	36
Outer Mongolia	-	-	4	-	4
North Vietnam	-	74	-	-	74
Total	26 938	1 590	2 214	2 628	33 370

Source: JRC Society Report, 1953–56 (Tokyo, 1956), p. 7.

The international wing of the Red Cross Society in Japan busied itself with the serious problem of repatriating Japanese citizens who, for one reason or another, were visible to the authorities but remained abandoned in Asia. It was not until the early 1950s that the Red Cross was sufficiently in control to begin to arrange repatriation. These relatively small numbers, coming back home several years after the war ended, take no account of the mass return of Japanese organised earlier by government agencies. Nevertheless the negotiations between the Red Cross Societies of Japan, China, the Soviet Union, North Korea, and so on was valuable not only for those returned to their homeland, but also to enable the humanitarian societies to re-establish links previously broken.

THIRTY YEARS ON; THE JAPANESE RED CROSS IN 1977

By 1977[21] over thirty years had passed since the disastrous end of the war in 1945. Looking at the JRC at that time it is possible to see an extraordinary range of flourishing activities bringing Red Cross ideas to every part of Japan. It is also the case that very many of the pre-1945 Red Cross services, no doubt re-organised and developed to take account of peace-time conditions, had also become very important.

JRC work can be examined under seven heads: disaster relief; medical services; the training of nurses; traditional skills training; social welfare; blood transfusion services; and volunteer services.

The Red Cross Society of Japan is part of the national disaster relief arrangements. By 1977 there were 453 relief teams, each consisting of 1 doctor, 3 nurses, 1 administrator and 1 driver, the members of which were paid a small retaining fee. There were also volunteer groups, 86 amateur radio volunteer groups and over 450 flying volunteer groups with 74 aircraft.

The medical services provided by the JRC adds over 34 000 beds to the country's national provision, and these are to be found in 96 hospitals. Ninety-two of these are general, to be found in all the main centres in Japan, and there are two maternity hospitals as well as hospitals in Hiroshima and Nagasaki for victims of the two atomic bombs.

The use of nuclear weapons had been a matter of great concern to all humanitarian movements, including the JRC. Japan was the only country to have suffered in this way and the toll of victims who, apparently untouched, later succumbed to leukemia, cancers and other major disorders was bound to involve the Red Cross.

Early in November 1954 the JRC mounted at their headquarters in Tokyo an exhibition designed to alert visitors to the 'multitude of disasters' caused by atomic explosions. A service was offered, organised by the staff of various medical colleges in Tokyo, of a free medical examination and advice about possible diseases.

It was resolved to open hospitals for 'atomic bomb diseases' both at Hiroshima and Nagasaki. The former hospital, opened in August 1956 and built adjacent to the Red Cross hospital, can accommodate 120 patients from all over Japan. The Nagasaki hospital was constructed in 1957. Both hospitals have developed a special expertise in dealing with those diseases associated with exposure to radiation.

As a pioneer in the training of women as nurses the Red Cross maintains two Junior Colleges of Nursing, thirty-six Schools of Nursing, one Institute of Post-Graduate Nursing and three Schools of Midwifery. Most of the cost of nurses' training is borne by the Red Cross and in general the girls trained continue to serve in Red Cross hospitals. Other skills which the Red Cross is eager to disseminate throughout the community are first aid, home nursing and life-saving; this work links up with the social welfare programme which provides assistance for children, old people and the physically handicapped.

The Red Cross Society is the principal provider of blood donations in Japan; it maintains nearly 200 blood centres and branches throughout the country, provides 'blood-mobiles' to collect blood from outlying areas, and had (in 1976) over 4 000 000 Japanese as blood donors.

As a volunteer organisation the Red Cross can call on nearly 4 000 000 members for community work. It also maintains registers of volunteer specialists who are available for a wide variety of services, from duties like that of Braille translation, language translation and ski-patrolling.[22] There can be no doubt about the versatility of the new peacetime Red Cross.

The JRC, resurrected after 1945, has again become an enormous organisation. Many people are committed to its work in Japan from their school days in the Junior Red Cross through to other activities in later life. Sachiko Hashimoto, herself a new recruit to Red Cross work after the war and who gave a lifetime's work especially to the Junior Red Cross, in her survey of 1975 urged all Japanese to become Red Cross minded.[23] In Japan large numbers, amounting to millions, have taken her advice.

THE JAPANESE RED CROSS SOCIETY OVERSEAS

The Red Cross, a Society belonging to a worldwide network with strong international obligations, has always been a rarity in chauvinist Japan. In the post-war world, for some twenty years, Japan's commitment of overseas aid was small. In 1963 the international Red Cross movement celebrated its centenary and this was the occasion in Japan to review overseas commitments. From 1966 Japan was spending about one billion yen annually, and in the 1980s these figures have again risen substantially. Japan's increased contributions reflect the country's greater prosperity.

Most of the Japanese money has gone to emergency assistance or development programmes. In times of crises (that is, drought, floods, cyclones and earthquakes) Japan has sent help to Chad, Ethiopia, Mauritania and Mozambique in Africa, Bangladesh, Nepal and the Philippines in Asia. Refugee programmes in Cambodia, Afghanistan and Vietnam have also been mounted.

Development programmes which have a longer term impact have also been launched in Asia and Africa. In Bangladesh, for example, primary health care schemes have been set up in both urban slums and rural areas. A scheme in Bangladesh to provide blood was also set up, involving the provision of equipment and the training of personnel. Japan with its knowledge of cyclones has also undertaken a lot of work in Bangladesh, India, the Philippines and the South Pacific islands in preparing for cyclones and therefore reducing the damage. Like Red Cross Societies elsewhere the Japanese run a missing persons bureau; this originated after the last war, and still has calls on its expertise.

In recent years the JRC has taken its full share of international duties as a humanitarian organisation. The appointment of Mrs Sadako Ogata as Director of the United Nations Refugee Organisation, although nothing directly to do with the Red Cross, is an indication of how Japan has taken her place as a country concerned with humanitarianism.

14 In the Emperor's Name

THE RED CROSS IN JAPAN: AN IMPERIAL AGENCY

The humanitarian movement in Japan, as demonstrated by the Red Cross Society, was an astonishingly precocious development, embarked upon in the Emperor's name by a powerful Japanese government, determined to legitimise itself as far as possible on the world stage. By ratifying the Geneva Agreement on 6 June 1886, it became the first Asian country to do so.[1]

No Red Cross Society has been so extravagantly praised[2] as during the Russo–Japanese War of 1904–5, and none has been so humiliated by its failure internationally as the Japanese Society during the Pacific War, 1941–5.

At least until the Pacific War the JRC was a government agency. The millions of Red Cross members, often minor civil servants dragooned into service, were easily recruited as patriots because, in Japan, the Red Cross was purely an arm of the military. The spirit of 'voluntaryism' which motivated 'Red Crossers' elsewhere was, until introduced by the Americans after 1945, rarely present in JRC circles. Was it relevant that the JRC was organised in a non-Christian country? The strong traditions of Christian charity, care and consideration for others, were emphasised by many, including St Paul, who wrote, 'And now abideth faith, hope and charity, these three, but the greatest of these is charity.'[3]

Were similar duties of concern for others laid upon Japanese? What role did religion play in Japanese attitudes to organisations such as the Red Cross Society? Eastern religions, which included Confucianism, Buddhism and Taoism (from which Shintoism developed) have, when adapted for use in Japan, played a part in Japanese lives. But the emphasis, far from encouraging the individual, was on using the power of religion to legitimise the regime. The Meiji oligarchs, who overthrew the Bakufu forces in 1868, did so in the name of an older unity which would, in the name of the Emperor, strengthen the power of the state.

The 'Emperor regime', *tennosei*, was specifically designed to make Shinto the religion of government and in particular of the Emperor, its role being 'to sanctify the lineage of the ruling tribe or tribes'.[4] In this sense the Meiji Restoration, which brought a new group of thrusting lower rank *samurai* to power, merely reinforced the function of religion as a weapon for state control. There was no place for the individual and none for internationalism. There was no place for humanitarianism either, except when, during the Russo–Japanese War, it was deliberately and consciously espoused to make a statement about Japanese maturity to the outside world.

THE EMPEROR MEIJI

Initially there was a strong case in Japan in favour of the Red Cross Society for the Emperor, as Commander-in-Chief, could appreciate the necessarily close relationship between the Red Cross and the military forces. In Europe also, the Red Cross was closely associated with the armies of the kings, kaisers, emperors and tsars then in power, and with their acolytes, the armigerent aristocracy. In Japan support for the Red Cross society operated strictly on hierarchical lines and became a popular activity for the aspiring classes.

With patriotism as its motivation the JRC faced its first challenge during the Sino–Japanese War[5] of 1894–5. This campaign, in which the Meiji Emperor took a personal interest, was but a preliminary to the triumph of the Japanese during the Russo–Japanese War.[6] Caring humanely for nearly 70 000 Russian prisoners of war, the first time any nation had coped on their own territory with such numbers of the enemy, was an extraordinary achievement. It brought sustained and enthusiastic praise from all the Western nations.[7]

Although the Emperor Meiji, his government and his people had indeed, in one sense, embraced humanitarianism towards the enemy, the terrible toll of casualties on both sides during the bitter fighting resulted in the sacrifice of many thousands of lives. On 27 June 1904,[8] with the war but four months old, Count Leo Tolstoy published in *The Times* of London a long, furious polemic against the evils of war, and especially of the Russo–Japanese War.

As Tolstoy wrote, 'the Russian Tsar, the same man who exhorted all the nations in the cause of peace, publicly announces that notwithstanding all his efforts to maintain peace so dear to his heart, he, owing to the attack of the Japanese, commands that the same shall be done to the Japanese, . . . that they should be slaughtered' (Chapter 11).

Neither did Tolstoy spare the Japanese, writing: 'the same thing is going on in Japan. The benighted Japanese go in for murder with yet grander fervour, owing to their victories, the Mikado also reviews and rewards his troops; various generals boast of their bravery imagining that having learned to kill they have acquired enlightenment' (Chapter 12).

Tolstoy's cry was 'Bethink Yourselves' and he quoted from St Luke, 'but this is your hour and the power of darkness'[9] when Jesus Christ was betrayed, accused and mocked. Tolstoy's outrage was echoed in Japan where a courageous woman poet, Akiko Yosano,[10] published in *Myojo* (*Morning Star*) in September 1904 the following poem, referring to her brother, then amongst the Japanese attacking Port Arthur.

> You should not be killed
> The Emperor himself never goes to war,
> Yet he allows the people to kill each other
> Yet he allows them to die like beasts
> Yet he allows them to feel honoured that they are killed like this
> If the Emperor had a warm heart
> He would feel this.[11]

There were strong reactions from the Japanese military but, perhaps because the original outburst had come from Tolstoy who was famous in Japan, the bitter criticism of Akiko Yosano was somewhat restrained.

As Commander in Chief the Emperor did not, apparently, find his position in any way inconsistent. National pride and honour demanded the sacrifice of thousands of young lives, while devoted teams of Red Cross and military orderlies scoured the battlefields to recover bodies and wounded casualties. The difficulties of the Emperor's position were real, as can be seen in the case of General Nogi, for example, and are a reminder of the complexities where old and new values must necessarily be in conflict.

GENERAL NOGI

The siege of Port Arthur ended on 1 January 1905 when the fierce and prolonged Japanese assault finally broke through the Russian defences. For months General Maresuke Nogi[12] had hurled thousands of Japanese as 'human bullets'[13] against the fortress of Port Arthur. The breakthrough came because of the efficacy of the siege guns organised by General Gentaro Kodama, sent to 'advise' General Nogi, whose two infantry officer sons were among the 60 000 Japanese lives lost in the attack. General Nogi begged the Emperor to allow him to atone for this disastrous loss of young life by sacrificing himself. The Emperor forbade such action. The General lived on; a hero to his fellow countrymen. The Emperor died on 30 July 1912. On the very morning of the imperial funeral, (13 September 1912), as they had previously agreed, General Nogi, magnificently attired in full military uniform, killed first his wife, herself splendid in full court dress, and then himself.

The ritual suicide electrified[14] Japan; Nogi was venerated for his loyalty and self-sacrifice. Even today the small wooden house in which General Nogi ended his life, set in quiet gardens, adjacent to the Nogi shrine and a haven in noisy Tokyo, is daily a place of pilgrimage.

But General Nogi's suicide did more. In linking the Emperor with *seppuku*, the ultimate act of loyalty of a *samurai* for his master, Nogi was applying, literally, the old ideas of the *bushido* code. This was also echoed in the Rescript on Education, then repeated by Japanese children in their schools:

'What is your dearest ambition?'
'To die for the Emperor'.[15]

At the time of Nogi's death the *Asahi Shimbun* in an editorial wrote:

General Nogi's death marked the completion of Japan's *bushido* of old. And while emotionally we express the greatest respect, rationally we regret we cannot approve. One can only hope that this act *will not long blight the future of our national morality* [author's italics]. We can appreciate the General's intention; we must not learn from his behaviour.[16]

Tragically *Asahi's* words on Nogi's suicide were only too prophetic.

General Nogi's life and death illustrate the theme of this book, which discusses the long struggle in Japan between the new humanitarianism and the old *bushido* traditions of war. The Emperor Meiji, accepting the new code, refused to allow the General to take the admired course and atone, by suicide, for his self-perceived failure. Once Meiji was dead it became imperative for Nogi to be true to his belief in *Junshi*, 'to follow his Lord in death' and so to the *samurai* code of honour.

In his novel *Kokoro*, Natsume Soseki summed up the feelings of a generation, writing: 'On the night of the Imperial funeral I sat in my study, listening to the booming of the cannon. To me, it sounded like the last lament for the passing of an age. Later, I realized, that it might also have been a salute to General Nogi'.[17] The outstanding achievements of the Meiji generation had brought Japan into the modern world; but they had created tensions within Japanese society which proved to be resolvable only through aggression and war.

THE EMPEROR SHOWA

The Emperor Meiji's son, the Emperor Taisho, of poor physical and mental health, died in 1926. It was Hirohito, the Emperor Showa, who, as a young man of twenty-five, came to the throne determined to emulate his grandfather, the Emperor Meiji. Unfortunately Hirohito, a quiet and unassuming man, was to be faced with challenges which he was temperamentally ill-equipped to meet.

Hirohito, born 29 April 1901,[18] had been removed from his mother at the age of three months to be brought up by senior figures in his own household. At the age of seven, Hirohito had started to attend the Peers School (*Gakushuin*), now Gakushuin University, of which, after the Russo–Japanese War, General Nogi had been put in charge.

When Hirohito came into the General's care, Nogi, still mourning his two dead sons, succeeded in forging a real bond between himself and the young prince. The timid little boy found in the battle-scarred old general the father figure which he had hitherto never known. How far Hirohito's character was moulded by his unnatural upbringing or by General Nogi's death, following immediately on that of his admired grandfather, cannot be known, but it was unfortunate that General Nogi's moral imperatives prevented him from remaining the guardian of the young Crown Prince.

It was the peace-loving Hirohito's personal misfortune that the early years of his reign, after 1926, were dominated by the pro-war factions as the army gradually tightened its grip on the Japanese nation. As a diffident man and still young, the Emperor, determined to serve as a constitutional monarch, was hindered by the barriers which kept him secluded from his people, and he proved to be no match for the unruly military.

It is important to remember that, despite being imprisoned in tradition, the Showa Emperor did take three difficult decisions: forcing the resignation of Giichi Tanaka, the prime minister, in July 1929, when he believed the organisers of an army coup had not been properly punished; insisting on suppressing an army revolt after the 26 February incident in 1936; and, ultimately, requiring the surrender of Japan in August 1945.

General Douglas MacArthur, the supreme commander for the Allied powers in Japan and who knew the Emperor in his official capacity, was impressed. On the occasion of the Emperor's first visit he said, 'I come to you General MacArthur to offer myself to the judgement of the powers you represent as the one to bear sole responsibility for every political and military decision made and action taken by my people in the conduct of war.'

MacArthur, fortunately, understood something of the Japanese people. He may not have recognised the Japanese belief in their uniqueness with a particularly strong sense of themselves as 'insiders' and everyone else as 'outsiders', but he appreciated that it was politically impossible to make the Emperor the scapegoat for Japanese war crimes.

MacArthur commented that, 'I found that he (the Emperor) had a more thorough grasp of the democratic concept than almost any Japanese with whom I talked. He played a major role in the spiritual regeneration of Japan and his loyal co-operation and influence had much to do with the success of the occupation.'[19]

It was Hirohito's tragedy that, himself peace-loving, he came to play a crucial part in the military aggression pursued in his name. It was a peculiar irony that the most vivid image of him in war-time Japan was his picture, in full military uniform, on his white horse, the Lippizaner *Shirayuki* (Snow White).

JAPAN AND THE REST: A STUDY OF RACISM?

No nation had moved more rapidly into the modern world from a kind of medieval feudalism than Japan, although the transformation during the life-time of two generations had necessarily imposed enormous strains.

These had been exacerbated by the Meiji government's policy of bringing to Japan over 4000 foreign experts, of whom some 2000 were British. The foreigners came to Japan to work, but their alien culture and their ready superiority[20] – the 'Japs', as some Westerners believed, were 'natives', yellow-skinned and inferior – bred resentment and was hard for the Japanese to bear.

Western assumptions, which smacked of racism, had always caused annoyance in Japan where many, including influential journalists like Soho Tokutumi (1863–1957), were angry at the price which they considered Japan had paid in the process of emulating Western societies. It was increasingly believed there that 'Western practices of individualism, extreme personal freedom, and the unbridled pursuit of self-interest undermined family, community, and national solidarity and fostered social alienation and discontent.'[21]

These attitudes, although by no means universal, were common throughout Japanese society; newspapers and periodicals increasingly urged the people to remember the *Yamato* spirit, which made them, as Japanese, unique. Elements of Japanese society were, by the 1920s, disillusioned; this played into the hands of those who were anxious to ensure that Japan protect herself by expanding her empire. Unfortunately Japan suffered a calamitous bank failure in 1927; by 1930, in the ensuing depression, there were 2 000 000 unemployed. Not only that but the rate of increase of the population, living in the relatively small Japanese islands, was frighteningly high. Neither did Japan have the necessary raw materials at home which could sustain an expanding industrialised society. These anxieties encouraged the army, over time, to assume power and embark upon dreams of a great Japanese East Asian empire.[22]

As the Japanese military grew ambitious in the 1930s and their plans for what became the East Asia Co-Prosperity Sphere developed, it became clear that there could be no role for internationalism in Japan's Red Cross movement, or indeed for any humanitarian organisation. The Japanese, themselves racists, and resentful of Western racism, were severe and overbearing in their treatment of other Asiatics. In fact Japanese behaviour in Asia has been described as 'puppet master to puppet'.[23] As Ba Maw, the Burmese nationalist leader explained, for the Japanese,

> there was only one way to do a thing, the Japanese way, only one goal and interest, the Japanese interest; only one destiny for the East Asian countries, to become so many Manchukuos or Koreas tied for ever to Japan. These racial impositions – they were just that – made any real understanding between the Japanese militarists and the people's [sic] of our region virtually impossible.[24]

BROTHERS ALL?

The use of the phrase *tutti fratelli* ('we are all brothers'), uttered by those at the Battle of Solferino in 1859, stems from the Western idea of universality and the brotherhood of man and suggests equality. In Japan, on the other hand, brotherhood implies a hierarchical relationship, the older brother having authority over younger. But the Japanese (in their own eyes, older brothers) were regarded outside Japan as younger brothers and immature. These perceptions were a recipe for confrontation.

Japanese attitudes to power had direct consequences for the Allies during the Pacific campaigns. The rank and file of Japanese soldiers, as 'younger brothers' and the subject of abuse when at home, were astonished to find themselves in a position of 'older brothers' and enhanced power when abroad. As has been explained, 'Men who at home were 'mere subjects' and who in the barracks were second-rank privates, found themselves in a new role when they arrived overseas; as members of the Emperor's forces they were linked to the ultimate value and accordingly enjoyed a position of infinite superiority.'[25]

When, however, the JRC (always closely linked to, and supported by the imperial family) was subverted and its international work shelved, there was no word of protest from a drafted, deferential membership, subject to tight social control. In this sense the Red Cross, and its members, can stand as a metaphor for Japan and the Japanese people. Obedient Red Cross workers who knew nothing of the Red Cross as an international body were incapable of protest against a narrowing of objectives, any more than the Japanese people knew how to control the military and achieve a greater role for themselves. It is unfortunate that the Japanese required outsiders – in effect, the Americans – to effect a change.

The 'brothers all' philosophy, which involved offering succour to one's enemies, was easily rejected by a xenophobic people, although not personally by the Showa Emperor himself. On 8 September 1941 in Tokyo, at one of the last cabinet meetings before the Pacific War started with the Pearl Harbor attack of 8 December 1941, Emperor Hirohito stunned his ministers (at whose deliberations he normally sat apart as silent observer) by taking from his pocket, with a white-gloved hand, a small slip of paper from which he read twice in 'a strong clear voice':

> Throughout the world
> we are all brothers
> Why then do the winds
> and the waves
> Rage so turbulently?

The Emperor continued: 'this poem by the Meiji Emperor (1852–1912) is one which I have always loved. That Great Emperor's love for peace is a feeling I have also held as my own.'[26]

In this way the forty-year old Emperor endeavoured to divert his cabinet, committed as it then was to war. The Emperor's ineffectual intervention, received deferentially but with intense embarrassment, was (as Allied POWs were to discover) useless, for the international principles of humanitarianism and of the Red Cross Society of Japan had been, deliberately and with forethought, betrayed.

Appendix A: Glossary of Japanese Terms

bushido	literally the Way (*do*) of the Warrior (*bushi*), developed over centuries in Japan as the ethical code of the warrior class. *Bushido* involved martial spirit, skill with weapons, absolute loyalty to one's lord, a strong sense of personal duty and honour and the courage to sacrifice one's life either in battle or in ritual.
Choshu	the clan or *han* (today Yamaguchi Prefecture), whose members played a decisive role during and after the *Meiji* era.
genro	senior statesmen, who advised the Emperor until c 1941.
Hakuaisha	Benevolent Society founded in 1877 at the time of the South-West rebellion, the precursor of the Red Cross Society in Japan, which rendered some aid both to imperial casualties and rebels in 1877.
hara-kiri	Japanese ritual suicide by self-disembowelment; see also *seppuku*, the term usually used in Japan.
hibachi	charcoal heating stove.
Junshi	'to follow one's lord in death', the ritual sacrifice, by *seppuku* of a *samurai's* life on the death of his lord; see General Nogi, Appendix B.
Kempetai	Military Secret Police.
Meiji	era, from 1868 to 1912; see Meiji Emperor, Appendix B.
Ronin	literally 'floating men', leaderless *samurai*, soldiers without masters, they had no function after 1868 (see *47 ronin*).
47 ronin	also known as Ako incident, is the most famous story of *samurai* loyalty and warrior ethics. On 31 January 1703 (in Japan the date was 14 December, Genroku era 15th year, 1702) the 47 *ronin* attacked the home of Yoshinaka Kira and assassinated him, because their lord Naganori Asano (1665–1701) had been wronged (by Yoshinaka Kira) and had been forced to commit suicide. His estates were also forfeited. After the revenge had been carried out the 47 marched the five miles to Sengakuji temple, Shinagawa, Tokyo, to present Kira's head at their master's grave. The Shogun ordered them to commit suicide which, in February 1703, they all did. They are buried beside their lord at Sengakuji temple, which is even now a place of pilgrimage.
samurai	feudal retainer; there were several ranks within this category, but used here as a generic term. Their pensions were commuted and finally abolished by the *Meiji* government.

Satsuma han	led by the *Shimazu* family; became important point of entry, often through the capital Kagoshima, of foreign innovation; eventually played leading role in the *Meiji* Restoration of January 1868.
seppuku	Japanese ritual suicide by self-disembowelment. The abdomen was believed to be the home of the soul, and the source of a man's will and determination. It became a way of death with honour for *samurai* convicted of doing wrong, and required immense courage and calm.
'*Speedo*'	quickly, the order given by the Japanese to POWs working.
TAMA	in military terms means bullet, but if being used in capital letters it could mean 'Things' that is material for experiments. The Japanese called their material (that is the human beings used) *Maruta*. Perhaps TAMA was a regimental name.
tennosei	'the Emperor system' existed for centuries, but was re-established from 1868 to 1945. It demanded an unquestioning loyalty from the individual Japanese to the Emperor and to those who ruled in the Emperor's name. The state was run by an oppressive bureaucracy, an intrusive police force and a conscripted army; under this system there was no place for democracy, liberty or human rights.
Yamato race	the Japanese race; usually, during the Pacific War, denoted a narrow pride and nationalistic view of Japan and the Japanese.
Yamato damashii	Japanese spirit, used until 1945 to refer to those who were constant in their absolute loyalty to Japan and to the Emperor. It became synonymous with *Sonno Joi* (Revere the Emperor, expel the barbarians) and so was taken up with enthusiasm by the militarists in the 1930s.
Zaibatsu	Industrial and financial combines of great power in Japan until 1945 officially dissolved during the occupation period, but re-established as *Keiretsu*.

Appendix B: Biographical Details of Japanese Leaders to whom Reference is Made

DOIHARA, Kenji (1883–1948) General, sentenced to death by Tokyo War Crimes tribunal and hanged, had commanded Kwantung Army in Manchuria, 1938–40, served on Supreme War Council and commanded in Singapore (1944–5), deeply involved with drug trafficking, which the Japanese Army ran in China, and responsible, as senior officer, for POW camps and internee camps in Malaya, Sumatra, Java and Borneo.

FUKUZAWA, Yukichi (1835–1901) influential educator and populariser of Western ideas, of *Nakatsu* domain, founder of *Keio Gijuku*, now Keio University, of the newspaper *Jiji Shimpo* and of the art of public speaking. Fukuzawa, stifled by the 'narrow stiffness' of clan life, made strenuous efforts as a young man to familiarise himself with Western learning. He not only learnt Dutch and later English, but succeeded in 1860 in joining the first Japanese expedition to America, followed in 1862 by a further mission to Europe during which he visited France, England, Holland, Russia and Portugal. On his return he published *Seiyo Jijo* (*Conditions in the West*) which made his reputation as an interpreter of foreigners and their countries to the Japanese. Throughout his life he continued to educate his fellow Japanese in the ideas behind Western progress, particularly the importance of science and the spirit of independence.

HIROTA, Koki (1878–1948) Baron, the only civilian sentenced to death by Tokyo War Crimes tribunal, former ambassador to Soviet Union, (1928–31), foreign minister (1933–6), prime minister (1936–7), was foreign minister at the time of the Rape of Nanking.

ITAGAKI, Seishiro (1885–1948) General, sentenced to death by Allies War Crimes tribunal in 1948, had served as Chief of Staff of Kwantung Army and Minister of War, committed to militarist cause, and was responsible for prison camps in Java, Sumatra, Malaya and Borneo, where his men terrorised prisoners and the civilian population.

ITO, Hirobumi (1841–1909) *Choshu* clan; student of Yoshida Shoin, made *samurai* in 1863, one of original '*Choshu* Five', studied in London, 1863–4, regarded as 'Western' expert, most powerful of Meiji Oligarchs as government minister, Prime Minister and *genro*; assassinated, by Korean, in Manchuria.

IWAKURA, Tomomi (1825–83) also known as Tomoyoshi, middle-rank court noble; although initially hostile to change, later associated with *Satsuma*, especially *Okubo Toshimichi*; after Restoration, key-member of *Meiji* government; led Iwakura Mission, 1871–3; became a senior minister and influential adviser.

JIMBO, Nobuhiko (n.d.) Lieut. Col. Japanese army, credited with saving life during war, of Manuel Roxas (1892–1948), 1st President of Philippines after 1945.

KATSURA, Taro (1847–1913) born Choshu (now Yamaguchi prefecture) Army general and politician, prime minister 1901–6, 1908–11, 1912–13, he carried through Anglo–Japanese Alliance, 1902, Russo–Japanese War 1904–5, and the annexation of Korea, 1910, making Japan an imperialist nation.

KIMURA, Heitaro (1888–1948) General, sentenced to death by Tokyo War Crimes tribunal, responsible for action towards POWs which brutalised, field commander in Burma during the building of the notorious Siam–Burma railway.

KODAMA, Gentaro (1852–1906) Army general, born Yamaguchi, closely linked with Klemens Meckel, a German military adviser, fought in all Japan's wars from the Boshin Civil War (1868) onward, promoted full General in 1904, is credited with General Nogi's success in capturing Port Arthur during the Russo–Japanese War.

KOTSUJI, Abraham (1899–19??) Japanese who became a Hebrew scholar and a Jew, involved with assisting Jews in Kobe in 1940s.

MacARTHUR, Douglas (1880–1964) American Army general who, until April 1951, was Supreme Commander of the Allied powers (SCAP) during the Allied occupation of Japan. He accepted the Japanese surrender on 2 September 1945 on *USS Missouri*.

MATSUI, Iwane (1878–1948), General, sentenced to death at Tokyo War Crimes tribunal, represented Japan at the Geneva Disarmament Conference (1932–7), in effect representing military interests; troops under his command were involved with Rape of Nanking. He retired in 1938.

MATSUKATA, Masayoshi (1835–1924) modest official career in *Satsuma han* before 1868; posts in local and central government; became financial expert responsible, after 1881, for severe but successful deflationary policies, which gave Japan stable currency; later Prime Minister and *genro*; President of Japanese Red Cross from 1902–12.

MEIJI Emperor (1852–1912) given name Mutsuhito; era name *Meiji* meaning 'enlightenment'; son of Komei, succeeded to throne, 13 February 1867; originally manipulated by young Meiji oligarchs but later became a powerful figure.

MUTO, Akira (1892–1948) General, sentenced to death by Tokyo War Crimes tribunal, army career in China, army commander Sumatra (1942–3), Philippines (1944–5). Troops under his command involved in Rape of Nanking (1937) and Rape of Manila; overall command of POW camps in Sumatra.

NOGI, Maresuke (1849–1912) Army general, Choshu clan, but born Tokyo, active in imperial army during Satsuma rebellion (1877) but when his regiment lost its battle standard, he took it as a personal disgrace and wished to commit *seppuku*. In Germany (1887–8), reinforced his *samurai* belief in discipline and self-sacrifice, during Russo–Japanese War was unable to achieve capture of Port Arthur without help, in attacking which his two sons were killed. Nevertheless regarded by the Japanese people as a hero. His ritual suicide, *seppuku*, on the morning of the Meiji Emperor's funeral (13 September 1912) stunned Japan.

OMURA, Masujiro (1824–69) Choshu man, military expert, much involved with learning foreign military methods, reputation for high military skills, assassinated 1869. Aritomo Yamagata took over the responsibility for creating a modern Japanese army.

SAIGO, Takamori (1827–77) born Satsuma (now Kagoshima), military leader before Restoration, *Meiji* leader after that, but had stormy career; was forced by circumstances to lead Satsuma rebellion 1877; defeated near Kagoshima, committed suicide on battlefield, nevertheless became a national hero by maintaining his faith in the traditional virtues of a *samurai*.

SANO, Tsunetami (1822–1902) born Saga domain, studied at Koan Ogata's celebrated school in Osaka, was trained as a navy man, but also had experienced life in Europe; was in Vienna, in 1873, to look after Japanese interests at the Exhibition; learnt about Red Cross affairs, probably encouraged by Hirobumi Ito and Tomomi Iwakura; founded *Hakuaisha* in 1877 which helped with first aid on battlefield and became the JRC; President of Society until death in 1902.

SHIDEHARA, Kijuro (1872–1951) Prime minister (October 1945–April 1946) after the war, but noted for his internationalist foreign policy, based on Japan's economic imperatives, between 1924–7 and 1929–31. His pro-Western views were (1920s and 1930s) unpopular in Japan, particularly with the military.

SHOWA Emperor, Hirohito (1901–89) the first heir apparent of Japan ever to travel abroad, influenced by British monarchy and aristocracy, ascended throne 1926, and attempted to fulfil his obligations as constitutional monarch, thus giving militarists much freedom of action. Severely criticised, outside Japan, as responsible for Japanese war-time behaviour, but his own actions, secluded as he was by his advisers, were severely circumscribed.

SUGIHARA, Senpo (Chiune) (1900–75) Japanese Consul in Kovno, Lithuania in 1940, who, without authority, issued up to 6000 transit visas for Japan to Jewish refugees.

TAISHO Emperor (1879–1926) a weak and sickly youth whose health deteriorated after he ascended the throne. On 25 November 1921, regency established under Crown Prince Hirohito.

TANAKA, Giichi (1864–1929) General, prime minister (1927–9), foreign minister, born Choshu (now Yamaguchi), trained for army, served in Manchuria in Sino–Japanese War, sent to Russia 1898–1902, came back believing Japan could win war against Russia, after war embarked on army re-organisation to Imperial Military, Reservists' Association, strongly pro-military, forced to resign over aggressive intervention in China.

TERAUCHI, Masatake (1852–1919) General and prime minister, born Choshu (now Yamaguchi prefecture), worked to systematise military education, became first governor-general of Korea on its annexation in 1910, was notorious for his regime crushing all anti-Japanese protest.

TOGO, Heihachiro (1848–1934) *Satsuma*; Fleet admiral in IJN, commanded at Battle of Sea of Japan or Tsushima, 27–28 May 1905 when IJN destroyed Russian Baltic Fleet.

TOJO, Hideki (1884–1948) General, sentenced to death by Tokyo War Crimes tribunal and prime minister (1941–4); born Tokyo of army officer father, lived in Switzerland and Germany, then various army posts, including in

Manchuria, in the 1930s, returned to Tokyo, 1938, served various governments, became Prime Minister October 1941, and prepared for war; remained in office until July 1944; regarded by Allies as chief war criminal; continued to shoulder responsibility for war, thus exonerating Emperor, hanged 1948.

TOKUGAWA Major warrior family in Japan who dominated Edo era, from 1600 to 1868; Edo, the Tokugawa capital, now Tokyo; founded Tokugawa Shogunate.

YAMAGATA, Aritomo (1838–1922) *Choshu*; organised conscripted Japanese army; Prime Minister and *genro*, committed to military regime.

Appendix C: Japanese Regulations for the Treatment of Russian Wounded and Prisoners of War, Russo–Japanese War, 1904–5

On 14 February 1904, within a week of the outbreak of hostilities, the Japanese government issued regulations under imperial ordinance for 'Treatment of Prisoners', 'Prisoners Intelligence Board'.

The Intelligence Board was thus constituted:

The chief of the Board to be of General's or Colonel's rank.

His subordinates shall be drawn from among military as well as naval officers, and he shall have civilian clerks also, as required.

The Chief to be under the supervision of the Minister for War.

The business to be transacted by the Board shall include:

(a) Investigating circumstances of detention or removal of prisoners, reception into hospital, or decease of any one of them, and the compilation of proper records concerning each.

(b) Correspondence with regard to condition of prisoners.

(c) Due attention to delivery or dispatch of money or other articles sent to or by the prisoners.

(d) Retention in safe custody of the testaments or other articles or money left by prisoners who die, and for the subsequent dispatch of this property to the families or relatives of the dead.

(e) Whenever information is acquired by army or naval authorities concerning a fallen enemy, or any property of those killed in battle, or who otherwise die, is recovered, the course pursued is to be similar to that followed in the case of a prisoner.

(f) The Board has authority to obtain from the naval, military, or hospital authorities, or any other kindred institution, all needful information that they may possess in order to enable the Board to perform its allotted functions.

Minute directions are likewise given for the rendering of reports (by the several authorities named above) to the Prisoners' Intelligence Board, upon all necessary matters in which the condition or welfare of the prisoners may be in any way concerned.

The regulations regarding the treatment of prisoners are lengthy, it is only necessary to refer to their salient features:

(a) The prisoners of war shall be treated with humane consideration: no insult or cruelty shall be perpetrated upon them.
(b) They shall be dealt with in careful conformity to their rank and position.
(c) Save where imposed by military discipline, they shall not be subjected to physical restraint.
(d) They shall enjoy freedom of conscience, and in virtue thereof shall be at full liberty to attend the religious services of their own Faith, so long as in doing so they do not infringe the requirements of military discipline.

Should a prisoner be insubordinate he naturally must be subjected to disciplinary measures, according to the circumstances of his offence, and so also must a prisoner who attempts to escape, or who may actually for a time contrive to get away and is retaken, but no criminal punishment shall be inflicted on account of such escape.

Offences of prisoners are dealt with and punished in conformity with the established rules of the Military Court.

The subjoined resumé of the Regulations are indicative of the care with which the rules have been framed to agree with the spirit of the injunctions (a), (b), (c) and (d) quoted above.

1. Arms, ammunition, and all articles of warlike character carried by the prisoners shall be confiscated, but other articles shall either be kept in safe custody on behalf of the prisoners or left with them to carry on their own persons as expediency may dictate.
2. Prisoners of officers' rank may be allowed to carry their swords, or even any other weapons, according to circumstances, but in the case of firearms, the powder and bullets used in them shall be removed for safety's sake.
3. The Commander of an Army Corps, or of a Division, may arrange with the enemy for the transfer of sick or wounded prisoners, or for their exchange, or he may discharge prisoners on parole of not again taking part in the present war.
4. Prisoners who may be possessed of officers' rank shall be transported to their place of internment separately from the common soldiers.
5. Prisoners captured by the Navy shall be handed over to the Army Authorities. [This regulation was introduced, no doubt, to save the trouble and expenses of caring for them separately, under a distinct organisation.]
6. The Army Authorities shall provide suitable places for the internment of prisoners; soldiers' barracks, temples, or other convenient buildings are to be used for this purpose.

7. Prisoners shall be suitably allotted to different rooms, not huddled together indiscriminately, a certain number to each apartment as may be convenient, and the rank and position of the prisoners shall be taken into consideration when thus allotting their quarters. Each room shall appoint from among its inmates one person to be their chief, who shall be responsible for peace and good order among them, and shall be spokesman for his fellow-prisoners.

8. Prisoners may purchase with their own money any articles that they may fancy or that may add to their comfort – subject, of course, to the approval of the Superintending Officer.

9. Prisoners may receive or send telegrams or letters, subject, of course, to the approval of the Superintending Officer, but no cypher or suspicious communication of any sort can be permitted to pass.

10. The postal matter sent to or from prisoners is free of charge, in accordance with the post convention rules.

11. Any article or money retained for safe custody by the authorities shall be returned to the prisoners on their discharge.

12. Any articles or money belonging to a prisoner who may die shall be forwarded to the Prisoners' Intelligence Board. Perishable goods shall be sold and the value in money so recovered shall be transmitted to the Board, to be dealt with in due course.

13. The testaments found on prisoners who die shall be treated in precisely the same manner as those found on Japanese soldiers, and are to be sent to the Prisoners' Intelligence Board.

14. The custody of prisoners may, by a special provision, be delegated to a legally established philanthropic association. (This is no other than the Red Cross Society of Japan.)

15. For each pair of prisoners having officers' rank, one common soldier shall be selected from among the prisoners to serve in the capacity of personal attendant.

16. Prisoners of officers' rank may be permitted to take an outdoor stroll regularly on their making solemn promise not to run away or to transgress the disciplinary rules. Common soldiers also may be given this degree of liberty provided that no difficulty is experienced in keeping them in order in consequence thereof.

17. The burial of dead prisoners is to be conducted with due military honours, according to the rank and position of the deceased. They shall be interred in one part of our military cemeteries, or a special plot of land shall be allotted for this purpose, according to circumstances.

18. The mode of burial shall, as a rule, be that adopted in the ordinary interment of a corpse. [Note – The qualifying phrase, 'as a rule,' here inserted appears to indicate that whereas under some conditions – such as when medical precautions demand special treatment, in cases of infectious disease – Japanese law requires that the bodies of persons who thus die shall be cremated; a similar rule shall apply to the corpses of prisoners of war.]

Source: Baron Suyematsu, *The Risen Sun* (London 1905), pp. 317–19.

Appendix D: Medical Experiences in Japanese Captivity

By Lieut.Col. E. E. Dunlop, M.S., F.R.C.S.[1]

The fruits of experience as prisoners of war in Japanese hands, though abundant, were exceedingly bitter. Herculean tasks were enforced upon semi-starved and enfeebled captives – for example, the construction of the Burma–Siam railway by slave labour with primitive hand tools. To medical personnel fell the scarcely less arduous task of clearing the Augean stables of sickness. The crude slave hovels used for the accommodation of prisoners were euphemistically termed 'hospitals' when allotted to the sick, and were provided with some slender medical staff. During the days of darkest savagery they were little more than crowded pest-houses where sick were conveniently segregated, though by no means allowed to die in peace.

I have been asked to record briefly some salient impressions of three and a half years of imprisonment in Java and Siam, involving prisoner-of-war command of a number of camps and hospitals, including railway construction camps. The medical problems of the scattered prisoner-of-war groups in the Far East, and the struggles of the medical services against great odds, are of historical interest. The circumstances militated against research or far-reaching discovery but sharpened the unaided senses to greater clinical acuity and necessitated resource and ingenuity of a high degree. It is obvious that many prisoners of war will suffer for the remainder of their lives from disabilities related to their grim ordeal. Those who witnessed their fortitude and unconquerable spirit under conditions of great suffering, slow starvation, and physical wretchedness hope that their disabilities will be fully comprehended and will receive generous consideration.

CONQUEST OF JAVA

In Java, as in other conquered regions, medical personnel together with sick and wounded shared in the general programme of attrition designed to teach a sharp lesson to 'criminals' and 'rabble' who had dared to oppose the Japanese Army. All the inmates of an Allied general hospital under my command were ejected at a few hours' notice, and the majority forcibly marched to a fantastically overcrowded native gaol with negligible medical arrangements,

---

1 Reprinted by kind permission of Sir Edward 'Weary' Dunlop and the editor of the *British Medical Journal*.

where calculated humiliation, gross under-feeding, and savage regimentation were the daily routine.

Only a few medical stores, widely dispersed and concealed, escaped confiscation. Defiance of international conventions was emphasized by the confiscation of Red Cross brassards, along with badges of rank, unit or service ribbons, decorations, etc. Under the compulsion all Red Cross markings were obliterated. Mass violence and beatings and some untidy public executions enforced obedience, under vigorous protest. Uniform clipping of the hair to the scalp was required, and the extravagant mass 'salutations' enforced by the humblest of Japanese soldiers produced spectacles not devoid of Gilbertian humour. Medical officers and padres spent considerable time and energy in the task of instructing in Japanese drill and ceremony. There was some alleviation of the harshness of treatment in the British P.O.W. camp under my administration at Bandoeng, where for a few months the prisoners carried on highly organized educational and recreational activity in the teeth of difficulties and misunderstandings.

Malnutrition and deficiency diseases were rife within six months, *pellagra* being excessively common and associated in approximately one-third of all troops with distressing burning of the feet. The ration at this time amounted to 2,000 calories daily. While much more adequate than that in some later camps, it consisted largely of low-grade rice or dried potatoes, and was thus markedly deficient in protein, fats, and vitamins, especially of the B complex. The Japanese paid little heed to protests, carefully documented requests, or demonstrations of cases, but following the official acceptance of the captives as 'prisoners of war' meagre pay for work was introduced. This pay together with some fortunate clandestine negotiation for money on credit enabled us to augment the diet of the sick with purchased foodstuffs according to need.

THE BURMA–SIAM RAILWAY

Late in 1942 the movement of Allied prisoners to Lower Burma and Siam commenced. Soon some 60,000 captives and a larger force of Asiatic coolies were given the gigantic task of cleaving a railway through 400 kilometres of jungle-clothed mountains and oppressive valleys between Thanbyuzayat (Burma) and Bampong (Siam). By the end of 1943 the main task was completed by the enfeebled remnant of the decimated force. Some 15,000 prisoners together with uncounted scores of thousands of Asiatic coolies had perished. While this major tragedy was largely due to calculated official brutality and inhumanity, Japanese medical officers contributed in lending what zeal they possessed to the support of medical enormity in search of further labourers, rather than in a co-ordinated medical plan of evacuation, hospital services, and supply of medical stores.

Indiscriminate treatment of prisoners led to my being placed in command of a working force of Java captives transferred as packed human freight in the holds of a tramp to Singapore, and subsequently by rail for four days in box-trucks to Siam, where in due course they marched into the Konyu–Hintok section of the line in dense jungle about the Kwa-Noi river. Some six months of command of working camps mixed with endless medical work and peripatetic surgery was followed by experience of command of jungle hospitals, including Kinsayok, Tarsau, and Chungkai, before I was transferred in June, 1944, with large numbers of sick of the Siam force to Nakom Patom. There I enjoyed the privilege of working under Lieut-Col A.E. Coates, A.A.M.C. [Australian Army Medical Corps], as O.C. surgical section of this large hospital devoted to men still broken in health by the railway construction in Burma and Siam. The grimmest battle for the lives of men had already been fought in the crudity of jungle areas, and the attitude of the Japanese left little doubt that improved conditions bore some relationship to the changed state of the war and to world knowledge of the treatment of prisoners.

WORKING CAMPS

During railway construction men worked under savage pressure up to sixteen hours a day for months without rest, so that they rarely saw their squalid huts and tents in daylight. Amid thorny jungle and rotting corruption, with ceaseless monsoon rain lashing their bodies and soaking their miserable accommodation, large numbers were soon bootless, with practically no bedding, and reduced to rags about their loins. The heat was in general excessive, and well-nigh intolerable to bare feet in rock cuttings, but the greatest load on men's spirits was the pouring monsoon rain, converting the whole area in to a quagmire of evil-smelling mud.

Pellagra, diarrhoea, irritable bladders, and massed overcrowding interrupted rest, and the urge was often uncontrollable as men floundered out into darkness, rain, and mud. Hunger, food deficiency diseases, malaria, dysentery, ulcers, and skin sepsis, and extreme exhaustion were woven into a dull fabric of suffering rent here and there by sharp outbreaks of cholera. Whatever reserves of physical strength or spirit a man might possess were in the long run exploited, so that the stronger suffered longer, only to pay the same relentless tribute in loss of life and broken health.

Apart from some capricious inoculation measures, preventive medicine, hygiene, and sanitation were negligible. Men and tools were grudgingly spared for the most primitive sanitary measures. Such materials as antimalarial oil or chloride of lime were absent or pathetically scarce. Often there were insufficient containers to supply boiled water. Until the belated supply of limited American Red Cross stores in mid-1944, medical supplies other than quinine were farcical. A typical monthly issue for a thousand men, mostly sick, consisted of 6 to 12 bandages, a small piece of gauze or cloth, 1 or 2 ounces of spirit or iodine solution, and a few dozen assorted tablets of dubious value. Non-expendable stores such as instruments and ward equipment, though freely confiscated in the early months, were afterwards only possessed by cunning or ingenuity, since no issues were made. Allied medical personnel were distributed with scant regard to either incidence of sickness or qualifications on a scale of one per cent of strength – doctors and orderlies combined – for all purposes. Where by faulty distribution the number exceeded this slender provision, as in Konyu and Hintok camps, they were compelled to do routine manual work and the sick were deprived of their services.

'MOST SHAMEFUL DEED'

As the working force deteriorated under semi-starvation, diseases, and illimitable exhaustion, ferocious pressure was exerted to secure from sick and dying men increased fortitude in the Japanese Imperial cause. As sickness was regarded as a crime, the sick were given no pay and a reduced ration scale. (Col. Nakomura on assuming command of prisoners of war in Siam in June, 1943: 'those who fail in charge by lack of health is regarded in Japanese Army as most shameful deed.')

Relentless insistence upon fixed figures of workmen daily, if defied, led to the sick being turned out of hospital with indiscriminate violence. Sick parades were endless, since the wretched condition of the men required daily assessment and comparison. They dragged on up to midnight or beyond, and attendance was again needed at works parades before dawn. Japanese N.C.O.s and privates frequently overruled medical officers and cut short argument with violence.

In the Hintok area works parades were a deplorable spectacle, featuring scores of men tottering with the support of sticks, or even being carried out bodily to meet fixed figures. Men unable to stand were carried, to work in a lying or sitting position. During the grimmer months of railway construction the sick were deliberately persecuted by works supervisors. For example, men with horribly festering bare feet were forced to work on sharp rocks or in thorny jungle hauling logs; disabling ulcers were struck or kicked; those collapsing were savagely handled; and sufferers from diarrhoea and dysentery were compelled to foul themselves working.

The engineer officer of this area, Lieut Hirota, led his men in ferocity by personal example, and on occasion flogging of the sick was followed by their demise. Lieut Osuki, POW camp commander, stated that he did not care if sick men died, since 'working percentage better'. Lieut-Col Ishii, in charge of 13,000 prisoners, when shown emaciated dysentery sufferers devoid of drugs, commented on the treatment by no food for two to three days with loud laughter and the retort: 'In future no food no food one week, better!' The pungent protests of medical officers against these conditions need hardly be instanced. Capricious evacuations of sick were by casual hitch-hiking on passing lorries or barges. The weak supported or carried the weaker. Frequently days were spent in transit with exposure and little food. Barges arrived at jungle hospitals with both the sick and the dead in the stench of gangrene and dysentery.

JUNGLE HOSPITALS

Typical of early base hospitals heroically evolved under the greatest difficulties in Burma were Thanbyuzayat, Lieut-Col. T. Hamilton, AAMC; and 55-Kilo hospital, Lieut-Col A. E. Coates, AAMC. In Siam, Tarsau, Lieut-Col W. G. Harvey, RAMC; Takanoun, Major T. M. Pemberton, RAMC; Chungkai, Majors Reed, RAMC, D. Black, IMS [Indian Medical Service], and

Lieut-Col J St.C. Barrett, RAMC; Kanburi, Lieut-Col J. Malcolm, RAMC; Tamarkan, Major A.A. Moon, AAMC; and Non Pladuk, Major Smythe, RAMC.

The conditions at Tarsau and Chungkai hospitals at the time I was first associated with them are illustrative. Each contained a constant population of approximately 2,500 very sick men as a citadel within a jungle city of sickness. The sick lay massed together on bamboo staging in decrepit collapsing huts. Bedding and hospital utensils were largely non-existent. No instruments and very few medicines were supplied by the Japanese. Lack of tools, materials, and fit men combined with overcrowding to create a nauseating lack of hygiene. Bugs, lice, and almost universal scabies infection produced minor torments and florid skin sepsis. Men were too weak to keep themselves clean, and there were few orderlies, or even containers for water.

Table A1   Chungkai POW hospital statistics

Diseases	Total treated	1943 Died	Case mortality rate (%)	Total treated	1944 Died	Case mortality rate (%)
Malaria	3 336	67	2.0	1 753	13	0.74
N.Y.D.	374	-	Nil	142	-	-
Bacillary dysentery	734	129	17.5	139	2	1.44
Amoebic dysentery	1 309	266	20.3	1 113	46	4.13
Enteritis	565	19	1.6	414	12	2.92
Cholera	134	54	40.3	8	-	-
Diphtheria	88	14	15.9	1	-	-
Lobar pneumonia	26	23	88.5	13	6	46.15
Broncho pneumonia	32	25	78.1	6	3	50.0
Bronchitis	32	-	Nil	47	-	-
Avitaminosis (mixed)	774	257	34.5	397	61	15.36
Pellagra	189	110	58.2	62	10	16.1
Beriberi	335	170	50.7	100	11	11.0
Tropical ulcer	1 353	37	2.7	1 129	-	-
Other skin diseases	851	-	Nil	674	-	-
All other diseases	1 496	89	5.9	795	24	3.02
Grand Total	11 628	1 260	10.7	6 793	188	2.70

The condition of tropical ulcer patients was pitiable, and these wards stank of the hospital gangrene of pre-Listerian days. Rags, papers, leaves, and locally picked kapok and cotton were employed as dressings. The blowflies hanging in clouds about the patients produced maggot infections with far from benign effect. Dysentery and avitaminosis wards were scarcely less distressing. Some crude operating and pathological facilities had arisen from POW resources. Discipline, supremely high morale, and the pooling of resources in foodstuffs, money, materials, and human ability were even more important than purely medical treatment. A duck's egg daily might be all that was needed to turn the scales of a man's life. Herculean labours improved sanitation and accommodation. Patients were trained as medical orderlies, others were employed in the mass production of improvised equipment, even if they were only able to whittle with a knife on their beds. Sick-welfare money from various national and unit sources was directed into a common pool, and used with the utmost economy in a planned series of standard special diets, or in the clandestine purchase of essential drugs from the Siamese. For example, at Chungkai from January to April of 1944 we raised 38,000 dollars from prisoners' meagre resources, largely from the officers' pay of 30 dollars a month. (On capitulation of the Japanese the rate of exchange was 60 dollars to one English pound.) In addition, friendly sources contributed 3,000 dollars a month. Emetine, iodoform, and other drugs were obtained by the risky venture of selling Nipponese quinine. Emetine cost 35 dollars for 1 grain (65 mg.), and iodoform for tropical ulcers several hundred dollars a bottle.

The relationship of equipment to special problems was well illustrated by the great fall in septic cross-infection after the introduction of a rigid 'forceps' technique, employing large irrigating cans and small portable sterilizers, made from the mess-tins of dead men and heated by charcoal stoves devised from biscuit tins and mud. Even this simple equipment was extremely hard to obtain, and the striking benefits of mass disinfection and scabies treatment involved stealing petrol drums to make steam disinfectors. Intensive surgical measures were employed to drain pus, remove sequestra, and graft raw areas; amputations were performed where necessary. The steep fall in mortality at this stage was most gratifying.

NAKOM PATOM POW HOSPITAL

This huge hospital situated on the paddy-fields some twenty miles (32 km) from Bangkok contained as many as 8,000 sick during its most active period. Little was provided for prisoners other than the buildings and some Red Cross stores, but with more static conditions, and comparatively greater material resources for improvisation, the scope of medical work was made to compare with that of a large civilian hospital. Had even the crude facilities of this hospital been made available at an earlier date, great loss of life might have been avoided. Pin-pricking regimentation and constant interference with medical officers and sick, day and night, made the work of the hospital very difficult, and parties of sick were constantly being transferred in the teeth of medical opposition.

Isolated parties transferred in this fashion were employed in railway maintenance, road construction, and bridge repair in areas harassed by Allied bombing, and some suffered terrible experiences recalling the tragic fate of 'H' and 'F' forces during railway construction. An epic story was a six-weeks march of 800 British soldiers for some 600 km. (375 miles) from Nakom Nyak to Pitsanloke carrying their sick on rice-sack stretchers. Due to the devoted work of the medical officers, Capt. C. J. Poh, S.S.U.F. [Straits Settlements United Force], and Capt. T. Brereton, A.A.M.C., only three died on the march.

RECORDS AND STATISTICS

All the diseases of the male adult were encountered, and in addition numerous tropical diseases, even those as remote from ordinary experience as yaws and leprosy. The main diseases are shown in tabular form. Chungkai POW hospital statistics (Table A.1), kept by Major A. L. Dunlop, R.A.M.C., are self-explanatory. Where multiple diseases were present only the main disease on admission was recorded. Australian figures (Table A.2) are taken for my seven working camps, since the records I retain of other nationals are less complete. The average camp population from which the Australian casualties quoted were drawn was approximately 1,000. Usually two medical officers and six to eight medical orderlies were available.

MALARIA

In the absence of adequate clothing, bedding, and mosquito nets, in jungle areas where there were debilitated troops and negligible larval and mosquito control, the disease was almost universal. B.T. infections predominated over M.T. and showed such phenomenal recurrence rates as twenty attacks in a year. Suppressive quinine in a dosage of 3 to 6 gr. (0.2 to 0.4 g.) daily in my experience was given too sporadically to have noticeable effect.

Blackwater fever was not common – e.g. a total of 17 cases at Nakom Patom among thousands of malarial subjects enduring repeated attacks. Cerebral malaria was not infrequent, and, with no ampoules of quinine suitable for injections, sterile solutions were made from any quinine available. I found Howards' 5-gr. tablets of quinine hydrochloride very effective given intravenously in a dosage of 10 gr. (0.65 g.).

MALNUTRITION AND AVITAMINOSIS

'Vitamins are luxuries', was the answer of a Japanese medical officer, Capt. Novosawa, to a request for an increase. Pellagra was the most common disorder, and exerted a sinister influence on the course of other diseases. The early symptoms of pellagra appeared after a few months of imprisonment – notably angular stomatitis, glossitis, pigmentary changes, and dry scaly skin. Scrotal dermatitis with erythema and loss of rugae rapidly progressed to exudation and scaly crusting. 'Burning feet', much in evidence after six

Table A2 Australian patients admitted to Col. Dunlop's camp hospitals, June 1942 to October 1943

Camp	Malaria	Dysentery	Enteritis	Cholera	Diptheria	Pneumonia	Bronchitis	Avitaminosis and Malnutrition	Injuries	Tropical Ulcers	Other Skin Diseases	Other Diseases	Totals	Deaths
Bandoeng, Java (June 14–Nov.7, 1942)	37	129	7	-	-	2	2	17	8	3	25	58	288	1
Makosura, Java (Nov.7, 1942–Jan.4, 1943)	14	28	1	-	-	-	2	18	1	2	20	27	113	-
Changi, Singapore, south area (Jan.7–June 20, 1943)	7	29	-	-	-	-	-	38	6	1	12	16	109	-
Konyu (Jan.25–Mar.12, 1943)	166	153	21	-	-	-	3	5	5	7	12	18	392	-
Hintok, Mountain Camp (Mar.13–Aug.23, 1943)	916	558	340	93	11	18	38	194	113	209	221	171	2882	57
Hintok, River Camp (July 20–Sept.18, 1943)	590	98	56	57	-	1	4	78	38	104	213	95	1334	25
Kinsayok (Sept.10–Oct.23, 1943)	288	17	22	-	-	1	-	2	26	49	31	10	446	-

Totals	2018	1012	447	150	11	22	49	352	197	375	534	395	5 564	83
Deaths	-	10	-	63	-	1	-	3	1	-	-	5	83	

Notes:

1. Most cases of enteritis were of pellagrous origin.
2. The figures bear little relaionship to total disease, since almost all troops worked through illness, and malaria and pellagra were almost universal.
3. Where several diseases were co-existent only the principal one was recorded.
4. Avitaminosis and malnutrition column: 50% were serious pellagra cases, the remainder cases of protein oedema and beri-beri.
5. The low death rate at this time was quite exceptional, and is in large measure due to the fact that most of these troops were seasoned Middle East veterans of very fine physique. Large numbers, however, died at a later date in base hospitals.

months, gave great distress at night, the sensation being most marked in the ball of the foot and passing forward to the toes. In some the legs and hands were affected. The circulation in the feet was excellent, but free sweating gave them a clammy feeling. The deep reflexes were hyperactive, and some patients had knee and ankle clonus. Rare cases progressed to spastic diplegia. Amblyopia was seen at the same time as the 'burning feet', and occasionally both conditions occurred in the same case.

Later experience showed the rapid response of scrotal dermatitis and most mouth lesions to riboflavin, 6 to 8 mg. daily for a few days. Nicotinic acid or nikethamide was effective for other symptoms, except the amblyopia. In my experience the diarrhoea associated with pellagra was not very evident until the second year of prisoner-of-war life, when it became common and distressingly uncontrollable. Mental derangement was seldom marked, though in the terminal phase some cases showed extreme mental apathy and evinced difficulty in swallowing any food, particularly rice.

Nutritional oedema or famine oedema was excessively common, some soldiers becoming horribly bloated. In severe cases alimentary absorption seemed poor, and deterioration continued despite large numbers of eggs daily. Beri-beri occurred in all forms, though in some instances it was confused with famine oedema. Scurvy and frank vitamin A deficiency were uncommon.

The basis of these disorders will be evident from the average ration recorded at Hintok camp in March 1943. (This particular ration is by no means indicative of lower levels.)

Average issue per man per day: sugar 16 g., salt 10 g., fresh vegetables (mostly Chinese radish) 23 g., dried vegetables 6 g., meat 16.5 g., dried fish 26.5 g., oil of coconut 3 g., rice 600 g. (poor quality, some musty and almost uneatable).

Many sources of vitamins were tried in the absence of vitamin concentrates, but none was so effective as fresh foodstuffs obtained by money or credit. The whole question of a man's survival frequently hinged on the provision of money from prisoners' meagre resources, and on purchase facilities. Fresh ducks' eggs and the *katchang idjoe* bean (a lentil favoured by the Dutch) were excellent for all purposes. Meat was more expensive; yeast excellent but difficult to produce economically in concentrated form. Grass extracts were freely employed, but suitable grass was rare in the jungle. Jungle 'spinach' was popular. The supply of ducks' eggs for purchase, always hazardous in the jungle, was a major consideration in sustaining life in Siam. Blood transfusions later became a valuable measure in the worst cases of malnutrition, and under all circumstances there was no dearth of volunteer donors.

CHOLERA

The severe outbreaks of cholera were due to squalid conditions and association with Asiatic coolies, who contaminated water supplies and camp areas. Water sterilization often presented great difficulties. The Japanese showed terror of the disease, and frequently compelled the patients to be attended in appallingly unsuitable jungle sites with little shelter – in the hope they would die quickly. One notorious case where a cholera sufferer was shot by Japanese order illustrates this attitude.

Typical cases showed dramatic prostration, with copious rice-water stools, vomiting, husky voice, cramps, ringing in the ears, weakness, and feebleness. As sterile saline and disinfectants were not supplied, many courageous improvisations were made, particularly for the replacement of fluids in the algid phase. Saline was prepared from kitchen salt and spring, river, or rain water distilled in curiously designed stills. In one instance a medical officer employed a drilled bamboo thorn as an improvised cannula, and on occasion the risk was taken of administering saline with boiled and not distilled water. The most severe epidemic I encountered was one with which Major E. L. Corlette, A.A.M.C., and I were concerned at Hintok, where in our own immediate camp of 1,000 men, 150 showed obvious infection, and there were 63 deaths. Hundreds of deaths occurred in the neighbourhood. The cases were nursed under leaking rags of tents, in an appalling morass in the jungle. Some early cases were given intraperitoneal saline injections of several pints. Three stills were hurriedly improvised from lengths of stolen petrol pipe surrounded by bamboo jackets, and irrigated by water brought in bamboo pipes from a spring. Some 120 pints (68 l.) were produced and given daily through a number of continuous saline sets manufactured from such oddments as our stethoscopes, bamboo tubing, saki bottles, etc. In cases with extreme fluid loss as much as 20 pints (11 l.) were given in twenty-four hours. Saline was very effective in the algid phase, but numbers passed into the stage of reaction (typhoidal state), rosy flush, and fever, or succumbed to other illnesses related to their gross debility.

Hypertonic saline was seldom employed owing to the crude clinical facilities. Capt. J. Markovitch, R.A.M.C., reported favourably on the use of double-strength saline. I found that potassium permanganate, in the usual 2-gr. (0.13 g.) dose as a pill wrapped in a cigarette paper, did not give relief commensurate with the burning discomfort caused.

DYSENTERY

Despite the appalling mortality and morbidity caused by this disease the Japanese refused to recognize its presence and compelled us to refer to it officially as 'colitis', or still more vaguely as 'other conditions'. Amoebic dysentery predominated, but emetine and other specifics were not supplied by the Japanese. The terrible severity of amoebic infections and the great shortage of emetine presented problems dealt with in a separate paper [1946]. Liver abscess was an infrequent complication, which under the circumstances required open drainage by the subcostal or transthoracic approach.

TROPICAL ULCER

This disease was highly prevalent in jungle areas among famished fever-ridden subjects exposed to blows and trauma. A distressing feature was massive spreading gangrene with acute exacerbations of spread. Frequently the deep fascia was penetrated and there followed gross involvement of bone, joints, muscle, tendon, vessels, and nerves. The type of evacuation and the practice of flooding ill-equipped hovels with these patients were disastrous. The base hospital sections receiving them became cesspools of 'hospital gangrene'. Waves of virulence spread about the wards, infecting other wounds – e.g. incisions for suppurative bursitis, septic scabetic lesions, and healing ulcers.

Ulcers were often multiple; three men seen in association with Capt. J. McConachie, R.A.M.C., were dying in agony from large ulcers arising from minor skin lesions all over the body and limbs. The pain, of which I have had personal experience, was very severe and caused muscle spasm, so that the lower limb frequently contracted with flexed knee and dropped foot. Natural healing, where the outcome was favourable, took months to years, and often resulted in severe deformity. Mild antiseptics were useless, and for effective action reagents were destructive to normal tissues – e.g. hyd. perchlor. solution 1 in 50, saturated solution of potassium permanganate, strong copper sulphate solution, pure phenol or lysol.

The best measure was removal of all gangrenous tissue by excision and curettage, followed by the application of pure phenol or lysol and a light sprinkle of iodoform powder. The latter was a specific for tropical infection, often effective even with such economy as 1 in 20 dilution. The distressing pain disappeared and the dressing could be left for days; the resulting granulating area was then skin-grafted. With this procedure, early cases could be healed in a month without deformity. The Japanese did not supply iodoform, but it could be bought in small quantities at high prices from the Siamese. It was the most economical of all purchased drugs, and the sight of it brought a glad smile to sufferers.

Many hundreds of men endured the agony of curettage of ulcers necessarily without anaesthesia. Necrosed tendon and muscle required wide incisions in fascial planes and formal excision. Huge sequestra were extracted when they loosened, some constituting the greater part of the shaft of the tibia. At Nakom Patom sequestrectomy was accompanied by large 'saucerizing' procedures. Amputation was often necessary to save life, and some patients begged for it, despite the crude knives and butchers' saws employed. Immediate mortality rates were surprisingly good – e.g. under 10% – but there were associated gross nutritional disorders often evidenced by running diarrhoea and famine oedema. Further depletion of body protein occurred with the copious discharges. Ultimately about 50% of amputation cases succumbed, many of them after good healing. Blood transfusion was a valuable measure. When hostilities ceased, 170 amputation cases surviving at Nakom Patom, including two with bilateral amputations, were already provided with useful artificial limbs.

Some hundreds of skin grafts in the hospitals with which I was associated showed gratifying results in healing and lessened deformity, compensating for great difficulties in arranging dressings and suitable firm pressure over graft areas. I found that a light dust of iodoform powder over the graft area gave considerable protection against recurrence of tropical infection.

SCABIES AND INFECTED SKIN LESIONS

In some hospitals over 90% of the population had scabies, many with florid skin sepsis. Mass treatment by wards was required, using improvised steam disinfectors for personal effects. Sulphur was largely purchased in a crude form. A very economical suspension with a minimum of oil was made by means of ox bile.

The feet of workmen employed without boots and constantly in mud and water became cruelly inflamed with gross septic tinea. Cure was difficult without rest.

GENERAL POINTS

Mental disorders were surprisingly infrequent, and neurosis uncommon among Anglo-Saxon prisoners. The hostility of the Japanese to the sick made their lot so unattractive that possibly a source of conflict was removed. Notwithstanding this fact, in well-led camps a heroic feature was the routine way men in the extremity of fatigue and debility lined up to take the place or bear the burden of those in worse case. A minor outbreak of hysterical palsies in the last year of imprisonment was predominantly among Netherlands East Indies soldiers. Suicide was uncommon and I personally know of only six cases. Possibly owing to lack of all privacy, and to the debilitating diet, sexual perversion was very inconspicuous. Though some men inevitably became morose and irritable, and quarrels arose, sanity, good humour, and optimism were predominant.

Ingeniously hidden wireless sets and news translations helped in sustaining morale, as did the organization of recreation, entertainment, and mental activities. Astonishing stage effects were obtained with rice matting, bamboos, rags of mosquito netting, etc., and symphonies were orchestrated from memory and played with impressive effect on instruments of great ingenuity. Fertile minds invented most diverting games. Formal religion appeared to have no enhanced appeal in camps of sickness and death. The maintenance of strict discipline was the greatest factor in preserving life and maintaining morale, and this was never questioned where officers set an example in unselfish devotion to duty.

JUNGLE SURGERY

The Japanese with characteristic interest in the dramatic and sadistic appeared to find a surgical operation a 'good show'. Shortly after arriving in the dense jungle in the Konyu area I performed a successful night operation for a perforated duodenal ulcer – on a hurriedly constructed bamboo table, lit by a bonfire and a borrowed hurricane lamp. Following this event I was freely allowed to visit other camps to perform operations, and incidentally effect medical and other liaison. In these areas only emergency operations were performed, such as those for acute abdominal lesions, wounds, and gross sepsis, and usually in the open or under a large mosquito net. Many penetrating wounds were seen from brittle fragments of steel drills (e.g. necessitating excision of the eye), and some severe dynamiting injuries.

In the absence of strapping for extension, fractured femurs were best treated by driving the cleanest nail that could be found through the upper tibia. Thomas splints were devised by twisting wire, and pulleys and cords were manufactured. The Hamilton Russell type of extension was used on occasion. It was found that good healing usually occurred in abdominal wounds, using well-washed hands and no gloves. All instruments, along with such drapings as were available, were sterilized by boiling.

Lack of anaesthesia was the greatest difficulty, and it was necessary to perform most minor operations in its absence. Minute amounts of chloroform were obtained from the Japanese and Siamese, and carefully conserved for special procedures. I was able to obtain small quantities of 'novocain' products, and this became the sheet anchor for spinal anaesthesia (1-2.5 ml. of freshly prepared 10% solution in distilled water). With variations of technique this sufficed for almost all operations on the abdomen and lower limb – e.g. gall-bladder surgery and amputations through the thigh. Local infiltration was much less economical but was necessary for the head or upper limb. Lieut-Col E. Coates did a most impressive series of 120 amputations of the lower limb at the 55-Kilo Hospital in Burma, employing a solution of cocaine (approximately 0.75 ml. of 2% solution intrathecally).

Catgut or other suture materials were rarely supplied by the Japanese, and numerous substitutes were used. I found cotton very useful, also silk obtained in quantity by unravelling the parachute cords carried by R.A.F. personnel. The most useful product was a locally prepared 'catgut' from the peritoneum of pigs and cattle, first introduced by an ingenious Dutch chemist, Capt. von Boxtel, working under Lieut-Col Coates. The peritoneum was trimmed in 6-metre ribbons of varying width, twisted on a winder and dried. Sterilization was effected at 130 F. (54.4 C.) for half an hour, after which it was put in ether for twenty-four hours, and finally in 90% alcohol and iodine.

Surgical instruments were most scarce, and ingenious improvisations were made. On occasion razors and pocket-knives were used to make incisions, while butchers' saws and carpenters' tools found useful employment.

SURGERY IN BASE HOSPITALS

In base hospitals the resources in tools, scraps of metal, and cherished oddments were greater, and some quite complex instruments were devised – for example, sigmoidoscopes, bowel clamps, rib shears, Cushing's silver clips and applying forceps, and optical apparatus. At Nakom Patom hospital, where the theatre was reasonably dust-proof and provided with a cement floor, a great range of surgical procedures were carried out under the enthusiastic direction of Lieut-Col Coates, who worked tirelessly at surgery in addition to administration. Major S. Krantz, A.A.M.C., has reviewed the surgical work of the hospital, in which he took an important part. Excluding very minor procedures, 773 surgical interventions were carried out, including such varied operations as brain and spinal-cord surgery, thyroidectomy, gastrectomy, enterectomy and anastomosis, abdomino-perineal resection, cholecystestomy, thoracic surgery, splenectomy, nephrectomy, laryngectomy, orthopaedic measures, and nerve sutures.

Appendicostomy, caecostomy, and ileostomy were allotted some place in the treatment of dysentery. Appendicectomy was carried out for appendicitis in 133 cases without mortality. Operations for hernia totalled 114, the majority being repaired with unabsorbable sutures. There were no deaths, 5 infected wounds, and 3 known recurrences. While it cannot be said that surgical procedures played a major part in the survival of prisoners of war, they represented considerable triumphs over unfavourable conditions.

IMPROVISATION

Necessity is indeed the mother of invention, and while the Japanese were in the main obstructive rather than helpful they paid Allied prisoners the compliment of expecting miracles of improvisation to replace normal supplies. In heartbreaking jungle areas devoid of the most commonplace materials, where even pieces of wire, nails, fabrics, empty tins, leather, etc., were prized possessions, and habitations were made of bamboo and palm leaf held together with jungle fibre, ingenuity was indeed tested.

Astonishing uses were made of bamboo, which served for such varied construction as beds, brooms, brushes, baskets, containers, water-piping, tubing, splints, etc. Timber was obtained by felling trees and splitting with wooden wedges, and used for many purposes, including footwear (clogs). Where solder could not be extracted from sardine tins and the like, water-tight tinsmithing was done by ingenious folding. Sources of hydrochloric acid included the human stomach. Flux was readily manufactured if sulphuric acid could be stolen from car batteries. Leather was prepared from buffalo or cow hide, and thread or string from unravelling webbing equipment, kit-bags, etc. It was necessary to equip jungle hospitals by the work of patients as well as staff, and they were organized in mass-production efforts with all available tools and resources.

Articles made by this 'cannibalization' of effects at Tarsau and Chungkai included urinals, bed-pans, commodes, surgical beds and pulleys, feeding-cups, wash-basins, irrigators, sterilizers, small portable charcoal stoves, disinfectors, stretchers and stretcher beds (with sack and bamboo), back-rests, leg-rests, oil-lamps, brooms, brushes, trays, tables, orthopaedic appliances, splints, surgical instruments, and artificial limbs and eyes (from mah-jongg pieces). The artificial limbs made at Nakom Patom under the direction of Major F.A. Woods, A.I.F., were designed from crude timber, leather cured from hide, thread from unravelled packs, iron from retained portions of officers' stretchers, and oddments of sponge-rubber, elastic braces, etc.

Part of an appeal to camp members at Chungkai was: 'The following articles are urgently needed: Tins and containers of all sorts, solder, flux, nails, wire, screws, sponge-rubber, scraps of clothing, hose-tops and old socks, string, webbing, scraps of leather, rubber tubing, glass bottles of all sorts, glass tubing (transfusion purposes), canvas, elastic, rubber bands or strips, braces, wax, mah-jongg pieces, and tools of all sorts. Nothing is too old, nothing is too small.'

TWO LIFE-SAVING ACHIEVEMENTS

A life-saving measure introduced by Major Reed, A.A.M.C., and developed by Capt. J. Markovitch, R.A.M.C., was the use of defibrinated blood for transfusion purposes. Using soldiers trained as technicians, thousands of transfusions were carried out by simply collecting the blood of a suitable donor into a container while stirring continuously with a spatula or whisk. Vigorous stirring was carried on for five minutes after clotting commenced on the spatula. The blood was then filtered through sixteen layers of gauze, and administered. Much help in the preparation of drugs and chemicals was given to medical officers by chemists, botanists, and scientists. Another life-saving achievement was the production of emetine from a limited quantity of ipeccacuanha by Capt. van Boxtel at the 55-Kilo Camp. Sgt. A.J. Kosterman and Sgt. G.W. Chapman did most valuable work in this respect.

Distilled water for intravenous use was prepared in numerous camps and hospitals. Alcohol for surgical and other purposes was obtained by the fermentation of rice with a suitable strain of fungus and distillation up to 90% strength. Grass extracts and other vitamin sources were exploited, and some useful items of materia medica were collected from local natural sources. From these, such products as essential oils – e.g. cloves and citronella – were obtained. Milk and bread made from soya bean lent some variety to the diet at times.

Products of minor importance included ink, paper, and cork substitutes. Major T. Marsden, R.A.M.C., provided an ingenious pathological service with improvised apparatus which satisfied most routine requirements. Colour indicators of pH were extracted from local flowers, and litmus paper was manufactured.

CONCLUSION

The treatment of sick prisoners by the Japanese left almost all civilized behaviour to be desired.

The fortitude and sustained morale of British soldiers under prolonged strain and suffering were most praiseworthy. The toll of long-continued strain and multiple debilitating diseases merits consideration and sympathy in the problems of post-war rehabilitation.

Appendix E: Report on the Repatriation of Koreans after 1959[1]

When Japan surrendered in August 1945, there were about two million Koreans living there. From 1945 to 1948, 1,400,000 of them returned to Korea. The remaining 600,000 stayed on, often living in difficult conditions, and it became increasingly obvious that something should be done to repatriate those who so wished.

Two ICRC delegates carried out a mission to Korea and Japan from 9 to 16 May 1956. They endeavoured to arrange the release of Japanese fishermen held in Pusan, in the Republic of Korea (hereinafter South Korea; the Democratic People's Republic of Korea will be referred to as North Korea) and Koreans interned in the Omura and Hamamatsu camps in Japan. Following their mission, the President of the ICRC sent a note to the Presidents of the Japanese, South Korea and North Korean Red Cross Societies on 16 July 1956 offering to act as intermediary in arranging for Koreans living in Japan or in Korea itself to make their homes in a place of their choice on Korean territory, if they so wished. One basic condition laid down by the ICRC was that the free choice of those involved must be guaranteed.

The ICRC asked the three Red Cross Societies to pass its proposal on to their respective governments.

The Japanese and North Korean Red Cross Societies replied favourably to the ICRC proposal but the South Korean Red Cross rejected it on the grounds that it would serve only to advance the political objectives of the Communists and the Japanese government which, it said, wanted to seize the property of Koreans living in Japan.

The ICRC then suggested that the three National Societies meet at its Geneva headquarters. The Japanese and North Korean Societies accepted but the South Korean Society refused and the meeting did not take place. On 12 December 1956, the ICRC sent another note to the three Societies repeating its proposal.

On 26 February 1957, the ICRC wrote again to the three Societies setting out a number of practical steps that could be taken for the repatriation of Koreans living in Japan.

On 31 December 1957, Japan and South Korea reached an agreement relating in particular to the Koreans interned in the Omura camp in Japan and the Japanese fishermen detained in Pusan, South Korea. As a result, a

---

1 Report prepared by Florianne Truninger, archivist of the ICRC in Geneva, printed by kind permission.

number of the Koreans held in Omura were released and those who expressed the desire to do so were repatriated to South Korea.

In early 1958, 922 Japanese fishermen held in Pusan were repatriated.

However, a number of Koreans remained interned in the Omura camp and the ICRC delegate in Tokyo visited them several times during 1958. Among them were about a hundred internees who wished to go to North Korea.

On 20 January 1959, the Central Committee of the Japanese Red Cross Society adopted a resolution calling for the Koreans' repatriation. Several months previously, the government of North Korea had announced that it was willing to provide boats and cover the cost of repatriating them.

On 30 January 1959, the Japanese Ministry of Foreign Affairs announced at a press conference that it intended to ask the ICRC to verify that the Koreans who decided to go to North Korea were doing so of their own free will. On 14 February, the Japanese government asked the Japanese Red Cross to convey this request to the ICRC which it was also asking to act as intermediary in the repatriation operation. The latter request was sent to Geneva the same day. A short time later, Tokyo made it public.

At the end of February, a delegation from the Japanese Red Cross arrived in Geneva.

The Republic of Korea National Red Cross immediately contacted the ICRC in an attempt to persuade it not to agree to the Japanese request. In March three South Korean representatives (two from the government and one from the Red Cross Society) arrived in Geneva to give the ICRC a more detailed explanation of their country's attitude to the proposed repatriations.

Other leading figures representing various groupings within South Korea opposed to the Japanese proposals also went to Geneva where they were received by the ICRC. They too urged the ICRC to refuse to take any part in the repatriations.

However, the Japanese Red Cross had endeavoured to arrange for a North Korean Red Cross delegation to be sent to Geneva so that the two Societies could meet there under the auspices of the ICRC. But the North Korean Red Cross then made known its opposition to the principle of screening repatriation candidates and refused to attend in the proposed talks under ICRC auspices.

On 13 March 1959, the ICRC set out its position in a press release, which stated: 'Guided by humanitarian principles and the Resolutions of the International Conferences of the Red Cross, the ICRC feels that every individual should be free to return to his country of origin, to the place of his choice, if he so wishes'. In early April, the North Korean Red Cross finally accepted the Japanese proposal of a meeting in Geneva and sent a delegation there. On 13 April, negotiations began.

The ICRC provided the two delegations with a meeting room but made it clear that it would not take part in their talks. It further advised them that it would remain silent on the conditions under which it might take part in any repatriation or even if it would take part at all, until such time as the two parties had reached agreement on the subject.

The negotiations went on until 24 June. On that date, the delegations from the Japanese and North Korean Red Cross Societies reached an agreement 'based on the principle of freedom to choose one's place of residence and on the Red Cross principles, to enable Koreans living in Japan to return to their country according to the free expression of their own wishes'.

The agreement set out what was required to be eligible to request repatriation (Article 1), the general procedure for making (Article 2a) or withdrawing (Article 2b) applications and the role as observer and advisor to the Japanese Red Cross which the two Societies now planned to entrust to the ICRC (Article 3). Other provisions concerned departure formalities (Articles 4 and 5), exemption from travel costs, baggage transport costs and customs duties (Article 6) and the conditions under which representatives of the North Korean Red Cross would be present at the port of departure. Finally, it was agreed to publish the text of the accord (Article 8), the duration of which was fixed at one year and three months to begin at its signing (Article 9).

The agreement was initialled in Geneva and officially signed in Calcutta on 13 August 1959.

A short time before, the ICRC had informed the Japanese Red Cross that it was willing to assist in preparations for the repatriation of Koreans living in Japan who expressed a wish to go to the place of their choice in their country of origin. It pointed out, however, that this willingness implied neither approval nor disapproval of the agreement of 24 June between the Japanese and North Korean Red Cross Societies. This was because the ICRC felt that it was not required to give an opinion on an agreement reached independently of it and by which it was in no way bound. It merely pointed out that the two parties had formally recognized that the agreement was based on the principle that each person must be free to choose his country of residence and return to his country of origin if he so desired.

In addition, the ICRC took note of the assurances it had received from the Japanese government and Red Cross on the steps that would be taken to guarantee freedom of choice for those concerned. These assurances also applied to the Koreans who preferred to stay on in Japan.

The ICRC further mentioned messages it had received from the Red Cross Society and government of South Korea concerning the repatriation of Koreans who expressed the wish to go to the southern part of their country of origin. The authorities in Seoul announced that they would be willing to receive them as soon as the necessary arrangements had been concluded with the Japanese government.

All these points were briefly made in an ICRC press release issued on 11 August. It summarized the ICRC's position in the matter and announced that a mission would soon leave Geneva for Japan.

This mission was carried out by Dr Marcel Junod, ICRC Vice-President, who arrived on 23 August in Tokyo where he immediately began talks with the Japanese Red Cross and government authorities to settle the conditions under which the ICRC would take part in the repatriation. Shortly before he returned to Europe he was joined by Dr Otto Lehner, who took over as head of the ICRC special mission.

In early September, the Japanese Red Cross published a 'Guide-Book for Mr Returnee' setting the repatriation procedure out in detail. It listed the guarantees ensuring that each person would be fully informed as to the choice being offered to him (going to North Korea, going to South Korea or staying in Japan) and would be able freely to state his choice.

It explained that any candidate for repatriation to North Korea would be called upon to confirm his decision in an interview alone with a Japanese Red Cross delegate and an ICRC delegate. This interview would take place at the transit centre in the port city of Niigata on the Sea of Japan, immediately prior to departure. The Guide-Book stated that in addition to this interview in offices specially set up for the purpose, anyone could at any time speak without witnesses to an ICRC delegate. The book, approved by Dr Junod, was very widely distributed throughout Japan.

Taking up an invitation received before his departure for the Far East, Dr Junod also went to the Republic of Korea. In Seoul, he was received by Mr Syngman Rhee, President of the National Red Cross Society, and several other leading figures, to whom he gave copies of the Guide-Book. During Dr Junod's visit, the South Korean leaders repeated their total opposition to any repatriation of Koreans to North Korea. A short time later, Dr Junod returned to Geneva.

On 21 September, the Japanese Red Cross opened 3,655 registration offices throughout Japan. Koreans wishing to go to the northern part of their country of origin were able to fill out application forms there. However, because of reservations expressed by certain members of the Korean community in Japan about some aspects of the procedure laid down by the Japanese Red Cross, departure applications were at first few in number; there were only 432 for the period from 21 September to 3 November.

In the meantime, the ICRC had organized its mission in Japan and Dr Lehner and some 20 Swiss delegates who had come from Europe or been recruited in Japan began visiting the main Japanese Red Cross registration offices. Accompanied by National Society representatives, the ICRC delegates checked that the registration centres were displaying notices informing Koreans of the choices open to them. They also checked that the offices were set up in accordance with the directives of the Japanese Red Cross and the principles laid down by the ICRC.

In the end, the Japanese Red Cross made several adjustments to the repatriation procedure. The number of applications then rose sharply (4,500 on 4 and 5 November), and reached 6,200 by 15 December.

In early November, Dr Lehner was replaced as head of the special ICRC mission by Mr André Durand who had already carried out a number of important missions in the Far East.

In early December, special trains escorted by ICRC delegates brought the first Koreans who had applied for repatriation to the North from several regions of Japan to Niigata. There they were received at the Japanese Red Cross transit centre and asked to confirm, in the presence of a Japanese Red Cross representative and an ICRC delegate, their wish to go to the Democratic People's Republic of Korea. Each individual then received an emigration certificate and went through police and customs formalities. Those who so desired were also able to receive visits at the centre from relatives or to talk to ICRC delegates without witnesses.

On 14 December 975 Koreans, escorted by a large police force, were taken from the transit centre to the docks where they made their final farewells to a large number of their compatriots. They then boarded the two Soviet ships chartered by the North Korean Red Cross and the following day arrived in Chongjin on north-east coast of Korea.

On 21 December, another group of 976 Koreans left Niigata in the same way. On this occasion, the need for a final interview without witnesses before departure was demonstrated when a 16-year-old girl declared that she had been registered against her will and stated that she wished to remain in Japan. She was sent home without incident. In addition, the head of the ICRC mission postponed the departure of two unaccompanied children under 16 years of age until it was possible to place them in the care of either their parents or a guardian.

A third group, this time numbering 991, left in the same way on 28 December. This time the head of the ICRC mission prevented the departure of one person who had not been properly registered.

By the end of 1959, almost 3,000 Koreans had been repatriated in accordance with the rules laid down by the Japanese Red Cross. All the people concerned had been quite free to change their minds at any point before the final confirmation of their wishes at the interview in Niigata. And indeed some 60 applicants failed to appear at the first three departures. The departures continued in 1960.

The repatriation of Koreans wishing to go to South Korea was worked out in negotiations between the South Korean mission in Tokyo and the Japanese Government. The ICRC took no part in these.

The special ICRC mission continued throughout 1960 to assist the Japanese Red Cross in preparing and carrying out repatriations to North Korea.

The repatriation of children under the age of 16 presented the most difficult of problems. In such cases the Japanese Red Cross and the ICRC mission endeavoured to act in the best interests of the children concerned, taking into account both Japanese legislation and Korean customs and making sure that the children were not separated from their families.

The ICRC delegates further checked to ensure that the candidates for repatriation were not under any pressure either to go to North Korea or to stay in Japan. Such cases were few and only a small number of applications with irregularities were turned down.

Before each departure, the ICRC mission studied the documents presented to it, mostly to prevent children under 16 being separated from their parents or leaving unaccompanied.

In Niigata, ICRC delegates continued to take part in the final interviews with the Koreans. Asked by a representative of the Japanese Red Cross to confirm that they wished to leave, a small number of them said that they had changed their minds, usually for family reasons. A much larger number (a sizeable proportion of the number registered for each ship) simply failed to turn up for the departure. Thus, ships chartered to take a thousand passengers sometimes left with as few as 800 or even 700.

These changes of heart were probably due, at least in part, to the uncertainty created by the talks begun in September in Niigata aimed at renewing the agreement reached between the North Korean and Japanese Red Cross Societies in Calcutta on 13 August 1959 for a period of 15 months. In the end, however, the agreement was renewed on 27 October for a further period of one year beginning on 13 November. Representatives of the two Societies then agreed, on 24 November, to accelerate the repatriations by allowing the departure, beginning on 1 March 1961, of 1,200 people per week instead of 1,000.

By the end of 1960, 52,000 people (including 4,000 Japanese citizens) had left Japan for North Korea in 51 shiploads.

The repatriation of Koreans living in Japan continued in 1961, and ICRC delegates continued to monitor registration and departures throughout the year.

The delegates once again travelled to all regions of Japan to study with local officials the problems raised by the departure applications. These visits made it possible to clear up a number of cases, most of them involving unaccompanied children under 16 years of age.

But the number of people leaving each week decreased considerably over the year. Following an interruption of more than two months requested by the North Korean Red Cross because of the influenza epidemic in Japan at the beginning of the year, the number of people leaving, which had been 1,000 to 1,100 per week in June 1961, dropped to about 500 in early October. Another suspension of operations was requested by North Korea from 11 September to 2 October in order to repair the ships. On 16 December, the 85th group to leave, the last of the year, numbered 124 people, bringing to about 75,000 the number that had left Japan for North Korea since December 1959. About 23,000 people left in 1961 as against 52,000 from December 1959 to December 1960. The vast majority of those leaving had Korean nationality but there were some Japanese and Chinese citizens.

The departures resumed in 1962 but at a slower pace. The 86th group numbered less than 100 persons whereas at the beginning of the operation over 1,000 Koreans were leaving Japan each week. The groups that followed comprised an average of only 200 to 300 people. In view of this situation, the Japanese and North Korean Red Cross Societies decided at the end of the year to renew the 1959 Calcutta agreement, which would otherwise have run out on 12 November 1962, for another year. The ICRC agreed to a request from the Japanese Red Cross to keep its special delegation in Japan for one more year.

By the end of December 1962, about 78,000 people had been repatriated, as compared with 75,000 at the end of 1961 and 52,000 at the end of 1960.

Repatriations continued in 1963, bringing to 80,500 the number of people who had left. In 1964 it reached 82,655 and, at the end of 1965, 84,920.

In 1966, the Japanese Red Cross informed the ICRC that the Calcutta agreement had been renewed for another year and asked the ICRC to maintain special mission in Japan. The ICRC agreed.

By the end of 1966, 86,780 people had been repatriated and by the end of 1967 the number had reached 88,611. Despite opposition from the North Korean Red Cross, the Japanese decided not to renew the Calcutta accord and applications for departure to North Korea were not accepted after 11 August 1967. The last boat allowed to dock in Japan under the agreement left Niigata for North Korea on 13 October 1967.

Delegations from the Japanese and North American Red Cross Societies met in Moscow in late August and in Colombo at the end of November to discuss how Koreans who had not been able to leave Japan before the 12 November deadline set by the Calcutta accord could go to North Korea. These talks concerned in particular the 17,000 Koreans who had applied for repatriation before 12 August, the closing date for applications set by Japan. The two Societies agreed that an extra boat would be allowed to enter Niigata on 18 December 1967 to take on board a fresh contingent of Koreans, whose departure had been organized in compliance with the 1959 Calcutta agreement. The boat left on 22 December. Meanwhile, the North Korean and Japanese Red Cross Societies continued their talks in Ceylon.

But there were still some 17,000 Koreans in Japan who wished to go to North Korea and had followed the proper application procedure before the deadline set by the agreement.

On 2 April 1968, the ICRC called on the two Red Cross Societies to do what was necessary to allow these people to be repatriated. The ICRC received a favourable reply from the Japanese but nothing from the North Korean Red Cross. It therefore repeated its appeal on 10 September.

On 5 February 1971, the Japanese and North Korean Red Cross signed a new agreement in Moscow allowing repatriation operations to be resumed for a period of six months beginning in May. Following the signing of this agreement, the Japanese Red Cross asked the ICRC to send a delegate to Niigata to help with the departure of Koreans who wished to go to North Korea and who had applied before the deadline set by the Calcutta agreement. It was the intention of those involved to complete the operation begun in 1959.

Six departures were organized between May and October for 1,081 people. This brought to 89,692 the total number of Koreans who had left Japan for North Korea under ICRC auspices since 1959. Repatriation continued until 1972.

Notes and References

Full details of authors' works to which reference is made here will be found in the Bibliography.

The place of publication is London, unless otherwise stated.

1 The Red Cross in Japan

1. See Kokuryu Kai (ed.), *Seinan ki den* (Chronological Accounts of the S.W. War), 6 Vols., (Tokyo, 1908–11).
2. Takamori Saigo (1827–77) see K. Inoue, *Saigo Takamori* (1970); I. Morris, *The Nobility of Failure* (1975), especially Chapter 9 on 'The Apotheosis of Saigo the Great', pp. 217–75, and Appendix B.
3. In general, traditional Japanese battlefield behaviour, of killing off any enemy, wounded or prisoners, was condemned in the West as barbaric. For the Japanese, *seppuku*, killing oneself by disembowelling, must be 'an excruciatingly painful form of self-torture which served as conclusive evidence that . . . here was a man who could be respected by friend and enemy alike, for his physical courage, determination and sincerity': I. Morris, *The Nobility of Failure* p.15. But note that Takayoshi Kido (1833–77), one of the ablest early Meiji leaders, was severely critical of the old *bushido* code of military honour: see S. D. Brown and A. Hirota, *The Diary of Kido Takayoshi*, Vol. III (3 September 1874), pp. 69–70.
4. On 18 August 1877, when the Satsuma soldiers at Nagai surrendered, Medical Superintendent Hayashi was ordered by Yamagata, the chief of staff, to treat as many rebels as possible. In addition, rebel Satsuma doctors, already captured, were released so that they could give aid: *Seinan ki den* (S. W. War), Vol. 2–1, p. 777. It would appear that at least one female nurse was also working on the battlefields. She was Saha Masuda, whose husband was fighting on Saigo's side, but she served also in 'police hospitals'. With thanks to Seibi Ota.
5. Early in 1877 (the dates 6 April and 8 June 1877 are given) Tsunetami Sano's initiative of the *Hakuaisha* Society was agreed by Prince Arisugawa, the Commander in Chief, and approved by the Emperor. Another account suggests that Sano, with the help of Josen Matsudaira, Tadako Sakurai and Nobumasa Matsudaira petitioned Iwakura, who approached Prince Arisugawa and *Hakuaisha* was founded on 1 May 1877: see R. Honma, *Sano Tsunetami Den* (Tokyo, 1943), pp. 181–3, with thanks to Isao Fujiwara. It was felt that the *Hakuaisha* was important because 'the number of dead and wounded in the Satsuma army is double that of the government army . . . Although these men are rebels and against the Emperor, they are still our people, and still the Emperor's subjects. It is intolerable to let them die': *Seinan ki den* (S. W. War), Vol. 2–1, p. 771.

214

6. Yasukuni Jinja, Shinto shrine in central Tokyo, to honour all the Japanese war dead, originally established (1869) to pay respects to those who had sacrificed themselves to make Japan safe for the Emperor Meiji.

7. C. Z. Rothkopf, *Jean Henri Dunant, Father of the Red Cross* (1971); E. Hart, *Man Born to Live, Life and Work of Henry Dunant, Founder of the Red Cross* (1953); M. Gumpert, *Dunant, the Story of the Red Cross or the Knight Errant of Charity* (1939).

8. G. I. A. Draper, *Red Cross Conventions* (1958), p. 2.

9. Henri Dunant (1829–1910) *A Memory of Solferino* (British Red Cross Reprint, 1947), *A Proposal for Introducing Uniformity into the Conditions of Prisoners of War on Land* (1872).

10. D. Schindler and J. Toman, *The Law of Armed Conflict* (Leyden, 1973), p. vii.

11. Dr Rutherford was not encouraging about the Red Cross initiative in Geneva. He believed that following the Crimean War, the British, by increasing and improving army medical services, were able to provide all that was necessary on the field of battle. Rutherford did not mention, in his address, societies for the relief of wounded; he clearly felt they were superfluous: see P. Boissier, *From Solferino to Tsushima* (Geneva, 1985), p. 74.

12. Although the Japanese accepted the + as symbol it has not, in the twentieth century, been universally accepted. Muslim countries in general have Red Crescent Societies.

13. See C. Woodham Smith, *Florence Nightingale* (1950); F. B. Smith, *Florence Nightingale, Reputation and Power* (1982); M. E. Baly, *Florence Nightingale and the Nursing Legacy* (1986).

14. B. Oliver, *The British Red Cross in Action* (1966).

15. F. R. Dulles, *The American Red Cross Society, a History* (New York, 1950).

16. See M. Keswick, *The Thistle and the Jade* (1982) and O. Checkland, *Britain's Encounter with Meiji Japan, 1868–1912* (1989).

17. Tsunetami Sano (1822–1902) was a politician trained in Western learning, who was involved with founding the Japanese navy. He is credited with founding the JRC on his own initiative but he may have acted at the request of Iwakura and Ito. He remained President of the Red Cross Society until the end of his life. See Appendix B.

18. Sano was Japanese Chargé d'Affaires in Vienna from 31 January to 30 September 1873; he had duties concerning the Japanese display at the Vienna Exhibition.

19. The Iwakura Mission members met Sano in Rome in 1873; it is not known whether he accompanied the Mission on their Swiss tour: see Shinpo Ko Tsuitokai (ed.), *Ito Hirobumi Den*, Vol. I, p. 720.

20. *Bulletin International de Sociétés de secours aux militaires blessés publié par le Comité International*, No. 17 (October 1873), p. 13.

21. *Bulletin International . . .*, No. 17 (October 1873), p. 15.

22. C. Z. Rothkopf, *Jean Henri Dunant*, and E. Hart, *Man Born to Live*.

23. J. J. Rousseau, *Contrat Social* (Geneva, 1762), Book I, Chapter IV.

24. F. B. Freidel, *Francis Lieber, Nineteenth Century Liberal* (1947). See also *The Mississippi Valley Historical Review* (1945–6), pp. 541–56.

25. U.S. Army General Order No. 100, Washington (24 April 1863); see also G. F. A. Best, *Humanity in Warfare* (1980), p. 155.
26. G. F. A. Best, *Humanity in Warfare*, p. 156.
27. G. F. A. Best, *Humanity in Warfare*, p. 157.
28. G. I. A. Draper, *Red Cross Conventions* (1958), p. 4.
29. G. F. A. Best, *Humanity in Warfare*, p. 345.
30. Y. Komatsu, personal letter to author, 11 March 1992.
31. J. Suzuki, 'The Japanese Red Cross Mission to England', *JSL* (*Japan Society of London*), Vol. 14 (1915–16), p. 29; see also M. C. Fraser, *A Diplomat's Wife in Japan* (Tokyo, 1982), p. 311.
32. J. Suzuki, 'The Japanese Red Cross Mission to England', p. 29.
33. N. Ariga, *The Japanese Red Cross Society* (St Louis, 1904), p. 10.
34. N. Ariga, *The Japanese Red Cross Society*, p. 11.
35. Masayoshi Matsukata (1835–1924) had had a distinguished career as Finance Minister who had been remarkably successful in creating a modern banking system for Japan. In 1883 he was ennobled and became Count, while in 1905, in recognition of his financial services during the Russo–Japanese War for the JRC, he became a Marquis; see Appendix B.

2 The 'Emperor's Children': Army and Navy Health Care

1. 'In Japan the Emperor is the personal leader of the nation in arms and the soldier are his soldiers, not in theory only, but by the fact of historical tradition. Hence the nation which loves and respects the Emperor, literally as children do their fathers, naturally loves the soldiers whom the Emperor cherishes and does everything in his power to help them. We owe to the Emperor the independence and prosperity of the empire, which he maintains by means of his soldiers, and the best way of paying back this immeasurable debt is to give aid to his soldiers while risking their lives on the field of battle': Dr Nagao Ariga, Professor of International Law and leading Japanese Red Cross member, quoted in L. L. Seaman, *The Real Triumph of Japan* (New York, 1906), p. 144.
2. L. L. Seaman, *The Real Triumph of Japan*, p. 143. Dr Seaman was an American who, in praising Japan's care of her soldiers and sailors, severely criticised American practice. See L. L. Seaman, 'Some of the Triumphs of Scientific Medicine in Peace and War in Foreign Lands', *New York Medical Journal*, 9 June 1906, Vol. LXXXVII, No. 8, Whole No. 1525, pp. 335–43.
3. P. D. Curtin, *Death by Migration, Europe's Encounter with the Tropical World in the Nineteenth Century* (Cambridge, 1989).
4. For British sources, see F. N. L. Poynter, 'Evolution of Military Medicine' in Robin Higham (ed.), *A Guide to the Sources of British Military History* (Berkeley, 1971).
5. See *XIII International Congress of Medicine* (1913), Section XX, Part I and II, Naval and Military Medicine, where there are several articles on the health and hygiene of the soldier and sailor. The papers given by Japanese include Isao Nishi, Surgeon Inspector, IJN, 'Hospital Ships and the Transport of Wounded', pp. 17–32 and I. Hirano, Fleet-Surgeon,

Imperial Japanese Navy, 'Brief Notes on Sanitation in the Japanese Navy and on the classification and treatment of wounds, during the late wars', pp. 86–102.

6. C. Woodham Smith, *Florence Nightingale, 1820–1910* (1950).
   L. R. Seymer, *Florence Nightingale's Nurses, St. Thomas' Hospital Nurse Training School, 1860–1960* (1960).

7. L. L. Seaman, *The Real Triumph*. . . Chapter XIV, 'Lest we forget', pp. 254–78.

8. Dr Louis Livingston Seaman subtitled his book *The Conquest of the Silent Foe*, a reference to the difficulties of dealing with disease in the tropics. Because of his polemical writing extolling Japan for her achievements in the Russo–Japanese War he was highly regarded by the Japanese.

9. E. McCaul, *Under the Care of the Japanese War Office* (1905); 'The Red Cross in Japan', *JSL*, Vol. VII (1905–7), pp. 211–25.

10. P. D. Curtin, *Death by Migration*, p. 130.

11. See R. Ross, *Studies in Malaria* (1928); G. Macdonald, *The Epidemiology and Control of Malaria* (1957).

12. S. A. Waksman, *The Conquest of Tuberculosis* (Berkeley, 1966); and R. E. McGrew, *Encyclopedia of Medical History* (New York, 1985), pp. 336–50.

13. S. Kitazato (1853–1931) bacteriologist, *Clostridium tetani*. Institute of infectious diseases (f.1892) discovered *Pasteurella pestis* bubonic plague (1894), first Dean of Medicine, Keio University (1915), served House of Peers, 1st President Japan Medical Association.

14. K. Shiga (1870–1957), capillary dysentery, *shigella dysenteriae*, studied Germany, Professor at Keio (1920).

15. L. L. Seaman, *The Real Triumph* . . ., Chapter VIII.

16. L. L. Seaman, *The Real Triumph* . . ., Chapter VIII.

17. A. B. Cottell, 'Water Conservancy in War', *JRAMC*, Vol. IV (1905), pp. 174–7.

18. A. B. Cottell, 'Water Conservancy in War', p. 177.

19. C. J. Burnett, *British Officers' Reports*, Vol. II (1907), p. 662.

20. T. Sakurai, *Human Bullets, a Soldier's Story of Port Arthur* (1907), p. 72.

21. T. Sakurai, *Human Bullets* . . ., p. 113.

22. A. Hino, *War and Soldier* (1940), p. 62.

23. R. R. Williams and I. D. Spies, *Vitamin B₁ (Thiamin) and its Use in Medicine* (New York, 1939), for thiamin contents of foods see p. 236; also S. Davidson, R. Passmore, I. F. Brock and A. S. Truswell, *Human Nutrition and Dietetics* (1979), and J. Marks, *Vitamins in Health and Disease* (1968).

24. Before the knowledge of essential nutrients and vitamins, *c.*1910, there were innumerable articles written in medical journals, particularly those dealing with white men overseas, on the incidence of beri-beri. One example is H. E. Winter, 'Observations on beri-beri', *JRAMC*, Vol. V (1905) pp. 178–81.
   L. L. Seaman, *The Real Triumph* . . ., devotes Chapter XIII to beri-beri, pp. 233–53. Seaman, writing in the aftermath of the Russo–Japanese War, did understand that in some way beri-beri was a deficiency disease, and that barley or lentils added to the rice would 'supply the necessary deficiencies' (p. 249). He believed it might be nitrogen which was missing.

25. P. D. Curtin, *Death by Migration*, p. 77–9.
26. R. J. Bowring, *Mori Ogai and the Modernisation of Japanese Culture* (Cambridge, 1979), pp. 12–16.
27. E. McCaul, *Under the Care of the Japanese War Office*, p. 116.
28. C. J. Burnett, *British Officers' Reports*, Vol. II (1907), p. 665.
29. H. Conroy, *The Japanese Seizure of Korea* (1960), and H. F. Cook, *Korea's 1884 Incident* (Seoul, 1972).
30. Dr K. Takaki (later Baron) was, because of his training in England, well-known. See Baron Takaki, FRCS Eng, DCL, 'The preservation of health amongst the personnel of the Japanese Army', *JRAMC*, Vol. VI (1906), pp. 54–62. See also report of lectures, 'The preservation of health amongst the personnel of the Japanese Navy and Army', *The Lancet*, Vol. I (19 May 1906), pp. 1369–74; (26 May 1906), pp. 1451–5; (2 June 1906), pp. 1520–3; see also Baron K. Takaki, 'Military Hygiene of the Japanese Army', *New York Medical Journal*, Vol. LXXXIII, No. 23 (New York, 9 June 1906), Whole No. 1436, pp. 1161–6, with thanks to M. M. Lamb for her help.
31. L. L. Seaman, *The Real Triumph* . . ., p. 238.
32. See D. Hamilton and M. Lamb, Chapter 5, 'Surgeons and Surgery' in *Health Care as Social History, The Glasgow Case* (Aberdeen, 1982); A. J. Youngson, *The Scientific Revolution in Victorian Medicine* (1979).
33. E. McCaul, *Under the Care of the Japanese War Office* p. 156–8.
34. T. Sakurai, *Human Bullets* . . ., p. 164–5.
35. T. Sakurai, *Human Bullets* . . ., p. 112.
36. T. Sakurai, *Human Bullets* . . ..
37. Isao Nishi (IJN), 'Hospital Ships and the Transport of Wounded', *XVII International Conference of Medicine* (1913), Section 20, Part 2, Naval and Military Medicine, pp. 17–32.
38. P. Boissier, *From Solferino to Tsushima* (Geneva, 1985), p. 372.
39. P. Boissier, *From Solferino* . . ., p. 323.
40. *Hakuai Maru* and *Kosai Maru*, the business records of Messrs Lobnitz, Shipbuilders, are held at the University Archives, the University of Glasgow, Scotland.
41. N. Ariga, *The Japanese Red Cross Society and the Russo–Japanese War* (1907), p. 31.
42. N. Ariga, *Japanese Red Cross Society* . . ., p. 149.
43. N. Ariga, *Japanese Red Cross Society* . . . , pp. 149–51.
44. N. Ariga, *Japanese Red Cross Society* . . ., p. 147.
45. See I. Nishi (IJN), 'Hospital Ships and the Transport of Wounded', pp. 17–32.
46. N. Kovlovski, 'Statistical data concerning the Losses of Russian Army from sickness and wounds in the war against Japan, 1904–5', *JRAMC*, Vol. 18 (1912), pp. 330–46.

3   The Red Cross and Health Care for the Nation

1. In the nineteenth century in Western Europe and North America, charitable concern led to the provision of general hospitals in the cities

and later to small 'cottage hospitals' in country towns. Specialist hospitals were also established, usually under the care of a particularly enthusiastic doctor, especially as medical science made great progress in certain specialities. In addition there were also important public health initiatives intended to control infectious diseases. See O. Checkland and M. Lamb, *Health Care as Social History, the Glasgow Case* (Aberdeen, 1982).

2. From 12 February 1881, there was *Seiikai* (Society for Training Physicians), set up by Kenkwan Takagi: see Vol. 5, p. 276, *Meiji Tenno Ki* (Imperial Household) (Tokyo, 1968–77); later, 28 May 1883, the Emperor gave ¥6,000 to Takagi's *Yushi Kyoritsu Byoin* (Volunteers' Co-operative Tokyo Hospital): see Vol. 6, p. 62. Then on 19 January 1887 the hospital came under the patronage of the Empress and was renamed *Tokyo Jikeiin Byoin* (Tokyo Benevolent Hospital) with Takagi at its head (Vol.6, p. 682). See also H. Cortazzi, *Dr Willis in Japan, 1862–1877, British Medical Pioneer* (1985).

3. *Red Cross in the Far East*, Bulletin No. 4 (1912), p. 34.

4. Baron Dr Hashimoto served until his death, reported in *The Red Cross in the Far East* (Tokyo, May 1904), p. 50.

5. N. Ariga, *The Japanese Red Cross Society* (St Louis, 1904), pp. 15–18.

6. *The Japanese Central Red Cross Hospital* (Tokyo, 1934).

7. *The Japanese Red Cross Maternity Hospital* (Tokyo, 1934).

8. . . . *Maternity Hospital*, p. 1–2.

9. . . . *Maternity Hospital*, p. 3.

10. See M. Otis Poole, *The Death of Old Yokohama* (1923), and E. Seidensticker, *Tokyo Rising* (Cambridge, Mass., 1991).

11. . . . *Maternity Hospital*, p. 6.

12. . . . *Maternity Hospital*, p. 6–7.

13. . . . *Maternity Hospital*, p. 13

14. M. E. Baly, *Florence Nightingale and the Nursing Legacy* (1986).

15. For nurses' training in Scotland see O. Checkland, *Philanthropy in Victorian Scotland* (Edinburgh, 1980), Chapter 13, 'The Nursing Revolution', pp. 219–28.

16. L. R. Seymer, *Florence Nightingale's Nurses, St. Thomas' Hospital Nurse Training School, 1860–1960* (1960).

17. Before nurse training was introduced the Japanese also had the problem of 'saucy and debased women, who had known men well' offering themselves as nurses; see M. Kameyama, *Kindai Nihon Kango Shi* (History of Nursing in Modern Japan) (Tokyo, 1983–5), Vol. 2, p. 14; see also O. Checkland and M. Lamb, *Health Care as Social History*, Chapter 9, Note 11.

18. From *Jindo, Sono Ayumi* (Steps to Humanity, 100 year History of the Japanese Red Cross Society) (Tokyo, 1977), and thanks to Seibi Ota for his careful research.

19. Paper prepared on Tokushi Kango Fujin Kai (Women's Voluntary Nursing Association) by Seibi Ota, to whom many thanks.

20. Yuji Otabe, *Nashimoto no Miya Itsuko Hi no Nikki* (Diary of Princess Itsuko Nashimoto) (Tokyo 1991), p. 44, 4 May 1900, 1 p. m., Meeting of *Tokushi Kango Fujin Kai* (see n. 19) went to the hospital at Hiroo. As usual the princesses were in attendance, also 40 to 50 girls of *Kazoku*

Joggako (the Peers School). 'We all went to the operating theatre with the surgeon', p. 44, also on 15 March 1901 'our first practice at the Red Cross', p. 44.
See also M. C. Fraser, *A Diplomat's Wife in Japan* (Tokyo, 1982), pp. 311–12.

21. N. Ariga, *Japanese Red Cross Society*, p. 14.
22. *Japanese Red Cross Report* (Tokyo, 1912), p. 12.
23. N. Ariga, *Japanese Red Cross Society of Japan*, p. 38.
24. *Jindo, Sono Ayumi* (Tokyo, 1977).
25. *Jogaku Zasshi* (Women's Magazine) (Tokyo, 21 July 1884).
26. For other women in nursing see J. Hunter (ed.), *Japanese Women Working* (1993), especially Chapter 7, 'Japanese Care Assistants in Hospital, 1918–88' by Eiko Shinotsuka, pp. 149–80.
27. The Nurses College today is housed in a modern, but not lavish, building on the Red Cross site at Shibuya. The girls, hurrying to classes and the library, seem hard-working and earnest.
28. See . . . *Maternity Hospital*, p. 20–33, and *Jindo, Sono Ayumi*, Seibi Ota's report, p. 8.
29. See . . . *Maternity Hospital*, p. 22–3, and *Jindo, Sono Ayumi*, Seibi Ota's report, p. 8.
30. Baron Ozawa, *Moral Education*, p. 3 (copy in British Red Cross Archives, Barnett Hill, ref. R.C.Lib.Acc. B6/190, n.d. but 1912?).
31. Baron Ozawa, *Moral Education*, p. 4.
32. *Fujo Shinbun*, No. 275 (14 August 1905).
33. *Red Cross in Far East* (1912), p. 5.

4   Japan, Humanitarian World Leader, 1894–1905

1. D. Schindler and J. Toman, *The Law of Armed Conflict* (Leyden, 1973), pp. 205–6.
2. P. Boissier, *From Solferino to Tsushima*, Letter from Gustave Moynier (Geneva, 1985), p. 318–19.
3. Apart from Argentina (1879), Bolivia (1879) and Chile (1879), Japan was the first country, other than those in Europe and the United States of America, to adhere to the Geneva Convention: see Schindler and Toman, *The Law of Armed Conflict*, pp. 205–6.
4. P. Boissier, *From Solferino . . .*, p. 319 and *Bulletin International des Sociétes de Secours aux militaires blessés* (Geneva, 1873–75), pp. 11–16.
5. P. Boissier, *From Solferino . . .*, p. 319.
6. P. Boissier, *From Solferino . . .*, p. 320.
7. P. Boissier, *From Solferino . . .*, p. 329.
8. E. Ashmead Bartlett, *Port Arthur, the Siege and Capitulation* (Edinburgh, 1906), p. 401–2.
9. The meetings between Generals Nogi and Stoessel were friendly; Stoessel left his white horse as a gift for Nogi and between them they composed a song, *Suishiei*, famous in Japan, extolling chivalry and bravery.
10. E. Ashmead Bartlett, *Port Arthur . . .*, p. 398.
11. E. Ashmead Bartlett, *Port Arthur . . .*, p. 405.

12. N. Ariga, *The Japanese Red Cross Society and the Russo–Japanese War* (presented at the eighth international conference) (1907), p. 209.
13. N. Ariga, *The Japanese Red Cross Society* . . ., p. 210.
14. N. Ariga, *The Japanese Red Cross Society* . . ., p. 210.
15. Figures relating to prisoners, war casualties and so on, cannot be relied upon: N. Ariga, *The Japanese Red Cross Society* . . ., p. 211.
16. E. Ashmead Bartlett, *Port Arthur* . . ., p. 246.
17. The Russians' decision to use the *Orel* and the *Kostroma* was the first time anyone had used hospital ships as part of a naval force: see P. Boissier, *From Solferino* . . ., p. 331.
18. Ian Hamilton, *A Staff Officer's Scrap-Book during the Russo–Japanese War* (1905–7), Vol. II, p. 363.
19. See G. Phillips, *Best Foot Forward, Chas. A. Blatchford & Sons Ltd. (Artificial Limb Specialists), 1890–1990* (Granta editions, Cambridge, 1990); *In Celebration of the 100th Birth of Otto Bock, founder of Orthopadische Industries* (Dunderstadt, 1988), details the growth of German interest in the limbless which dates from the First World War.
20. For a history of artificial limbs see G. Phillips, *Best Foot Forward*, Chapter 3, pp. 25–43.
21. Sakura FineTechnical (Sakura Seiki, K. K. Nihonbashi, Tokyo), with thanks to Ken'ichi Matsumoto, the Chairman.
22. N. Ariga, *The Japanese Red Cross Society* . . ., p. 213.
23. Thanks to the tenacity of Seibi Ota it has proved possible to trace the manufacture of artificial arms and legs, at this time, to Sakura FineTechnical in Tokyo. It is not known where the artificial eyes which the Japanese used during and after the Russo–Japanese War were made.
24. P. Boissier, *From Solferino* . . ., p. 328.
25. P. Boissier, *From Solferino* . . ., p. 329.
26. A. Novikoff-Priboy, *Tsushima* (1936), p. 386.
27. A. Novikoff-Priboy, *Tsushima*, p. 389.
28. P. Boissier, *From Solferino* . . ., p. 329.

5 Russian Prisoners of War, 1904–5

1. The first Geneva Prisoners of War Convention was agreed in 1929. Prior to that the rules relating to prisoners of war relied on Convention No. IV which emerged from the Second Hague Peace Conference of 1907. The original statement regarding prisoners of war was based on the Brussels Declaration of 1874, but had been brought together as a coherent set of rules at the First Hague Convention of 1899. See G. I. A. Draper, *Red Cross Conventions* (1958), pp. 4–5.
2. Baron Suyematsu, *The Risen Sun* (1905), p. 319. See also Appendix C, Japanese Regulations for the treatment of Russian Wounded and Prisoners of War.
3. P. Boissier, *From Solferino to Tsushima* (Geneva, 1985), p. 326.
4. S. Okamoto, *The Japanese Oligarchy and the Russo–Japanese War* (Tokyo, 1970); J. A. White, *The Diplomacy of the Russo–Japanese War* (Princeton, 1964).

5. Until the Pacific War, Army day was celebrated in Japan on the anniversary of the Battle of Mukden (March 1905) and Navy day on that of the Battle of Tsushima (May 1905).
6. The Japanese stated: 'In the Russo–Japanese War the total number of Russian prisoners of war was over 84,450 of whom more than 72,300 were transported to Japan and 1,700 died on the battlefield': N. Ariga, *The Japanese Red Cross Society and the Russo–Japanese War* (1907), p. 212. According to one Russian source, almost 60 000 Russians became prisoners of war. N. Kozlovski, 'Statistical Data concerning the losses of the Russian Army from sickness and wounds in the war against Japan, 1904–5', *JRAMC*, Vol. 18 (1912), p. 336. For convenience, the figure of 70 000 Russian prisoners of war has been used throughout.
7. *The Times*, 11 and 30 November 1905.
8. 'Two Russian Surgeons caputred by Russians', *Russo–Japanese War*, Vol. III (Tokyo, 1905), pp. 1395–1404.
9. *The Times*, 18 December 1905.
10. The most detailed account of Japanese work with the Russian prisoners of war is contained in N. Ariga, *The Japanese Red Cross Society . . .*, see Chapter XIII, pp. 198–218.
11. N. Ariga, *The Japanese Red Cross Society . . .*, p. 216.
12. N. Ariga, *The Japanese Red Cross Society . . .*, p. 213.
13. See K. Odagawa (ed. F. Kaputinski), *Matsuyama Horyo Shuyojo Nikki; Rosia-jui Shoko no mita Meiji Nihon* (Diary of a Russian officer in Matsuyama prison camp in Meiji Japan) (Tokyo, 1988).
14. See K. Odagawa (ed. F. Kaputinski), *Matsuyama Horyo Shuyojo Nikki*, pp. 231–2.
15. See K. Odagawa (ed. F. Kaputinski), *Matsuyama Horyo Shuyojo Nikki*, pp. 206–7.
16. See A. Novikoff-Priboy, *Tsushima* (1936), Epilogue, pp. 378–90.
17. A. Novikoff-Priboy, *Tsushima*, pp. 380–82.
18. Sophia von Theil's story, translated into Japanese by R. and M. Ogiso, *Nichi-Ro Senso Ka no Nihon – Rosia gunjin horyo no tsuma no nikki* (Tokyo, 1991), pp. 52 and 219–20.
19. N. Ariga, *The Japanese Red Cross Society . . .* (1907), p. 245.
20. T. E. Richardson, *In Japanese Hospitals During War-time* (Edinburgh, 1905), p. 122.
21. T. E. Richardson, *Japanese Hospitals . . .*, 1905), p. 125.
22. T. E. Richardson, *Japanese Hospitals . . .*, p. 126.
23. Treaty of Portsmouth, New Hampshire, 5 September 1905: see J. A. White, *The Diplomacy of the Russo–Japanese War*.
24. N. Ariga, *The Japanese Red Cross Society . . .*, pp. 256–9.

6 German Prisoners of War, 1914–18

1. The Japanese took part, as one of the victors, in the Versailles Peace Treaty negotiations.
2. J. Suzuki, 'The Japanese Red Cross Mission to England', *JSL*, Vol. 14 (1915–16), pp. 28–36.

3. F. Paravicini, *Bericht des Herr Dr F. Paravicini, über seinen Besuch der Gefangenenlager in Japan*, 30 June to 16 July 1918 (Account of Dr Paravicini's visits to prisoner of war camps in Japan) (Basle, 1919), pp. 1–43, with thanks to B. M. Hardie-Ramshauer.
4. *General Report of the Relief Work of the Japanese Red Cross Society during the last War 1914–1919* (Tokyo, 1919), p. 38.
5. Translation into English from Dr Paravicini's *Bericht des Herr Dr F. Paravicini, über seinen Besuch der Gefangenenlager in Japan*, 30 June to 16 July 1918 (Account of Dr Paravicini's visits to prisoner of war camps in Japan) (Basle, 1919).
6. *General Report of the Relief Work*, p. 39.
7. F. Paravicini, *Bericht des Herr Dr F. Paravicini*, p. 2.
8. In Kurume they were very proud of the Kurume Regiment, famous for its bravery.
9. F. Paravicini, *Bericht des Herr Dr F. Paravicini*, p. 8.
10. This curious incident may be related to the Japanese military intervention in Siberia in the wake of the Russian revolution of 1917. See J. A. Morley, *The Japanese Thrust into Siberia, 1918* (1950), and J. A. White, *The Siberian Intervention* (1950).
11. *General Description of the Relief Work of the Japanese Red Cross Society during the last war 1914–1919* (Tokyo, 1919), p. 40.
12. J. Suzuki, 'The Japanese Red Cross Mission to England', pp. 28–36.
13. J. Suzuki, 'The Japanese Red Cross Mission to England', p. 32.
14. J. Suzuki, 'The Japanese Red Cross Mission to England', p. 32.

7 Humanitarianism Abandoned

1. Japanese enthusiasm ensured that in addition to the commemorative literature, the XV International Conference Editions of *The Japan Advertiser*, *The Japan Times* and *The Asahi Mainichi* of 30 October 1934, special studies of various Japanese Red Cross institutions, including the Tokyo Red Cross Hospital and the Maternity Hospital, were commissioned. This material is held by the JRC at its headquarters in Shiba, Tokyo.
2. R. J. Bowring, *Mori Ogai and the Modernization of Japanese Culture* (Cambridge, 1979), p. 20. Bowring notes that although Ogai was supposedly interpreter, he was listed as the main delegate, instead of Tadanori Ishiguro, at the Karlsruhe meeting.
3. A. Durand, *From Sarajevo to Hiroshima* (Geneva, 1984), p. 290.
4. *Japan Advertiser*, 30 October 1934, p. 3.
5. Judge Barton Payne, Report to Cordell Hull, 30 December 1934. USA National Archives Gift Collection (NAGC), Record Group 200, 041, Folder 6.
6. *Rough Estimate of Travelling Expenses to Japan for the XV International Red Cross Conference*, JRC, Tokyo, August 1933. USA NAGC, Washington, No. D.41 NNRC.
7. There were 70 persons in the American group; some were accompanying persons.
8. *Japan Advertiser*, 30 October 1934, p. 2.

9. Cordell Hull to J. B. Payne, 3 August 1934, USA NAGC, Washington, WE 514.2 A15.31 NNRC.
10. J. B. Payne, Report to Cordell Hull, 20 December 1934, p. 2, NAGC, Civil Research Group 200, Record Group 2, 8 Folders on Tokyo Conference, 1934.
11. *Japan Advertiser*, 30 October 1934, p. 4.
12. *Japan Advertiser*, 30 October 1934, p. 4.
13. J. B. Payne to Cordell Hull, 30 December 1934, USA NAGC, Record Group 200, 041, Folder 6.
14. *Japan Advertiser*, 30 October 1934, p. 4.
15. Letter to the author from Florianne Truninger, Research Officer, ICRC, Geneva, 15 August 1991.
16. For the creation of the Modern Japanese Army see R. F. Hackett, *Yamagata Aritomo in the Rise of Modern Japan, 1838–1922* (Cambridge, Mass., 1971); M. and S. Harries, *Soldiers of the Sun* (1991); see also Inazo Nitobé, *Bushido, the Soul of Japan* (1905).
17. Yamagata was in Europe in 1870 and was deeply impressed with the Spartan way of life of the Prussians in Berlin; see I. Tokutumi, *Koshaku Yamagata Aritomo Den* (Biography of Yamagata), 3 vols., Vol. 2, pp. 13, 31.
18. Y. Mishima, *The Sea of Fertility* (Penguin edn, 1985), p. 345.
19. R. J. Smethurst, *The Social Basis for pre-war Japanese Militarism, the Army and the Rural Community* (Berkeley and Los Angeles, 1974), p. 2.
20. R. J. Smethurst, . . . *pre-war Japanese Militarism*, p. 27.
21. R. J. Smethurst, . . . *pre-war Japanese Militarism*, p. 28.
22. It was re-named *Dai Nihon Kokubo Fujin Kai* (Great Japan Women's National Defence Association) in December 1932.
23. R. J. Smethurst, . . . *pre-war Japanese Militarism*, p. 28 and C. Sugiyama, in personal letter to the author.
24. R. J. Smethurst, . . . *pre-war Japanese Militarism*, p. 47.
25. R. J. Smethurst, . . . *pre-war Japanese Militarism*, p. 48.
26. JRC, *Jindo: sono Ayumi* (Humanity, its footsteps), pp. 117–18.
27. T. Marks, 'Life in war-time Japan', *Japan and the Second World War*, LSE, ICERD (1989), p. 3.
28. Perhaps an exaggeration but, as one Japanese explained: 'Twice a year Japan cleaned house . . . everything had to be moved into street or garden . . . nothing could be put back until a police inspector found the place to his satisfaction and posted a certificate. He looked especially at my books . . . and wrote something in his notebook . . . it had become a method for the police to ferret out any signs of radicalism in the household': T. Matsumoto, *A Brother is a Stranger* (1947).
29. Y. Mishima, *The Sea of Fertility*, p. 479.
30. Y. Mishima, *The Sea of Fertility*, p. 409.

8   Shame and the War Prisoner

1. T. Matsumoto, *A Brother is a Stranger* (1947), p. 51.
2. See R. S. Baker, *Woodrow Wilson, Life and Letters*, 8 Vols (New York, 1927–39).

3. Quoted in N. Bamba, *Japanese Diplomacy in a Dilemma* (Kyoto, 1972), p. 196.
4. H. Gordon, *Die like the Carp* (Sydney, 1978), p. 13.
5. I. Morris, *The Nobility of Failure* . . . (1975), p. 14–15.
6. Toshiko Marks, 'Life in War-time Japan' in *Japan and the Second World War*, International Studies, LSE, IS/89/197 (1989), p. 3.
7. See I. Morris, *The Nobility of Failure* (1975), pp. 14–15.
8. J. Grew, *Report from Tokyo* (1943), p. 20.
9. GHQ S.W. Pacific area, Allied Translator and Interpreter Section, Interrogation Reports, No. 161 (Australian War Memorial 312.11); these reports relate to R. Matsuoka, captured 2 February 1943.
10. R. Benedict, *The Chrysanthemum and the Sword* (Boston, 1946), p. 38.
11. C. Carr-Gregg, *Japanese Prisoners of War in Revolt* (Queensland, 1978), p. 35.
12. ICRC, *Inter Arma Caritas* (Geneva, 1947), p. 104.
13. R. Benedict, *The Chrysanthemum and the Sword*, p. 39.
14. See W. W. Mason, *Prisoners of War* (Wellington, 1954), pp. 256–361 and C. Carr-Gregg, *Japanese Prisoners of War in Revolt*, see pp. 38–56.
15. T. Matsumoto, *Brother is a Stranger*, p. 141.
16. W. W. Mason, *Prisoners of War*, p. 357.
17. W. W. Mason, *Prisoners of War*, p. 358.
18. Proceedings of a Court of Enquiry on the Mutiny of Japanese POWs at Featherston, 25 February 1943 (in Australian Archives, MP 729/663/401/634).
19. Papers relating to the Cowra Breakout are held by Australian Archives, and Australian War Memorial, Canberra. There were various official enquiries, see also C. Carr-Gregg, *Japanese Prisoners of War in Revolt* (1978) for events at Cowra, pp. 56–79; see also H. Clarke, *Breakout* (Sydney, 1965), H. Gordon, *Die like the Carp*; and K. S. Mackenzie, *Dead Men Rising* (Sydney, 1971).
20. K. S. Mackenzie, *Dead Men Rising*, p. 85 and p. 236.
21. Australian War Memorial, Canberra, CRS A2663 item 780/3/2.
22. Proceedings of (HQ NSW L of C Area) Court of Enquiry on the Meeting at No. 12 PW Group, Cowra (Australian Archives AA 1977/461, known as the Christison Enquiry).
23. C. Carr-Gregg, *Japanese Prisoners of War in Revolt*, p. 204.
24. C. Carr-Gregg, *Japanese Prisoners of War in Revolt*, p. 203.
25. C. Carr-Gregg, *Japanese Prisoners of War in Revolt*, p. 204

9 Prisoners in Travail

1. The Japanese had already negotiated with the French government at Vichy.
2. On the 50th anniversary of the Fall of Singapore, 15 February 1992, the Australians gave the number of their war prisoners as follows:

   Australians captured 20 969, died 5990

   The military tribunal of the Far East (Transcripts, p. 40 537) in 1946, gave the number of Australian prisoners as 29 138, of whom 7412 died.

Captured	Thailand	2336
	Borneo	1783
	Ambon	718
	Malaya	284
	New Britain	200
	Japan	190

See *Fall of Singapore Memorial Service*, 15 February 1992, Canberra, Australia. The discrepancy between the figures is a reminder of the difficulties of achieving accuracy.

3. See Sir J. Smyth, *Arthur E. Percival and the Tragedy of Singapore* (1971).
4. The figures given are approximate; there is no general agreement on these.
5. In addition to servicemen, there were large numbers of civilian internees who were held by Japan during the war years.
6. See *Report of the ICRC on its activities during the Second World War*, Vol. 1 (Geneva, 1948), pp. 459–63.
7. See H. Tasaki, *Long the Imperial Way* (1951), p. 30–31.
8. H. Tasaki, *Long the Imperial Way*, p. 44.
9. There is a commemorative plaque, a replica of the 70 kg bronze, already in place at the crossing of the River Kwai on the Burma–Siam railway, presented to the Imperial War Museum, Duxford, on the 50th anniversary of the beginning of work, 2 October 1942. Report in *The Times*, 2 October 1992.
10. R. Parkin, *Into the Smother, a Journal of the Burma–Siam Railway* (1963).
11. R. Parkin, . . . *a Journal of the Burma–Siam Railway*, p. 66.
12. R. Parkin, . . . *a Journal of the Burma–Siam Railway*, p. 77.
13. R. Parkin, . . . *a Journal of the Burma–Siam Railway*, p. 98.
14. O. Wynd, *The Forty Days* (1972).
15. R. Parkin, *The Sword and the Blossom* (1968), p. 75.
16. R. Parkin, *The Sword and the Blossom*, p. 101.
17. H. Tasaki, *Long the Imperial Way*, p. 193.
18. For another account (unpublished) see J. D. (Jock) McEwen, 'The Mine at Ohama', with thanks for the use of the Diaries.
19. R. Parkin, *The Sword and the Blossom*, p. 141.
20. R. Parkin, *The Sword and the Blossom*, p. 152.
21. F. Bell, *Undercover University* (Cambridge, 1990), with thanks to Elisabeth Bell.
22.

A. General Subjects	Pupils
Navigation	7
Military Law	7
Book-keeping (advanced)	5
Book-keeping (intermediate)	7
Book-keeping (elementary)	6
History	16
Public Speaking	17
Chess	11

General Commercial Knowledge	40
Pig Farming	20
Poultry Keeping	21
Civics	30

B. Modern Languages

German (intermediate)	12
German (elementary)	5
French (intermediate)	19
French (elementary)	6
French conversation	15
Spanish (advanced)	3
Spanish (intermediate)	8
Spanish (elementary)	9
Italian (elementary)	5
Dutch (elementary)	5
Urdu (elementary)	5

Source: F. Bell, *Undercover University*, p. 78.

23.

Term 1	15 September–15 December 1943	Half-term test and end of term examination
Term 2	9 January–1 April 1944	No examination
Term 3	1 May–31 August 1944	Test papers
Term 4	15 September–15 November 1944	'Final' examinations
Term 5	1 January–1 April 1945	No examination
Term 6	1 May–August 1945	End of War

Source: F. Bell, *Undercover University*, p. 85.

24. Frank Bell's 'text books' are now deposited at the Imperial War Museum, London.

25.

Artes in Arduis
University Kuching – Diploma Holders

Capt. J. A. Bailie, RA [Royal Artillery]
Lt. F. E. Bell, RA
Lt. A. E. H. Bulford
Lt. D. F. Campion
Lt. L. E. Coleman, MM, RA
Capt. A. D. Dant
Lt. D. Davies, R Sigs [Royal Signals]
Lt. S. V. B. Day
Lt. D. H. Dewar, RA
Lt. D. P. Glasgow
Capt. H. B. Hare Scott, RA
Flt./Lt. E. I. Lee, RAF
Lt. P. G. Lovely, RA
Capt. J. B. Machie
Lt. A. D. Mason, RA
Lt. E. M. Nicholas, RA
Capt. I. C. Paterson RA
Capt. J. Temple
Lt. V. N. Wade, RNVR
Lt. A. Wearing, RA
Lt. J. Wilson
Capt. H. D. A. Yates, REME [Royal Electrical and Mechanical Engineers]

Source: F. Bell, *Undercover University*, p. 107.

26. 'Spud' Spurgeon's Diary, C. H. Spurgeon, Deakin, Canberra. With thanks to C. H. Spurgeon for his help.
27. The inclusion of barley in the ration would be an attempt to limit the occurrence of the deficiency disease, beri-beri (see Chapter 2 above). Barley, a temperate crop, was not normally grown in South-East Asia.
28. 'Spud' Spurgeon's Diary.
29. James (Jock) McEwan, Edinburgh.
30. 'Spud' Spurgeon's Diary.
31. G. Murray, 'Oswald Wynd, a novel life', *Intersect*, March 1991, p. 36.
32. E. Norbeck, 'Edokko, a narrative of Japanese prisoners of war in Russia', *Rice University Studies*, Vol. 57 (1971), p. 31.
33. E. Norbeck, 'Edokko . . .', p. 27.
34. E. Norbeck, 'Edokko . . .', p. 27.
35. E. Norbeck, 'Edokko . . .', p. 27–28.

10 Ultimate Weapons, Drugs and Disease

1. See P. Williams and D. Wallace, *Unit 731, the Japanese Army's Secret of Secrets* (1990).
2. See A. C. Brackman, *The Other Nuremberg, the Untold Story of the Tokyo War Crimes Trials* (1989), Chapter 16, pp. 205–17.
3. P. Williams and D. Wallace, *Unit 731*, entries under Ishii, Shiro.
4. A. C. Brackman, . . . *Tokyo War Crimes*, Chapter 16, p. 211.
5. Summary Report on biological warfare investigations, *Mita Gakkai Zasshi* (Mita Journal of Economics) Vol. 84, No. 2 (July 1991), pp. 294–7.
6. J. W. Powell, 'Japan's Germ Warfare, the US cover-up of a war crime', *Bulletin of Concerned Asian Scientists* (December 1980), pp. 2–17, and 'A Hidden Chapter in History', *The Bulletin of the Atomic Scientists* (October 1981) pp. 45–53.
7. A. C. Brackman, . . . *Tokyo War Crimes*, Chapter 16, p. 215.
8. A. C. Brackman, . . . *Tokyo War Crimes*, Chapter 16, pp. 237–42; P. Williams and D. Wallace, *Unit 731*, Chapter 16, pp. 326–40 and other references in index.
9. J. W. Powell, 'Japan's Germ Warfare', p. 3.
10. P. Williams and D. Wallace, *Unit 731*, p. 40.
11. P. Williams and D. Wallace, *Unit 731*, p. 41.
12. The Hippocratic oath did not, however, prevent German doctors from experimental work on Jews.
13. Sadao Araki (1877–1966), A.C. Brackman, . . . *Tokyo War Crimes*, pp. 454.
14. A. C. Brackman, . . . *Tokyo War Crimes*, p. 206.
15. A. C. Brackman, . . . *Tokyo War Crimes*, p. 206.
16. A. C. Brackman, . . . *Tokyo War Crimes*, p. 207.
17. P. Williams and D. Wallace, *Unit 731*, references to plague.
18. P. Williams and D. Wallace, *Unit 731*, pp. 102–16.
19. J. W. Powell, 'A Hidden Chapter in History . . .' p. 50.
20. J. W. Powell, 'A Hidden Chapter in History . . .', p. 50.
21. *New York Times*, 26 November 1969.

11 Keeping the Humanitarian Flame Alight

1. (Sir) Selwyn Selwyn-Clarke, *Footprints* (Hong Kong, 1975), p. 71.
2. There is a Japan–Philippine Cultural Exchange Center in Tokyo, which together with the Rizal Society of Japan has collected material relating to Col. Jimbo and Manuel Roxas; thanks to Seibi Ota.
3. With thanks to Mamoru Tsunashima, former Director, International Relations Department, Red Cross Society of Japan, *Sankei Shimbun*, 25 December 1992.
4. See D. Kranzler, *Japanese, Nazis and Jews, Shanghai, 1938–45* (Hoboken, NJ, 1988).
5. Senpo (Chiune) Sugihara left the diplomatic service after the war but his reputation has recently been restored and he has become something of a hero. My thanks to Seibi Ota for his help.
6. See C. Adler, *Jacob H. Schiff, his Life and Letters* (New York, no date).
7. Korekiyo Takahashi (1854–1936), financial expert and politician, who, with his family, became friends of the Schiff family: see C. Adler, *Jacob H. Schiff*, pp. 37–9, 213–30, 235–41, 247–51, 253–59, 247–8.
8. M. Tokayer and M. Schwartz, *The Fugu Plan, the Untold Story of the Japanese and the Jews during the World War II* (1979).
9. M. Tokayer and M. Schwartz, *The Fugu Plan . . .*, p. 9.
10. M. Tokayer and M. Schwartz, *The Fugu Plan . . .*, p. 9.
11. P. Shatzkes, 'Kobe, a Japanese Haven for Jewish Refugees', *Japan Forum*, Vol. 3, No. 2 (October 1991), p. 264.
12. P. Shatzkes, 'Kobe, a Japanese Haven for Jewish Refugees', p. 265.
13. A. Kotsuji, *From Tokyo to Jerusalem* (Jerusalem, 1964).
14. Yosuke Matsuoka (1880–1946), Japan's chief delegate to the League of Nations, in 1933, president South Manchurian Railway, 1935–9, foreign minister 1939–40, jingoistic, arraigned as war criminal but died during trial.
15. ICRC Report, International Congress (Stockholm, 1948), p. 443.
16. A. Durand, *From Sarajevo to Hiroshima, History of the International Committee of the Red Cross*, (Geneva, 1984), p. 525–6.
17. For a more detailed discussion of the role of the ICRC, see O. Checkland, 'A perilous neutrality, Military Japan and the International Committee of the Red Cross, 1941–45', prepared for *Records of the British War Crimes Trials in the Far East, 1946–48* (Garland Publishing, New York; forthcoming 1994).
18. Dr Fritz Paravicini (1874–1944), surgeon, physician, Swiss diplomat, medical adviser to British Embassy, Tokyo; see *Who's Who in Japan* (Tokyo, 1925), p. 398. Dr Paravicini lived at 772 Honmoku, 3-chome, Yokohama; see *Chronicle Directory* (1940) published by *The Japan Chronicle*, Kobe, alphabetical list of foreign residents. 'Spud' Spurgeon noted that 'Dr Paravicini was of part Portuguese parentage, married to a Japanese and resident for many years in Japan. He was subsequently replaced by Dr Angst.' ('Spud' Spurgeon's Diary, 4 June 1943. With thanks to C.H. Spurgeon, Canberra, Australia.)
19. Max Pestalozzi, 127 Takinoue, Yokohama, worked for Charles Rudolph of Yokohama, who were agents for the Sun Insurance Office, London. See *Chronicle Directory* (1940) list of foreign residents (published by *The Japan Chronicle*, Kobe). Pestalozzi was accredited to the Japanese

Foreign Ministry, 25 August 1942 and in March 1943 started visiting POW camps; he became assistant delegate in June 1943 and on 16 July 1943 was approved by the Japanese.

20. Harry Angst, 40 Yamamoto-dori, 3-chome, Kobe, worked for Siber Hegner and Co., Kobe. See *Chronicle Directory* (1941) list of foreign residents (published by the *Japan Times*, Kobe).

21. *JRC, Annual Report 1943* (translated from the Japanese).

22. *Revue International de la Croix-Rouge* (March 1944), p. 108.

23. *Revue International de la Croix-Rouge* (March 1944), p. 108.

24. See O. Checkland, 'A perilous neutrality . . .'. *British War Crimes Trials in the Far East* (forthcoming, 1994).

25. Personal letter from Lieutenant Henling Wade, Loyal Regiment, 2nd Battalion, 24 September 1990.

26. W. E. Brougher, *South to Bataan, North to Mukden* (Athens, GA, 1971), pp. 67–8.

27. M. Junod, *Warrior without Weapons* (1951), reprinted ICRC, 1982.

28. Correspondents who have written on these matters include Lieutenant Henling T. Wade (Camps in Seoul, Korea, and at Omori, Tokyo), Sgt Harry Blackham, RA (Camp in Taiwan), Howard Williams (Camp at Muroran, Hokkaido), N. S. Vickerstaff (Camp at Taihoku, Taiwan), Lieutenant Colonel John Montresor (Camp at Heito, Taiwan) and G. P. Adams (Camp at Omuta, Kyushu, Japan).

29. M. Junod, *Warrior without Weapons*, p. 253.

30. *ICRC Report, Second World War*, Vol. I, p. 465.

31. Copies of the *Revue International de la Croix Rouge*, usually in French, are available at the library of the ICRC, Geneva, and at the Archives of the BRC at Barnett Hill, Wonersh, Surrey. The British, who published a small magazine sent free to the families of POWs, called *The Far East*, drew some of their information from Red Cross Sources.

32. M. Junod, *Warriors without Weapons*, p. 263.

33. M. Junod, *Warriors without Weapons*, p. 267.

34. M. Junod, *Warriors without Weapons*, p. 268.

35. M. Junod, *Warriors without Weapons*, p. 269.

36. M. Junod, *Warriors without Weapons*, p. 270.

37. 'There was Wainwright. He was haggard and aged. His uniform hung in folds on his fleshless form. He walked with difficulty and the help of a cane. His eyes were sunken and there were pits in his cheeks', General Douglas MacArthur's description of Wainwright, see D. MacArthur, *Reminiscences* (1964), p. 271.

38. M. Junod, *Warriors without Weapons*, for an account of a prisoner of war camp on Omori Island, Tokyo Bay, see part 4, Chapter III, 'Omori Camp', pp. 272–85.

39. M. Junod, *Warriors without Weapons*, for Hiroshima, immediately after the bomb, see part 4, Chapter IV, 'The Dead City', pp. 286–300.

40. Vice-President Tadatsugu Shimazu, of the former ruling Satsuma family, eased the way for whatever international humanitarian work was done by the Japanese. The President of the Japanese Red Cross, Prince Kuniyuki Tokugawa, was also active in interceding, on behalf of the ICRC, with the military authorities.

41. *Annual Report JRC*, 1944.
42. *ICRC Report During Second World War*, Vol. I, p. 466.
43. Y. Aida, *Prisoner of the British, a Japanese Soldier's Experience in Burma* (1966), p. 151.
44. The reference is to Seibi Ota to whom thanks are due; he has been an invaluable 'volunteer' research assistant.
45. S. Selwyn-Clarke, *Footprints*, p. 72.

12 'The Face of War is the Face of Death'

1. H. L. Stimson, 'The Decision to Use the Atomic Bomb', *Harper's Magazine*, Vol. 194, No. 1161 (February 1947), p. 98.
2. A. C. Brackman, *The Other Nuremberg, The Untold Story of the Tokyo War Crimes Trials* (1989), p. 38.
3. J. W. Dower, *War Without Mercy, Race and Power in the Pacific War* (1984), p. 297.
4. D. MacArthur, *Reminiscences* (1964), pp. 272–4.
5. A. C. Brackman, . . . *Tokyo War Crimes Trials*, p. 43.
6. A. C. Brackman, . . . *Tokyo War Crimes Trials*, p. 44.
7. R. Pal, *Crimes in International Relations* (Calcutta, 1955).
8. B. V. A. Röling, *International Law in an Expanded World* (Amsterdam, 1960), and *Law of War* (Stockholm, 1976).
9. A.C. Brackman, . . . *Tokyo War Crimes Trials*, Appendix A, pp. 454–62.
10. Kodansha Encyclopedia (1983), Vol. 8, p. 223.
11. Kodansha Encyclopedia (1983), Vol. 8, p. 224.
12. See J. Bradley, *Cyril Wild, the Tall Man who Never Slept* (Fontwell, Sussex, 1991).
13. *Fall of Singapore Remembrance Service*, 15 February 1992, National Prisoner of War Memorial, Royal Military College, Duntroon, ACT, Australia.
14. J. Bradley, *Cyril Wild* . . ., p. 95.
15. J. Bradley, *Cyril Wild* . . ., p. 95–6.
16. Y. Aida, *Prisoner of the British, a Japanese Soldier's Experience in Burma* (1966).
17. Y. Aida, *Prisoner of the British* . . ., p. 49.
18. Y. Aida, *Prisoner of the British* . . ., p. 52.
19. L. Allen, *End of War in Asia* (1976), p. 194.
20. L. Allen, *End of War in Asia*, p. 201–9.
21. L. Allen, *End of War in Asia*, p. 184.
22. L. Allen, *End of War in Asia*, p. 185.
23. E. Norbreck, 'Edokko, a Narrative of Japanese Prisoners of War in Russia', *Rice University Studies* (1971), p. 42.
24. E. Norbeck, 'Edokko . . .', p. 67.
25. H. L. Stimson, 'The Decision to Use the Atomic Bomb', pp. 98–107.
26. M. Junod, 'Hiroshima Disaster', p. 6, a contemporary account but published long after Junod's death, *ICRC* (Geneva, September to December 1982).
27. M. Junod, 'Hiroshima Disaster', p. 6.
28. M. Junod, 'Hiroshima Disaster', p. 8.

29. M. Junod, 'Hiroshima Disaster', p. 14.
30. M. Junod, 'Hiroshima Disaster', p. 14.
31. *Japanese Red Cross Society, Report, 1953–56* (Tokyo, 1956), p. 8.

13   Phoenix Resurgent

1. *Japanese Red Cross Society, Report, 1953–56* (Tokyo, 1956), p. 18.
2. *JRC, Report*, p. 17.
3. *Re-establishment of Japanese Red Cross Society* (Tokyo, 1945–47), p. 17.
4. M. Duffy, Draft report, p. 1, from Mrs Duffy's private papers, with thanks.
5. S. Hashimoto, *Henry Dunant and Myself* (Tokyo, 1978), p. 17.
6. S. Hashimoto, *Henry Dunant* . . ., p. 17.
7. S. Hashimoto, *Henry Dunant* . . ., p. 18.
8. See also *Japanese Junior Red Cross* (July 1937), in JRC Archives, Shiba Park, Tokyo.
9. Although this initiative was publicised as being a Red Cross concern it may have had substantial backing from the Ministry of Education. 1970 was the year of renegotiation and renewal of the Japanese–US Security Treaty.
10. M. Duffy, 'Volunteering', *Mainichi Daily News*, 2 May 1977.
11. M. Duffy, 'Volunteering', *Mainichi Daily News*, 2 May 1977.
12. M. Duffy, 'Memoir', p. 3.
13. S. Hashimoto, *Henry Dunant* . . ., p. 305.
14. One of the Americans working in this field was Carmen Johnson, from whose correspondence with the author this comes, with thanks to Miss Johnson.
15. *JRC Law*, p. 21.
16. *JRC, Report*, p. 19.
17. *JRC, Report*, p. 19.
18. See *Comité International de la Croix-Rouge*, Report on the repatriation of North Koreans after 1959, letter to Dr Chung, Geneva, 4 September 1989 (Reference DDM/RECH 89/246 FT/av). See Appendix E.
19. The bitterness between the South and North Koreans had prevented any form of contact or dialogue between the two countries.
20. Mr Seibi Ota was part of the Japanese Red Cross delegation.
21. See S. Hashimoto, *Henry Dunant* . . ., which gives 'A Glimpse of the Japanese Red Cross', pp. 291–313.
22. S. Hashimoto, *Henry Dunant* . . ., p. 213.
23. S. Hashimoto, *Henry Dunant* . . ., p. 213.

14   In the Emperor's Name

1. D. Schindler and J. Toman, *The Law of Armed Conflict, a Collection of Conventions* (Leyden, 1973), pp. 205–6, which shows that other than the European countries, the USA, Argentina, Bolivia and Chile, Japan was the first country to register.
2. For one example among many, see Lady Lawson, *Highways and Homes of Japan* (1910), Chapter XXIV, pp. 266–76.

3. *The Bible*, St Paul, 1st letter to the Corinthians, Chapter 13, Verse 13.
4. M. Morishima, *Why has Japan 'Succeeded'? Western Technology and the Japanese Ethos* (Cambridge, 1982), p. 194.
5. The Sino-Japanese War demonstrated, among other things, the unpreparedness of the JRC. There were also reports of atrocities, on both sides.
6. See N. Ariga, *The Japanese Red Cross Society and the Russo-Japanese War* (1907).
7. See L. L. Seaman, *From Tokio through Manchuria with the Japanese* (New York, 1905), and *The Real Triumph of Japan* (New York, 1906).
8. *The Times*, 27 June 1904, pp. 4 and 5.
9. *The Bible*, St Luke's Gospel, Chapter 23, Verse 53.
10. Y. Akatsuka, *Yosano Akiko Kenkyu* (Studies of Yosano Akiko) (Tokyo, 1990).
11. A. Yosano, *Collected Works* (Tokyo, 1981), Vol. 9, pp. 159–62.
12. General Maresuke Nogi (1849–1912), a Choshu man, commissioned in 1871 as major in new Japanese army; during the Satsuma Rebellion (1877) his regiment lost its battle standard, which he took as personal disgrace. A tour in Germany in 1887–8 re-affirmed his belief in the traditional *samurai* values; see Appendix B for further biographical details.
13. T. Sakurai, *Human Bullets, a Soldier's Story of Port Arthur* (1907).
14. See I. Morris, *The Nobility of Failure* (1975), pp. 14–15, for the Japanese attitude to *seppuku*, and appreciation of the immense courage needed for such action.
15. T. Crump, *Death of an Emperor* (1992), p. 83.
16. T. Crump, *Death of an Emperor*, p. 83; *Asahi Shimbun*, 15 September 1912.
17. Soseki Natsume, (trans. E. McLellen), *Kokoro* (The Heart of Things) (1968), p. 246.
18. In *Japan's Imperial Conspiracy* (1971), David Bergamini suggests that Hirohito may have been born one year earlier, before the marriage of his parents, see also J. M. Packard, *Sons of Heaven* (1987), pp. 234–235.
19. D. MacArthur, *Reminiscences* (1964), p. 288.
20. See O. Checkland, *Britain's Encounter with Meiji Japan, 1868–1912* (1989).
21. J. D. Pierson, *Tokutomi Soho, 1863–1957, a Journalist for Modern Japan* (Princeton, 1980), p. 362.
22. See W. G. Beasley, *Japanese Imperialism, 1894–1945* (Oxford, 1987), and I. Nish (ed.), *Anglo-Japanese Alienation, 1919–52* (Cambridge, 1982).
23. J. W. Dower, *War without Mercy: Race and Power in the Pacific War* (1984), p. 286.
24. Maw Ba, *Breakthrough in Burma* (Yale, 1968), p. 185.
25. M. Maruyama, *Thought and Behaviour in Modern Japanese Politics* (1969), p. 19.
26. T. Kawahara, *Hirohito and his Times* (Tokyo, 1990), p. 109.

Select Bibliography

(The place of publication is London, unless otherwise stated.)

Ackerknecht, E. H., *History and Geography of the most Important Diseases* (New York, 1965).

Adler, C., *Jacob H. Schiff, his Life and Letters* (New York, n.d.).

Aida, Y. (trans. L. Allen), *Prisoner of the British, a Japanese Soldier's Experience in Burma* (1966).

Akatsuka, Y., *Yosano Akiko Kenkyu* (Studies of Yosano Akiko) (Tokyo, 1990).

Allen, L., *Burma, the Longest War* (1966).

—— *Japan, the Years of Triumph* (1971).

—— *End of War in Asia* (1976).

—— *Singapore 1941–1942* (1977).

Almond, G. A. and Coleman, J. S., *The Politics of the Developing Areas* (Princeton, 1960).

Anon., *Disabled Soldiers' Handbook* (1918).

Ariga, N., *The Japanese Red Cross Society* (St Louis, 1904).

—— *The Japanese Red Cross Society and the Russo–Japanese War* (1907).

—— *La Chine et la Grande Guerre Européene* (Paris, 1920).

—— *La Guerre Russo-Japonaise* (Paris, 1908).

Asada, T., *The Night of a Thousand Suicides* (Sydney, 1970).

Ashmead Bartlett, E., *Port Arthur, the Siege and Capitulation* (Edinburgh, 1906).

Aston, W. G., *Shinto, the way of the Gods* (1905).

Ba, Maw, *Breakthrough in Burma. Memoirs of a Revolution, 1939–1946* (Yale, 1968).

Bacon, A. M., *Japanese Girls and Women* (1891).

Bacque, J., *Other Losses* (1989).

Bailey, S. B., *Prohibitions and Restraints in War* (1972).

Baker, M. N., *The Quest for Pure Water, the History of Water Purification from the Earliest Records to the Twentieth Century* (New York, 1948).

Baker, R. S., *Woodrow Wilson, Life and Letters*, 8 vols (New York, 1927–39).

Ballhatchet, K., *Race, Sex and Class under the Raj: Imperial Attitudes and Politics* (1980).

Ballon, R. O., *Shinto, the Unconquered Enemy: Japan's Doctrine of Racial Superiority and World Conquest* (1945).

Baly, M. E., *Florence Nightingale and the Nursing Legacy* (1986).

Bamba, N., *Japanese Diplomacy in a Dilemma, New Light on Japan's China Policy, 1924–1929* (Kyoto, 1972).

Batchelder, R. C., *The Irreversible Decision 1939–50* (Boston, 1962).

—— *Humanitarian Law or Humanitarian Politics?* (1974).

—— Diplomatic Conference on Humanitarian Law, *Harvard International Law Journal*, Vol. 16, (1975), pp. 1–16.

Baty, J. A., *Surgeon in the Jungle War* (1979).

Beasley, W. G., *Modern History of Japan* (1973).
—— *Japanese Imperialism, 1894–1945* (Oxford, 1987).
Bell, F., *Undercover University*, Privately printed (Cambridge, 1990).
Bell, L., *Destined Meeting* (1959).
Bellah, R. N., *Tokugawa Religion* (Glencoe, 1957).
Benedict, R., *The Chrysanthemum and the Sword, Patterns of Japanese Culture* (Boston, 1946).
Bennett, J. W. and Nagai, M., 'The Japanese Critique of the Methodology of Benedict's Crysanthemum and the Sword', *American Anthropologist*, Vol. 55, Part 3 (August 1953), pp. 404–11.
Bergamini, D., *Japan's Imperial Conspiracy* (1971).
Bernadotte, F., *Instead of Arms* (1949).
Best, G. F. A., *Humanity in Warfare* (1980).
Best, G. F. A. and Wheatcroft, A. (eds), *De Solferino à Tsoushima Histoire du Comité International de la Croix Rouge* (Paris, 1963).
—— *War, Economy and the Military Mind* (1976).
Blomberg, C., *Samurai Religion I and II* (Uppsala, 1976).
Boissier, P. , *From Solferino to Tsushima, a History of the International Committee of the Red Cross* (Geneva, 1985).
Bowring, R. J., *Mori Ogai and the Modernization of Japanese Culture* (Cambridge, 1979).
Boyle, J. H., *China and Japan at War* (1972).
Brackman, A. C., *The Other Nuremberg, the Untold Story of the Tokyo War Crimes Trials* (1989).
Braddon, R., *The Other Hundred Years' War, Japan's bid for supremacy* (1983).
Bradley, J., *Cyril Wild, the Tall Man who Never Slept* (Fontwell, Sussex, 1991).
Brazell, K., 'Mori Ogai in Germany', *MN* (Monumenta Nipponica) (Summer 1971).
Brereton, J. M., *The British Soldier, A Social History from 1661 to the Present Day* (1986).
Brindle, E., *With the Russians, Japanese and Chunchuse* (1905).
British Officers Reports, *The Russo–Japanese War*, Vols. I, II and III (1907).
British Red Cross Society, *Reports First World War, 1914–1919* (1921).
Broca, A. and Ducroquet, *Artificial Limbs* (1918).
Brooks, L., *Behind Japan's Surrender* (New York, 1968).
Brooks, S. M., *Civil War Medicine* (Springfield, Illinois, 1966).
Brougher, Brig. Gen. W. E., *South to Bataan, North to Mukden* (Athens, GA, 1971).
Brown, D. M., *Nationalism in Japan: An Introductory Historical Analysis* (Berkeley, 1965).
Brown, S. D. and Hirota, A., *Diaries of Kidoe Takayoshi* Vols. I, II and III (Tokyo, 1983–6).
Browne, C., *The Last Banzai* (1967).
Brownlie, I. (ed.), *Basic Documents on Human Rights* (Oxford, 1971).
Buell, R. L., *The Washington Conference* (New York, 1922).
Burleigh, B., *Empire of the East* (1905).
Burnett, C. J., 'Daily Life of Japanese Infantry Soldier in time of War', in *British Officers' Reports, Russo–Japanese War*, Vol. II (1907), pp. 662–65.

Burnett, J., *Plenty and Want: A Social History of Diet in England from 1815 to the Present* (1966).

Bush, L., *The Road to Inamura* (1961).

Butow, R. J. C., *Japan's Decision to Surrender* (Stanford, 1954).

—— *Tojo and the Coming of War* (Stanford, 1961).

Byas, H., *The Japanese Enemy, his Power and his Vulnerability* (New York, 1942).

—— *Government by assassination* (1943).

Byrnes, J., *All in One Lifetime* (New York, 1958).

Caidin, M., *Winged Samurai, Saburo Sakai and the Zero Fighter Pilots* (Mesa, Arizona, 1986).

Calvocoressi, R. and Wint, G., *Total War* (1972).

Cambray, P. G. and Briggs, G. G. B., *Red Cross and St John's War Organisation 1939–1947* (1949).

Cantile, N., *A History of the Army Medical Department*, 2 Vols (Edinburgh, 1974).

Carew, T., *Hostages to Fortune* (1971).

Carpenter, K. J., *The History of Scurvy and Vitamin C* (New York, 1986).

Carr, E. H., *Britain, a Study of Foreign Policy from the Versailles Treaty to the Outbreak of War* (1939).

Carr, Gregg, C., 'Japanese prisoners of war in Australia, the Cowra outbreak, August 1944', *Oceania*, Vol. XLVII, No.4 (June 1977), pp. 253–64.

—— *Japanese Prisoners of War in Revolt* (Queensland, 1978).

Carter, N., *G-String jesters* (Melbourne, 1966).

Checkland, O., *Britain's Encounter with Meiji Japan, 1868–1912* (1989).

Clarke, H., *Breakout* (Sydney, 1965).

Cole, A., *Japanese Society and Politics, the Impact of Social Stratification and Mobility in Politics* (Boston, Mass., 1956).

Connors, L., *The Emperor's Adviser, Kinmochi Saionji* (1987).

Conroy, H., *The Japanese Seizure of Korea* (1960).

Cook, H. F., *Korea's 1884 Incident* (Seoul, 1972).

Cooper, G. with Holman, D., *Ordeal in the Sun* (1963).

Cortazzi, H., *Dr. Willis in Japan, 1862–1877, British Medical Pioneer* (1985).

Costello, J., *The Pacific War, 1941–45* (1981).

Cottell, A. B., 'Water Conservancy in War', *JRAMC*, Vol. IV (1905), pp. 174–7.

Craig, A. M. and Shively, D. H., *Personality in Japanese History* (Berkeley, 1971).

Craig, G. A. and Gilbert, F., *The Diplomats, 1919–1939* (Princeton, 1953).

Craig, W., *The Fall of Japan* (1968).

Craigie, R., *Behind the Japanese Mask* (1946)

Creveld, M. van, *Supplying War* (Cambridge, 1977).

Crosby, A. W., *Ecological Imperialism: The Biological Expansion of Europe 900–1900* (New York, 1986).

Crump, T., *Death of an Emperor* (1992).

Curtin, P. D., *Death by Migration, Europe's Encounter with the Tropical World in the Nineteenth Century* (Cambridge, 1989).

Davidson, S., Passmore, R., Brock, I. F. and Truswell, A. S., *Human Nutrition and Dietetics* (1979).

De Bary, W. T., *Sources of the Japanese Tradition* (New York, 1958).

De Vos, G. A., *Socialization for Achievement, Essays on the Cultural Psychology of the Japanese* (Berkeley, 1973).
De Vos, G. A. and Wagatsuma, H., *Japan's Invisible Race, Caste in Culture and Personality* (Berkeley, 1966).
Doi, T., *The Anatomy of Dependence* (Tokyo, 1973).
Dore, R. P., *City Life in Japan* (1958).
—— *Land Reform in Japan* (1959).
—— *Education in Tokugawa Japan* (1965).
—— (ed.), *Aspects of Social Change in Modern Japan* (Princeton, 1971).
Dower, J. W., *Mori Ogai, Meiji Japan's Eminent Bystander* (Cambridge, Mass., 1963).
—— *Empire and Aftermath: Yoshida Shigeru and the Japanese Experience 1878-1954* (Harvard, 1979).
—— *War Without Mercy: Race and Power in the Pacific War* (1984).
Draper, G. I. A., *Red Cross Conventions* (1958).
—— 'The Geneva Conventions of 1949', *Recueil des Cours de l'académie de droit international*, Vol. 14 (I) (1965), pp. 61-165.
—— 'Implementation of International Law in Armed Conflicts', *International Affairs*, Vol. 48 (1972), pp. 46-59.
—— 'Military Necessity and Humanitarian Imperatives', *Revue de droit pénal militaire et de droit de la guerre*, Vol. 12 (1973), pp. 129-42.
Duffy, M., 'Volunteering', *Mainichi Daily News*, 2 May 1977.
Dulles, F. R., *The American Red Cross, a History* (New York, 1950).
Dunant, H., *A Proposal for Introducing Uniformity in the Conditions of Prisoners of War on Land* (1872).
—— *A Memory of Solferino* (1947).
Dunlop, E. E., 'Medical Experiences in Japanese Captivity', *British Medical Journal*, Vol. II (5 October 1946), p. 481-46.
—— *The War Diaries of 'Weary' Dunlop* (Melbourne, 1988).
Durand, A., *From Sarajevo to Hiroshima, History of the International Committee of the Red Cross* (Geneva, 1984).
Fall of Singapore, 50 year remembrance service (Canberra, 15 February 1992).
Fearey, R. A., *The Occupation of Japan. Second phase 1948-50* (New York, 1980).
Fliegel, O. and Feuer, S. G., 'Historical Development of Lower-Extremity Prostheses', *Archives of Physical Medicine and Rehabilitation*, Vol. 47 (1966).
Forbis, W. H. , *Japan Today* (New York, 1975).
Forsythe, D. P., *Humanitarian Politics: The International Committee of the Red Cross* (Baltimore, 1977).
Fraser, M. C. (ed. H. Cortazzi), *A Diplomat's Wife in Japan* (Tokyo, 1982).
Fraser, T. G. and Lowe, P. , *Conflict and Amity in East Asia* (1992).
Freidel, F. B., 'General Orders 100 and Military Government', *The Mississippi Valley Historical Review* (1945-46), pp. 541-56.
—— *Francis Lieber, Nineteenth Century Liberal* (1947).
Fuchida, M. and Okumiya, M., *Midway, the Battle that Doomed Japan* (1957).
Gayn, M., *Japan Diary* (New York, 1948).
Gibney, F., *Five Gentlemen of Japan* (1953).
—— *Japan, the Fragile Superpower* (1975).
Giovannitti, L. and Fried, F., *The Decision to Drop the Bomb* (New York, 1965).

Glahn, G. von, *The Occupation of Enemy Territory* (Minneapolis, 1957).

Glover, E., *War, Sadism and Pacificism: Further Essays in Group Psychology and War* (1946).

Gluck, C., *Japan's Modern Myths, Ideology in the late Meiji Period* (Princeton, 1985).

Gluck, C. and Graubard, S. R. (eds), *Showa, the Japan of Hirohito* (New York, 1990).

Goodwin, R., *Passport to Eternity* (1956).

Gordon, E., *Miracle on the River Kwai* (1963).

Gordon, H., *Die like the Carp* (Sydney, 1978).

Gower, E. S. (compiler), Queen Mary's Hospital, Roehampton, General Hospital and Limb Fitting Centre (1966) (outline duplicated typescript history).

Greenfell, R., *Main Fleet to Singapore* (1951).

Greenspan, M., *The Modern Law of Land Warfare* (Berkeley, 1959).

Grew, J. C., *Report from Tokyo* (1943).

—— *Ten Years in Japan* (New York, 1944).

—— *Turbulent Era, a Diplomatic Record of Forty Years* (1953).

Guillain, R., *Le peuple Japonais et la guerre* (Paris, 1947).

—— *The Japanese Challenge* (1970).

—— *I saw Tokyo Burning* (1981).

Gumpert, M., *Dunant, the Story of the Red Cross or the Knight Errant of Charity* (1939).

Hackett, R. F., *Yamagata Arimoto in the Rise of Modern Japan 1838–1922* (Cambridge, Mass., 1971).

Haggie, P. , *Britannia at Bay* (1981).

Haldane, E. S., *The British Nurse in Peace and War* (1923).

Hamilton, I., *A Staff Officer's Scrap-Book during the Russo–Japanese War* (1905–7).

Harries, M. and S., *Sheathing the Sword* (1987).

—— *Soldiers of the Sun* (1991).

Hart, E., *Man Born to Live: Life and Work of Henri Dunant, Founder of the Red Cross* (1953).

Hashimoto, S., *Henry Dunant and Myself* (Tokyo, 1978).

Hasluck, p. , *The Government and The People* (Canberra, Australian War Memorial, 1952).

Havens, T. R. H., *Valley of Darkness, the Japanese People and World War Two* (New York, 1978).

Hino, Ashihei (pseud.), trans. Lewis Bush, *War and Soldier* (1940).

Hirano, I., 'Sanitation in the Japanese Navy and on the Classification and Treatment of Wounds, during the late war', *International Congress of Medicine* (1913), Section 20, Part II, *Naval and Military Medicine*, pp. 87–102.

Holtom, D. C., *Modern Japan and Shinto Nationalism: A Study in Present Day Trends in Japanese Religions* (New York, 1963).

Howard, M., *War and the Liberal Conscience* (1978).

—— *Restraints on War* (Oxford, 1979).

Hudson, M. O., *International Legislation*, Vol. V (Washington, 1936).

Hull, C., *The Memoirs of Cordell Hull* (New York, 1948).

Humphreys, C., *Via Tokyo* (1948).
Hunter, J., *Japanese Women Working* (1993).
Ibuse, M., *Black Rain* (1969).
Ichihashi, Y., *The Washington Conference and After* (Stanford, 1928).
Ienaga, S., *The Pacific War, 1931–1945* (1978).
Ike, N., *Japan's Decision for War* (1967).
International Committee of the Red Cross, *Inta Arma Caritas* (Geneva, 1947).
Report of the ICRC on its activities during the Second World War, 3 Vols (Geneva, 1948).
—— *The Geneva Conventions of 12 August 1949* (Geneva, 1949).
—— *International Congress of Medicine* (1913).
Ion, H., *The Cross and the Rising Sun: The Canadian Protestant Movement in the Japan Empire, 1872–1931* (Waterloo, 1990).
Iritani, T., *Group Psychology of the Japanese in War-time* (1991).
Iriye, A., *Pacific Estrangement, Japanese and American Expansion 1897–1911* (Cambridge, Mass., 1972).
—— *Mutual Images, Essays in American–Japanese Relations* (Cambridge, Mass., 1975).
—— *Power and Culture* (Cambridge, Mass., 1981).
Ishimaru, T., *Japan Must Fight Britain* (New York, 1936).
James, D. H., *The Rise and Fall of the Japanese Empire* (1951).
Jannetta, A. B., *Epidemics and Mortality in early Modern Japan* (Princeton, 1987).
Jansen, M. B., *The Japanese and Sun Yat Sen* (Cambridge, Mass., 1954).
—— (ed.), *Changing Japanese Attitudes toward Modernization* (Princeton, 1965).
Japan, Ministry of Education, *Cardinal Principles of National Entity in Japan* (Kokutai no Hongi), trans. by G. O. Gauntlett, ed. by R. K. Hall (Cambridge, Mass., 1949).
Japanese Central Red Cross Hospital (Tokyo, 1934).
Japanese Central Red Cross Maternity Hospital (Tokyo, 1934).
Japanese Junior Red Cross (Tokyo, 1937).
Japanese Red Cross, College of Nursing Principles and Curriculum (Tokyo, 1990).
Japanese Red Cross Society, General Description of the Relief Work during the Last War, 1914–19 (Tokyo, 1919).
Japanese Red Cross Society, 1953–56 (New Delhi, 1957).
Jindo, Sono Ayumi (Steps to Humanity, 100 Years of the Japanese Red Cross) (Tokyo, 1977).
Jones, F. C., *Japan's New Order in East Asia* (1954).
Joyce, J. A., *Red Cross International and the Strategy of Peace* (New York, 1959).
Junod, M., *Warriors without Weapons* ICRC (Geneva, 1982) 'The Hiroshima Disaster' *International Review of the Red Cross* (Geneva, Sept.–Dec. 1982).
Kajima, M., *The Diplomacy of Japan 1894–1922* (Tokyo, 1976).
Kalshoven, F., *Materials on the Trial of Former Servicemen of the Japanese Army charged with Manufacturing and Employing Bacteriological Weapons* (Moscow, 1950).
—— *Belligerent Reprisals* (Leyden, 1971).

Kaputinski, F., *Matsuyama Horyo Shuyojo Nikki, Rosia-jui Shoko no mita Meiji Nihon* (Diary of a Russian Officer in Matsuyama prison camp in Meiji Japan), ed. K. Odagawa (Tokyo, 1988).

Karsten, P. , *Law, Soldiers and Combat* (Westport, Conn., 1978).

Kase, T., *Eclipse of the Rising Sun* (1951).

Katai, T., *One Soldier* (1956).

Kato, M., *The Lost War, a Japanese Reporter's Inside Story* (New York, 1946).

Kawahara, T., *Hirohito and his Times, a Japanese Perspective* (Tokyo, 1990).

Kawasaki, I., *Japan Unmasked* (Vermont and Tokyo, 1969).

Keene, D., *Japanese Discovery of Europe* (1952).

Kent Hughes, W. S., *Slaves of the Samurai* (1946).

Keogh, A., 'The results of Sanitation on the efficiency of Armies in peace and war', *JRAMC*, Vol. 12 (1909), pp. 357–785.

Kido, K., *The Diary of Marquis Kido, 1931–45*, selected translations into English (Tokyo, 1966).

Kirby, S. W., *Singapore: The Chain of Disaster* (1971).

Knox, E. Blake, 'Some medical notes on war', *JRAMC*, Vol. 4 (1905), pp. 440–6, 580–6, Vol. 5 (1905) pp. 616–22, 703–14.

Kokuryu, Kai (ed.), *Seinan ki den* (Chronological Accounts of the S. W. War), 6 vols (Tokyo, 1908–11).

Kotsuji, A., *From Tokyo to Jerusalem* (Jerusalem, 1964).

Kozlovski, N., 'Statistical data concerning the losses of the Russian Army from sickness and wounds in the war against Japan, 1904–05', *JRAMC*, Vol. 18 (1912), pp. 330–46.

Kranzler, D., *Japanese, Nazis and Jews, Shanghai, 1938–45* (Hoboken, New Jersey, 1988).

Large, S. S., *Emperor Hirohito and Showa Japan: A Political Biography* (1992).

Lawson, Lady, *Highways and Homes of Japan* (1910).

Lea, Homer, *The Valour of Ignorance* (1909).

Lebra, J. C., *Japan's Greater East Asia Co-Prosperity Sphere in World War II. Selected readings and documents* (1975).

Lebra, T. S., *Japanese Patterns of Behaviour* (Honolulu, 1976).

Lee, B. A., *Britain and the Sino-Japanese War 1937–39* (Oxford 1973).

Lee, H. G., *Nothing But Praise* (Culver City, California, 1948).

Lindsay, O., *At the Going Down of the Sun* (1981).

Long, G., *The Final Campaigns*. Australian War Memorial (Series 1, Army V7) (Canberra, 1946).

Lu, D. J., *From The Marco Polo Bridge to Pearl Harbour: Japan's entry to the Second World War* (1961).

Lumiere, C., *Kura* (Brisbane, 1966).

Mabire, J. and Breheret Y., *The Samurai* (1975).

MacArthur, D., *Reminiscences* (1964).

McCaul, E., *Under the Care of the Japanese War Office* (1905).

—— 'The Red Cross Society in Japan', *JSL*, Vol. VII (1905–7), pp. 211–25.

McCulloch, T., 'The Field Service Filter Water Cart', *JRAMC*, Vol. 6 (1906), pp. 449–54.

Macdonald, G., *The Epidemiology and Control of Malaria* (1957).

McGrew, R. E., *Encyclopedia of Medical History* (New York, 1985).

MacKenzie, K. S., *Dead Men Rising* (Sydney, 1971).

MacLeod, R. and Lewis, M. (eds), *Disease, Medicine and Empire: Perspectives on Western Medicine and the Experience of European Expansion* (1988).

McLoughlin, G. S., 'Notes on the Organisation and methods of the medical services of the Russian Army in time of War', *JRAMC*, Vol. VII (January to June 1907), pp. 590–608.

McNeill, W. H., *Plagues and Peoples* (New York, 1976).

McNeill, W. H., *Survey of International Affairs, America, Britain and Russia, their Co-operation and Conflict 1941–46* (Oxford, 1953).

McPherson, W. G., 'The Medical Organisation of the Japanese Army', *JRAMC*, Vol. VI, No.3 (March 1906), pp. 219–250.

—— 'Organisation and Resources of the Red Cross Society of Japan', *JRAMC*, Vol. VI, No.3 (March 1906), pp. 467–478.

Manning, P. , *Hirohito, the War Years* (1986).

Marks, J., *Vitamins in Health and Disease: a modern re-appraisal* (1968).

Marks, T., 'Life in war-time Japan', *Japan and the Second World War*, LSE, ICERD, IS/89/197 (1989).

Maruyama, M., *Nationalism and the Right Wing in Japan* (1960).

—— *Thought and Behaviour in Modern Japanese Politics* (1969).

Mason, W. W., *Prisoners of War. Official history of New Zealand in the Second World War, 1939–45* (Wellington, 1954).

Matsumoto, T., *Stories of Fifty Japanese Heroes* (Tokyo 1929).

Matsumoto, T., with M. O. Lerrigo, *A Brother is a Stranger* (1947).

Matsumura, T., 'Summary report on biological warfare investigations', *Mita Gakkai Zasshi* (Mita Journal of Economics), Vol. 84, No.2 (July 1991), pp. 294–97.

Matsunami, N., *The National Flag of Japan* (Tokyo, 1928).

Maxon, Y. C., *Control of Japanese Foreign Policy* (Berkeley, 1957).

Miller, R. I. (ed.), *The Law of War* (Lexington, Mass., 1975).

Mine, W. G., 'The influence of rice on beri-beri', *JRAMC*, Vol. 12 (1909), pp. 583–4.

Minear, R. H., *Victor's Justice, the Tokyo War Crimes Trials* (Princeton, 1971).

Mishima, Y., *The Samurai Ethic in Modern Japan* (1977).

—— *The Sea of Fertility* (1985).

Mitford, A. B., *Mitford's Japan, the Memoirs and Recollections, 1866–1906 of Lord Redesdale* (ed. Hugh Cortazzi) (1985).

Moore, C. H., *The Japanese Mind* (1973).

Morishima, M., *Why has Japan 'Succeeded'? Western Technology and the Japanese Ethos* (Cambridge, 1982).

Morley, J. A., *The Japanese Thrust into Siberia, 1918* (1950).

Morris, I., *Nationalism and the Right Wing in Japan* (Oxford, 1960).

—— *The Nobility of Failure: Tragic Heroes in the History of Japan* (1975).

Mosley, L., *Hirohito, Emperor of Japan* (1966).

Murakami, H., *Japan the Years of Trial, 1919–52* (Tokyo, 1982).

Murray, G., 'Oswald Wynd, a novel life', *Intersect* (March 1991), pp. 28–36.

Myers, R. H. and Peattie, M. R., *The Japanese Colonial Empire, 1895–1945* (Princeton, 1984).

Nakane, C., *Japanese Society* (1970).

Natsume, S (trans. E. McLellan), *Kokoro* (The Heart of things) (1968).

Nish, I., *Japanese Foreign Policy, 1869–1942* (1977).

—— (ed.), *Anglo-Japanese Alienation, 1919–52* (Cambridge, 1982).

—— *The Origins of the Russo–Japanese War* (1985).

—— (ed.), *Contemporary European Writing on Japan* (Ashford, Kent, 1988).

Nishi, I., 'Hospital Ships and the Transport of the Wounded', *XVII International Congress of Medicine* (1913), Section 20, Part II, Naval and Military Medicine, pp. 17–32.

Nitobé, I., *Bushido, the Soul of Japan* (New York, 1905).

Norbeck, E., 'Edokko, a narrative of Japanese Prisoners of War in Russia', *Rice University Studies, Essays in the Humanities*, Vol. 57, i (1971), pp. 19–67.

Norman, E. H., *Japan's Emergence as a Modern State* (New York, 1940).

Novikoff-Priboy, A., *Tsushima* (1936).

Nu, T., *Burma under the Japanese* (1954).

O'Brien, W. V., 'The Meaning of 'Military Necessity' in International Law', *World Polity*, Vol. 1 (1957), pp. 109–76.

—— 'Legitimate Military Necessity in Nuclear War', *World Polity*, Vol. 2 (1960), pp. 35–120.

—— 'Biological/Chemical Warfare and the International War of Law', *Georgetown Law Journal*, Vol. 51 (1962), pp. 1–63.

O'Connell, B., *Return of the Tiger* (1960).

Oe, Kenzaburo, *The Catch* (1959).

—— *A Personal Matter* (1969).

—— *The Silent Cry* (1974).

Offner, A., *American Appeasement* (1969).

Ogiso, R. and M (translators), *Nichi-Ro Senso Ka no Nihon – Rosiagunjin horyo no tsuma no Nikki* (Japan during the Russo–Japanese War, the Diary of Sophia von Theil, the wife of a Russian POW) (Tokyo, 1991).

Okamoto, S., *The Japanese Oligarchy and the Russo–Japanese War* (Tokyo, 1970).

Okuma, S., ed. M. B. Huish, *Fifty Years of New Japan* (1909).

Oliver, B., *The British Red Cross in Action* (1966).

Ooka, S., *Fires on The Plain* (1957).

Otis, G. A. and Huntingdon, D. L., *The Medical and Surgical History of the War of the Rebellion*, Vol. II, *Surgical History* (1876–83).

Pacific War Research Society, *Japan's Longest Day* (1968).

Packard, J. M., *Sons of Heaven* (New York, 1987).

Pal, R., *Crimes in International Relations* (Calcutta, 1955).

Paravicini, F., *Bericht des Herr Dr. F. Paravicini über seinen Besuch der Gefangenenlager in Japan*, 30 June to 16 July 1918 (Account of Dr Paravicini's visits to POW camps in Japan) (Basle, 1919), pp. 1–43.

Parkin, R., *Out of the Smoke, the Story of a Sail* (1960).

—— *Into the Smother, A Journal of the Burma-Siam Railway* (1963).

—— *The Sword and the Blossom* (1968).

Paskins, B. and Dockerill, M., *The Ethics of War* (1979).

Passin, H., *Society and Education in Japan* (New York, 1965).

Paull, R., *Retreat from Kokoda* (1953).

Pavillard, S. S., *Bamboo Doctor* (1960).

Peattie, M. R., *Ishiwara Kanji and Japan's Confrontation with the West* (Princeton, 1975).

—— *The Japanese Colonial Empire, 1895–1945* (Princeton, 1984).

—— 'The last Samurai, the military career of Nogi Maresuke', papers on E. Asian Studies 1, Japan 1 (Princeton, 1986).

Perrin, N., *Giving up the Gun* (1979).

Pictet, J., *The Principles of International Humanitarian Law*, ICRC (Geneva, 1966).

Pierson, J. D., *Tokutomi Soho, 1863–1957, a Journalist for Modern Japan* (Princeton, 1980).

Plomer, W., *Sado* (1931).

Pollock, C. E., 'Losses in the Russo–Japanese War, 1904–5', *JRAMC*, Vol. 17 (1911), pp. 50–4.

Post, L. van der, *The Night of the New Moon* (1970).

Powell, J. W., 'Japan's Germ Warfare, the US cover-up of a war crime', *Bulletin of Concerned Asian Scientists* (December, 1980), pp. 2–17.

—— 'A Hidden Chapter in History', *The Bulletin of the Atomic Scientists* (October 1981), pp. 44–52.

Poynter, F. N. L., 'Evolution of Military Medicine', in Higham, R. (ed.), *A Guide to the Sources of British Military History* (Berkeley, 1971).

Presseison, E. L., *Before Aggression: Europeans Prepare the Japanese Army* (Tucson, 1965).

Price, W. de M., *The Japanese Miracle and Peril* (1971).

Prior, M., *Campaigns of a War Correspondent* (1912).

Putti, V., *History of Artificial Limbs* (New York, 1930).

Rappaport, A., *Henry L. Stimson and Japan* (1963).

Reischauer, E. O., *Japan, the Story of a Nation* (1970).

Richardson, T. E., *In Japanese Hospitals during War-time: Fifteen Months with the Red Cross Society of Japan. April 1904 to July 1905* (Edinburgh, 1905).

Rimer, J. T., *Mori Ogai* (Boston, 1975).

Rivett, R. D., *Behind Bamboo, an inside story of the Japanese prison camps* (Sydney, 1946).

Roberts, A. and Guelff, R. K., *Basic Documents on the Laws of War* (Oxford, 1982).

Röling, B. V. A., *International Law in an Expanded World* (Amsterdam, 1960).

—— and Rüter, C. F. (eds), *The Tokyo Judgement, the International Tribunal for the Far East*, 2 Vols (Amsterdam, 1977).

Ross, H. C., 'A rapid means of Sterilizing Water for troops by using Thermite as fuel', *JRAMC*, Vol. 6 (1906), pp. 145–9.

Ross, R., *Studies in Malaria* (1928).

Rothkopf, C. Z., *Jean Henri Dunant, Father of the Red Cross* (1971).

Rousseau, J. J., *Contrat Social* (Geneva, 1762).

Lord Russell of Liverpool, *The Knights of Bushido* (1958).

Russo–Japanese War, 3 Vols (Tokyo, 1903).

Sadler, A. L., *The Life of Shogun Tokuyawa Ieyasu* (1937).

Sakurai, T., *Human Bullets, a Soldier's Story of Port Arthur* (1907).

Sanders, H.St G., *The Red Cross and the White* (1959).

Schindler, D. and Toman, J., *The Law of Armed Conflict: A Collection of Conventions* (Leyden, 1973).

Seaman, L. L., *From Tokio through Manchuria with the Japanese* (New York, 1905).
—— *The Real Triumph of Japan* (New York, 1906).
Seidensticker, E., *Tokyo Rising* (Cambridge, Mass., 1991).
Selwyn-Clarke, S., *Footprints* (Hong Kong, 1975).
Seymer, L. R., *Florence Nightingale's Nurses, St Thomas' Hospital Nurse Training School, 1860–1960* (1960).
Shigemitsu, M., *Japan and Her Destiny* (1958).
Shillony, Ben-Ami, *Politics and Culture in War-time Japan* (Oxford and New York, 1981).
Shinpo Ko Tsuitokai (ed.), *Ito Hirubumi Den* (Biography of Ito Hirubumi) (Tokyo, 1973–81).
Shiroyama, S., *War Criminal* (1974).
Sissons, D. C. S., 'The Cowra Break-out', *Rekishi to Jinbutsu*, No.165 (Tokyo, 10 September 1984).
Slim, Sir W., *Defeat into Victory* (1956).
Smethurst, R. J., 'The Creation of the Imperial Military Reserve', *Journal of Asian Studies (JAS)*, Vol. XXX, No. 4 (1971), pp. 815–28.
—— *The Social Basis for pre-war Japanese Militarism, the Army and the Rural Community* (Berkeley and Los Angeles, 1974).
Smith, F. B., *Florence Nightingale, Reputation and Power* (1982).
Smith, R., 'The Japanese Rural Community: Norms, Sanctions and Ostracism' in J. M. Potter *et al.* (eds), *Peasant Society: A Reader* (Boston, 1967). pp. 246–255.
Smith, R. C., *The Last Japanese Soldier* (1972).
Smith, R. J., *Ancestor Worship in Contemporary Japan* (Stanford, 1974).
Smith, W., *Japan at the Cross Roads* (1936).
Smyth, J. G., *Arthur E. Percival and the Tragedy of Singapore* (1971).
Spaight, J. M., *War Rights on Land* (1911).
Air Power and War Rights (1924).
Specter, R. H., *Eagle against the Sun: The American War with Japan* (1984).
Stead, A., *Japan, our new Ally* (1902).
—— *Japan by the Japanese* (1904).
—— *Great Japan* (1906).
—— *Japanese Patriotism* (1906).
Stimson, H. L., 'The Decision to use the Atomic Bomb', *Harper's Magazine*, Vol. 194, No.1161 (February 1947), pp. 98–107.
—— *The Far Eastern Crisis* (1971).
Stockholm International Peace Research Institute, *The Law of War and Dubious Weapons (*Stockholm, 1976).
Stone, J., *Legal Controls of International Conflict* (1959).
Storry, R., *The Double Patriots* (1957).
—— *Japan and the Decline of The West in Asia* (1979).
Stott, H., 'A Contribution to the Study of Aetiology of Beri-Beri', *JRAMC*, Vol. 17 (1911), pp. 231–44.
Suzuki, J., 'The Japanese Red Cross Mission to England', *JSL*, Vol. 14 (1915–16), pp. 28–36.
Takaki, K., 'The Preservation of health amongst the personnel of the Japanese Army', *JRAMC*, Vol. VI (1906), pp. 54–62.

—— 'The Preservation of health amongst the personnel of the Japanese Navy and Army', *The Lancet*, Vol. 1 (19 May 1906), pp. 1369–1374; (26 May 1906), pp. 1451–5; (2 June 1906), pp. 1520–3.

—— 'Military Hygiene of the Japanese Army', *New York Medical Journal*, Vol. LXXXIII, No.23 (New York, 9 June 1906), Whole No.1436, pp. 1161–6.

Takeda, K., *Dual Image of Japanese Emperor* (1988).

Takehara, M., *Senshisha no Kiseki* (In the footprints of the fallen soldiers) (Tokyo, 1984).

Tasaki, H., *Long the Imperial Way* (1951).

Timms, E. W., 'Blood bath at Cowra', *As you were* (Canberra, Australian War Memorial), pp. 175–180.

Titus, D. A., *Palace and Politics in Pre-war Japan* (1974).

Tokayer, M. and Schwartz, M., *The Fugu Plan: The Untold Story of the Japanese and the Jews during the World War II* (1979).

Tokyo Gazette, Field Service Code (Tokyo, 1941).

Toland, John, *The Rising Sun* (New York, 1970).

Tolishuro, O. D., *Tokyo Record* (1943).

Towle, P. , 'Japanese Treatment of Prisoners in 1904–5', *Military Affairs*, Vol. 39 (1975), pp. 115–17.

Tsuji, M., *The Singapore Version* (1960).

Tsunoda, R. W. T., de Barry, W. T. and Keene, D., *Sources of Japanese Traditions* (New York, 1968).

Tsurumi, K., *Social Change and the Individual* (Princeton, 1969).

Tuchman, B., *Sand against the Wind* (1971).

Varley, H. P. with I. and N. Morris, *The Samurai* (1970).

Vining, E. G., *Windows for the Crown Prince* (Philadelphia, 1952).

Von Theil, S., *Under the Hague Treaty* (New York, 1907).

Wainwright, J. M., *General Wainwright's Story* (1946).

Waksman, S. A., *The Conquest of Tuberculosis* (Berkeley, 1966).

Ward, R. E. and Shulman, F. J., *Allied Occupation of Japan 1945–1952*, An annotated bibliography of Western language material (Chicago, 1974).

Ward, R. S., *Asia for the Asiatics? The Techniques of Japanese Occupation* (Chicago, 1945).

Wasserstrom, R. A. (ed.), *War and Morality* (Belmont, California, 1970).

Weinstein, Alfred A., *Barbed Wire Surgeon* (New York, 1948).

Wheeler, G. E., 'Isolated Japan, Anglo–American Diplomatic Co-operation 1927–1936', *Pacific Historical Review*, Vol. XXX, No.2 (May 1961), pp. 165–78.

White, J. A., *The Diplomacy of the Russo–Japanese War: The Siberian Intervention* (Princeton, 1964).

Williams, P. and Wallace, D., *Unit 731, the Japanese Army's Secret of Secrets* (1990).

Williams, R. R. and Spies, I. D., *Vitamin B₁ (Thiamin) and its Use in Medicine* (New York, 1939).

Wohl, A. S., *Endangered Lives, Public Health in Victorian Britain* (Cambridge, Mass., 1983).

Woodham Smith, C., *Florence Nightingale, 1820–1910* (1950).

Woodhull, A. A., *Observations of the Medical Department of the British Army* (St Louis, Mo., 1894).

Woods, R. and Woodward, J. (eds), *Urban Disease and Mortality in Nineteenth Century England* (New York, 1984).

Wynd, O., *The Forty Days* (1972).

Yabe, Tatsusaburo, 'Disparition du Kakke (beri beri) dans la marine Japonais', *Archives du medicine navale* (1900), 73:58–551.

Yamashita, T., *Nihonjin Koko Ni Nemma* (Here lie the Japanese). Privately printed (1969).

Yanaga, C., *Japanese People and Politics* (New York, 1956).

Yokoi, S., *The Last Japanese Soldier* (1972).

Yosano, A., *Teihon Yosano Akiko Zenshu* (The Collected Works of Akiko Yosano) (Tokyo, 1979–81), 20 Vols.

Yoshida, K., *Japan is a Circle* (1975).

Yoshizawa, T., *Conspiracy at Mukden, the Rise of the Japanese Military* (New Haven, 1963).

Zimmern, A., *The League of Nations and the Rule of Law 1918–1935* (1936).

Index